MULTI-UNIT HOUSING IN URBAN CITIES

From 1800 to Present Day

This book investigates the development of multi-unit housing typologies that were predominant in a particular city from the 1800s to the present day. It emphasises the importance of understanding the direct connection between housing and dwelling in the context of a city, and the manner in which the city is an instructional indication of how a housing typology is embodied.

The case studies presented offer an insight into why a certain housing type flourished in a specific city and the variety span across cities in the world where distinct housing types have prevailed. It also pursues how housing types developed, evolved, and helped define the city, looks into how dwellers inhabited their dwellings, and analyses how the housing typologies correlate in a contemporary context. The typologies studied are back-to-backs in Birmingham; tenements in London; Haussmann Apartment in Paris; tenements in New York; *tong lau* in Hong Kong; perimeter block, linear block, and block-edge in Berlin; perimeter block and solitaire in Amsterdam; space-enclosing structure in Beijing; micro house in Tokyo; and high-rise in Toronto.

Katy Chey is an architect living, working, and teaching in Toronto. She lives in a multi-unit housing dwelling in the city.

MULTI-UNIT HOUSING IN URBAN CITIES

From 1800 to Present Day

Katy Chey

Routledge
Taylor & Francis Group

NEW YORK AND LONDON

First published 2018
by Routledge
711 Third Avenue, New York, NY 10017

and by Routledge
2 Park Square, Milton Park, Abingdon, Oxon, OX14 4RN

Routledge is an imprint of the Taylor & Francis Group, an informa business

Every effort has been made to contact and acknowledge copyright holders,
but the author and publisher would be pleased to have any errors or
omissions brought to their attention so that corrections may be published
at a later printing.

Library of Congress Cataloging-in-Publication Data
A catalog record for this book has been requested

ISBN: 978-1-138-18994-2 (hbk)
ISBN: 978-1-138-18995-9 (pbk)
ISBN: 978-1-315-64135-5 (ebk)

Typeset in Helvetica Light
by Florence Production Ltd, Stoodleigh, Devon, UK

CONTENTS

FOREWORD

Thousands of Cities, Millions of Acts

A pit bull on the Upper West Side noses open a refrigerator door. A Pomeranian obsessively rearranges her bedding. A rabbit in Greenpoint, Brooklyn, waits for his nightly bowl of oats. A bulldog in the East Village makes passionate love to a pillow.

This is how an article begins in *The New York Times,* published in the summer of 2016. It describes how pets live their domestic lives, unaware of being monitored by cameras, while their human companions are away. Most of the time there is not a lot going on. It turns out that pets sleep a lot when there is nobody around.

What pets do when they are home alone doesn't differ much from what humans do when they dwell: eating, cleaning, idling, having sex, sleeping. And just as with the secret life of pets, most of the time the human act of dwelling passes unnoticed. Even to dwellers themselves, who happen to dwell almost unselfconsciously. Precisely because it is so common to dwell, it is extremely hard to say what it is and how dwellers do it.

Most of the time, the act of dwelling exists in the domain of the infra-ordinary, as French writer Georges Perec has called it in a short essay written in 1973. The infra-ordinary is here, right in front of us, but we are unable to see it, unless, as Perec stated we start,

> to question that which seems to have ceased forever to astonish us. We live, true, we breathe, true; we walk, we open doors, we go down staircases, we sit at a table in order to eat, we lie down on a bed in order to sleep. How? Where? When? Why?

The same question applies to the dwelling itself. We can easily see the extraordinary, aspirational forms of habitation for a happy few, when they are published in lifestyle and architectural magazines for instance, but rarely can we discern the multitude of quotidian forms of living. How, where, when, and why we dwell often remains opaque. We just do it.

With more than half of the world's population living in urban environments, dwelling is deeply entangled with the city, a phenomenon which is often as hard to fathom as dwelling, and dwellings. The complexity of the city was succinctly defined by Egyptian architect Hassan Fathy during a conference in Persepolis back in 1974, when he said that "a city is not the stone and bricks of which its buildings are made. It's a million of acts that go into its making and the millions of acts that go on within it at every moment.' Many of those million of acts are related to housing, which, according to unsubstantiated by intuitively probable estimates, makes up around three quarters of cities.

As Fathy's statement elucidates, it is difficult to comprehend dwelling, dwellings, or the city in their entirety. Katy Chey's foray into the universe of urban housing is an ambitious attempt to deepen our understanding of what living in the cities means, and how in different times and places, the question of the big number of housing has been addressed and articulated in different building typologies, and how they have shaped the city.

Chey's *capita selecta* cover two centuries and a huge, and culturally diverse, territory which includes cities in Western Europe, North America, and Eastern Asia. The ten case studies in her book offer, in their breadth and depth, a wealth of knowledge and many great insights, yet they have an intriguing side effect, at least for this reader: the humbling realisation how many of the acts that go into the making of cities, even the ones I am familiar with, remain infra-ordinarily invisible. Not to mention the thousands of other cities I am *not* familiar with, and all their millions of acts that that go in their making and all the lives that take place in them. In that sense this book is as illuminating for what it contains, and for what it doesn't.

Hans Ibelings

Hans Ibelings is an architecture critic and historian. He is the editor and publisher of *The Architecture Observer* and author of numerous books on architecture and housing.

ACKNOWLEDGMENTS

Many people have contributed to the content of this book and I would like to take this opportunity to acknowledge them. I would like to first thank Brian Boigon, then Director of Bachelor of Arts and Architectural Studies Program at the University of Toronto, John H. Daniels Faculty of Architecture, Landscape and Design, for giving me the opportunity to teach the housing course. I need to thank Richard Sommer, Dean of the Daniels Faculty for his conversation, enthusiasm and support for my project. I would like to sincerely thank the multitude of colleagues who have shared their knowledge of my subject in the form of suggestions, advice, and feedback, and I have to extend a special thanks to Hans Ibelings for his insightful foreword. I would like to express my gratitude to my Routledge editors. To Wendy Fuller, then Commissioning Editor Architecture, for being interested in my topic and believing that it could be brought to a wider audience; Grace Harrison, then Editorial Assistant, for her assistance and guidance; and Katharine Maller, Commissioning Editor Architecture, for going above and beyond her role and coming to my rescue. I need to thank Zainab Abbasi, Bohden Tymchuk, Jiawen (Carmen) Lin, Xinting Fan, and Roseanne Imee Reyes Barbachano, my student assistants who drew and drew and drew some more. To friends and family who afforded me the use of their photos. To my parents, for simply everything. And finally, my deepest appreciation goes to Javier Viteri. There are not enough pages to describe all the support, encouragement, and patience provided unconditionally by him for this project. He is my house and home, and this book is to, for and because of him.

Katy Chey
Toronto, 2017

INTRODUCTION

This book investigates the development of multi-unit housing typologies that were predominant in a particular city from the 1800s to present day. It emphasises the importance of understanding the direct connection between housing and dwelling in the context of a city, and the manner in which the city is an instructional indication of how a housing typology is embodied. The case studies presented offer an insight into why a certain housing type flourished in a specific city. For example, why are there six-storey apartments in Paris, tenements in New York, block housing in Berlin, space-enclosing structures in Beijing, and high-rise towers in Toronto? It values the importance of learning the historical trace of the different housing types in order to influence new housing design that is coherent with the development of the city. This is the structure of my research on housing through my own comparative case studies, and this is how I based the housing course I teach at University of Toronto, John H. Daniels Faculty of Architecture, Landscape and Design, in Toronto, Canada, from where this book came to be.

The variety of different multi-unit housing typology case studies reviewed in this book span across cities in the world where distinct housing types have prevailed. The work also pursues how those housing types developed, evolved, and helped define the city, looks into how dwellers inhabited their dwellings, and analyzes how the housing typologies correlates in a contemporary context. The typologies studied are, back-to-backs in Birmingham; London tenements in London; Haussmann Apartment in Paris; New York tenements in New York; *tong lau* in Hong Kong; perimeter block, linear block, and block-edge in Berlin; perimeter block and solitaire in Amsterdam; space-enclosing structure in Beijing; *kyosho jutaku* in Tokyo; and high-rise in Toronto.

There are eleven chapters in the book. The first chapter provides an overview of multi-unit housing typologies, and the next ten chapters are organised by cities in chronological years starting with Birmingham, during the Industrial Revolution with worker housing, and ending present day in Toronto, analyzing the city's newly abundant high-rise towers. Each chapter includes architectural drawings, diagrams, and images to illustrate and compare how each multi-unit housing typology relates to its city. Each housing typology in each city begins with a characterisation of the multi-unit housing type; analyzes the typology's connection to the city; examines its housing policies, building codes, and laws; presents case studies of the housing type, its typical unit plan, access type, and construction materials; and each chapter ends with the housing typology's circumstance in the city at present day.

There are many different multi-unit housing typologies and many different types of multi-unit housing that can be found in one city. The typologies and case studies presented in the book are not absolute and do not represent all multi-unit housing types. The case studies provided are a small sample of the many examples that can help illustrate and establish the importance of understanding the direct connection between housing, dwelling, and the context of its city. Housing can be the framework of a city and has the ability to construct cities. Housing defines much of the city's presence and mood, and based on this premise, I hope my book can offer another view on housing and city dwelling.

Back-to-backs

London Tenement

Haussmann Apartment

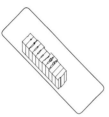

New York Tenement

Hong Kong *Tong Lau*

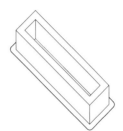

Perimeter Block

Linear Block

Block-Edge

Solitaire

Space-Enclosing Structure

Kyosho Jutaku

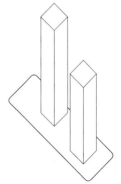

High Rise

Multi-Unit Housing Types

OVERVIEW
Multi-Unit Housing Typologies

Housing is a terminology that is used to describe any type of residence, dwelling domicile, or habitation planned for living, and multi-unit housing is a type of accommodation that can house many residents within one building or several buildings within one complex. Though the function is the same, there are many different types of multi-unit housing inhabited by many people across the world.

Housing typology refers to the classification of building types in terms of design, function, usage, and circumstance. It can be interpreted as the study of a shape or form of dwellings that evolves as a standard kind of habitable building, and social and spatial developments can affect the evolution of a housing type. Prevalent multi-unit housing types in certain cities have endured changes and have emerged and sustained as the multi-unit housing type we know today.

The term multi-unit housing is an interchangeable term. Multi-unit housing can also be known as multi-dwelling units, multi-unit dwelling, or multi-storey housing. Though all terms refer to the same housing typology, this book will use the term "multi-unit housing" throughout and the case studies, diagrams and drawings shown in the book are a small example of style and not conclusive of any one type of multi-unit housing.

Multi-Unit Housing Types

Back-to-backs

Back-to-backs are a type of row housing development dating back to the late 1700s. The name derives from rows of dwelling units that were constructed back to back from one another. The characteristics are:

- Economical housing solution to accommodate urban working poor in late-1700s and mid-1800s England

- Back of one house joined onto the back of another house

- Built at right angles to street and were separated from each other by narrow alleys or courtyards

- Dwelling units were attached on three sides to neighbouring units, except the end units

- Dwelling units stacked atop one another two or three storeys in height

- Communal sanitary facilities

London Tenement

A London Tenement is a single building five to six-storeys in height above a basement. The characteristics are:

- Built to house the urban working poor in mid-1800s London

- Sturdy masonry construction

- Communal sanitary facilities and kitchens on each floor

- Communal courtyard

- Moderately well lit and ventilated

Haussmann Apartment

A Haussmann Apartment form is six storeys in height with a 45° sloped mansard roof. The characteristics are:

- Building conforms to city's street pattern, orientation, height, style, and colour

- Each block forms a unified whole

- Neoclassical style clad with cream-coloured stone

- Shop on the street level

- Flat façades that are plain or elaborately detailed, with or without balconies

New York Tenement

The New York Tenement is a single development five to six storeys in height. The characteristics are:

- Economical housing solution to accommodate urban working poor

- Building attached to both sides of neighbouring tenement buildings

- Lot size usually 25 feet (7.6 metres) wide by 100 feet (30.5 metres) deep

- Four apartments on each floor

- Central shared staircase

- Communal sanitary facilities

Hong Kong *Tong Lau*

A Hong Kong *Tong Lau* is a single building three to five storeys in height and the ground floor accommodates a shop. The characteristics are:

- Usually built in continuous blocks with long, narrow units

- Built in rows of two to four buildings attached along streets with uniform façades

- Three to five storeys high with balconies or verandahs facing the street

- Load-bearing walls with timber floors

- Main entrances directly off streets

Perimeter Block

Perimeter Block buildings are single developments that occupy a city block. The characteristics are:

- Corresponds to individually developed parcel of land

- Building form conforms to the street pattern, height, depth, and other zoning regulations in the city

- Buildings can be single entity or fragmented and divided up by recessed openings or reveals

- Usually has two orientations: street and courtyard

- Courtyards are semi-private green spaces designated for use by residents of the building

- Ground floors can be zoned for retail

Linear Block

A building type that is linear in shape and stands free from adjacent buildings. The characteristics are:

- Not necessarily informed by aspects of the specific block

- Building appears as autonomous object multi-layered volume, whose presence can structure an entire urban area

- Usually cost-effective concrete slab building construction

- Comprises large number of dwelling units

- Usually stacked and systematic floor plans

- Units are arranged along a single or double-loaded internal access corridor

- Units usually face one orientation

Block-Edge

A Block-Edge is a building that completes one portion of an existing urban block or defines formerly undeveloped block edges. The housing type shares the same characteristics as the perimeter block typology.

Solitaire

A Solitaire is a fully detached building form. The characteristics are:

- Building form does not necessarily conform to characteristics of the existing block

- Building appears as autonomous object

- Building receives natural light from all orientations

- Voluminous urban presence usually on its own site

- Smaller in scale than linear blocks and high-rise towers

Space-Enclosing Structure

A Space-Enclosing Structure is a building or buildings that create and enclose open spaces. The characteristics are:

- A version of linear block that is bent, angular, sinuous or curved in building form

- Building form envelops a semi-public or private open, outdoor space

- Can be a single building that folds or contours to create one or many open spaces

- Can be a series of similar shape buildings that form an enclosure around one or many open spaces

- Building form does not necessarily conform to characteristics of the existing block

Kyosho Jutaku

A *Kyosho Jutaku* is a fully detached building form. The characteristics are:

- Not informed by characteristics of the specific block

- Building is autonomous object

- Single-family house found in Japan

- Small and often odd-shaped size lot and building footprint

- Building area of 100 square metres (1,000 square feet) or less

High-Rise Tower

A High-Rise Tower building form is vertical, high in storeys and stands free from adjacent buildings. The characteristics are:

- Building appears as autonomous object

- Building receives natural light from all orientations

- Comprises large number of dwelling units

- Stacks the highest possible number of identical or similar floor plans one above the other

- Units are grouped around a central core of elevators and stairwells

- Units usually face one, sometimes two, orientations

- Parking and amenities are generally integrated into the building

Unit Floor Plan Types

Unit floor plans are the organisation of domestic functions within a dwelling unit. The layout can occur in different arrangements and can be numerous in configurations. There are many unit floor plan types and many are flexible to interpret different ways to inhabit space and create ways of dwelling. The following list is not absolute and does not represent all the many different and diverse unit floor plan types.

Corridor

Corridor units are organised along a corridor. The characteristics are:

- Unit rooms are lined up on one or both side of a corridor
- Sole purpose of the corridor is to provide access to rooms

Dividing Elements

Dividing Elements are units that have a large, open space with a prefabricated dividing element to separate a space into two, and have an encircling circulation

Centre Living Space

Centre Living Spaces are units that have a living room at the centre of the plan. The characteristics are:

- All rooms circulate through the living room
- Living room gains in floor area due to absence of corridor access

Separated Rooms

Separated Rooms have separate areas for each different function and create very private spaces.

Circular Path

Circular Path units create pathways of access into all rooms. The characteristics are:

- Every room can be reached through more than one access route
- Users can circumnavigate the entire unit

Access Type (Interior Building)

The path that leads to each dwelling unit represents the internal access system for multi-unit housing.

Vertical

Vertical access is dwelling units that open around a common vertical circulation. The characteristics are:

- Access shared by one to four units

- Direct entry from access into one to four units

Horizontal

Horizontal access is exemplified by dwelling units that are grouped around a common horizontal circulation. The characteristics are:

- Corridor connects units to vertical circulation

- Access shared by multiple units

- Direct entry by way of corridor

Combination

Combination access is exemplified by dwelling units that are grouped around either a common vertical access or a horizontal access in the same building. The characteristics are:

- Vertical access shared by some units

- Horizontal access shared by some units

Corridors

Dividing Elements

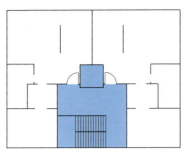

Vertical

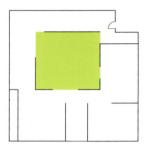

Centre Living Space

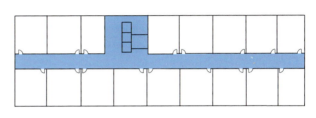

Horizontal

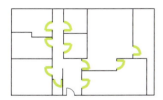

Separated Rooms

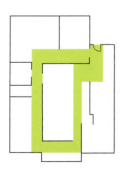

Circular Path

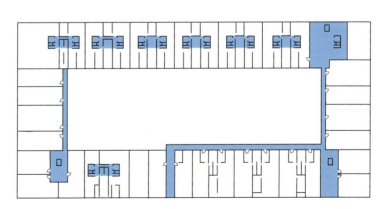

Combination

Unit Floor Plan Typology

Access Typology

Three-storey back-to-back at the rear of 12–13 Upper Priory, c.1872

BIRMINGHAM

Circa 1800 to 1880
Back-to-backs

The Industrial Revolution outfitted Britain with innovative advances in many economic sectors and the country was immensely transformed in all aspects of society. The most dramatic changes happened in the countryside, where many rural landscapes became modernised. The breakthrough developments resulted in new and different work opportunities, and lifestyles and living configurations for many of its inhabitants were drastically affected and altered.

During the Industrial Revolution, the invention of steam power remade manufacturing and mass production, and factories, factory work and factory workers, were abundant. During the intense industrialisation age, many rural areas grew into small towns and existing towns expanded and became small cities. As the accumulation of rural inhabitants migrated to cities in search of factory employment, so began the phenomenon of urbanisation—the rise of cities and the planning and constructing of new housing developments to accommodate the great change.

With the movement of people away from the countryside and into cities for factory work, there was now a decisive need to plan, organise and design dwellings to accommodate the new populations of workers and their families. New housing for factory workers was formulated by factory owners, who arranged for their labourers to live in close proximity to their workplace, or built by developers who perceived the need for housing as a business opportunity. The city of Birmingham was one of the first cities to experience a flux of migrant workers and the new type of housing stock that was created were back-to-backs. Birmingham was a developing metropolis where the emergence of city and housing forged a profound start.

Birmingham Back-to-backs Characteristics

Back-to-backs are a type of row housing development that dates back to the late 1700s. The name derives from rows of dwelling units that were constructed back to back from one another. The key characteristics are:

- Economical housing solution to accommodate urban working poor in late 1700s and mid-1800s England

- Back of one house joined onto the back of another house

- Built at right angles to street and were separated from each other by narrow alleys or courtyards

- Dwelling units were attached on three sides to neighbouring units, except the end units

- Dwelling units stacked atop one another two or three storeys in height

- Exterior communal sanitary facilities

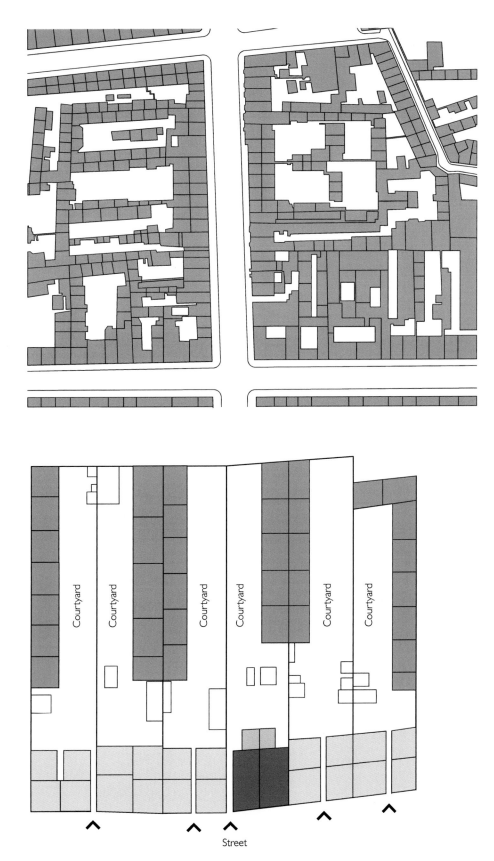

Courtyard Courtyard Courtyard Courtyard Courtyard Courtyard

Street

Three-Storey Back-to-Back Houses
Two-Storey Back-to-Back Houses
"Through" Houses

Urban Scale and Density

Court in Rupert Street, Nechells, 1908

During the late 1700s and mid-1800s, back-to-backs were a response to a particular housing need. The typology was the most economical and practical solution to housing; first, for the newly arrived workers and their families from the countryside into the city for employment, and later, for the urban working poor and their families who had settled themselves working in the city. The development of back-to-backs spread quickly and thousands of back-to-backs soon occupied the city's many vacant lots and back gardens.

Back-to-backs were extremely practical and economical to build in terms of land use and construction materials. The housing type was a group of two- or three-storey brick houses that surrounded a common courtyard on a piece of available land. The need to rapidly fabricate back-to-backs meant that little attention was made to properly prepare the building site and often the land was not adequately levelled. The inattentive construction practice resulted in unsanitary water seepage and collection into cellars and ground-level dwelling units.

Back-to-backs were constructed of brickwork for its cost-effectiveness and quick construction. The higher standards of country house construction were now replaced by inferior building practices to meet the growing demand for quick living accommodations. The economical use of the back-to-backs' tight building footprints and construction materials to create small, scant, and banal living quarters contrasted harshly with the idyllic single-family countryside houses the workers were used to. The severely reduced standards in housing resulted in bleak living conditions for the migrant workers and their families.

Building Components and Organisation

Courtyard

Back-to-back developments had a distinctive arrangement. The two- or three-storey brick houses surrounded a communal courtyard and were built upon a rectangular- or irregular-shaped lot. The housing type was adaptable to fit onto any shape land to better maximise development prospects in the city. The productivity, together with the asymmetrical configuration of the city blocks and streets, often led to irregular and different sized courtyard forms and layouts.

All back-to-backs were planned and built at right angles to a street and separated from each other by narrow alleyways or courtyards. These courtyards, also commonly known as "courts", were systematically numbered along a street and made up part of each back-to-backs postal address. The courts varied in size and had a few or many dwelling units on it depending on the number of units that shared it and the shape or confines of the building lot. One court would have as few as four dwelling units and accommodate a few families, while another court could have as many as twenty dwelling units and house up to a hundred families. The variations in court size, number of dwelling units, number of facilities and services, and proximity to facilities and services, were taken into consideration and reflected into the rental value of the properties. For example, a court at a corner site with many dwelling units facing the street would be considered valuable and the landlord who administered the rent would take account of this fact.

2

5

5

5

2

5 5 5 5

2

4 above

4 above

3

3

1
4 above

1
4 above

3

3

1
4 above

1
4 above

3

3

2

1
4 above

1
4 above

3

3

5

5

1
4 above

1
4 above

3

3

2

Courtyard

1
4 above

1
4 above

Courtyard

1
4 above

1
4 above

Courtyard

3

3

3

3

1
4 above

1
4 above

1
4 above

1
4 above

3

3

3

3

3

3

3

3

1
4 above

1
4 above

1
4 above

1
4 above

Street

Ground Floor

1 Living Room
2 Toilets
3 Kitchen
4 Bedroom
5 Wash House

Two-Storey Back-to-backs

Layout

Each back-to-back dwelling unit had a cellar and a ground floor, with another one or two storeys above, making back-to-backs totalling two or three storeys in height. Each unit shared a common brick wall with its neighboring units on three sides–left, back, and right sides. The brick walls were constructed of single wythe brick masonry and used as both external and internal wall construction. Door and window openings for light and air were only on the front side of each unit, either facing the street or the courtyard, making natural day lighting, air ventilation, and circulation barely sufficient. Dwelling units had dim lighting levels and stagnant air movement.

There were two types of two- or three-storey stacked dwelling units: multiple units and single units. The multiple units housed one individual or one small family per floor and access to each unit was by a common and narrow wooden staircase in the hallway. These units did not offer their occupants much privacy, as they were comprised of one, un-partitioned room where eating, living, and sleeping areas overlapped. Usually these units had enough space for a table, two chairs or a bench, and a bed. The single units were designed and intended to house one large family. There was more privacy and space in these units because the floors separated their eating, living and sleeping areas. Each dwelling unit, regardless of whether it was multiple or single, had fireplaces built in as a source for heating the room and for boiling hot water.

Alongside two- and three-storey back-to-back houses, some courts often had a through house. The through house unit had a door that faced the street and another that faced the courtyard so there was through access from street to courtyard through the unit. These units were usually larger in size and rented by one large family or shared by different families.

Alley Passage

The way into the communal courtyard, and to the units that entered from the courts, was through a narrow, arched passageway, commonly known as an alley or alleyway, which was formed between two front units. The entryway was very slender, usually less than a metre (approximately 3 feet) wide and was the only entry into and out of the courtyard. Some courts had the alley passage entrance secured with a wood door, while in others it was left open. The single, tight pathway made it difficult for inhabitants to quickly evacuate to the street for safely in events of emergencies. Fires in the courtyard or in units accessed through the courtyard were often fatal.

Big Yard

The external communal courtyard was also known as the "big yard". It was paved in brick and served a variety of functions. It housed the shared sanitary facilities—bathing and laundry wash houses and dry earth toilets, water pump, water pipe, drain, ash pit, clothes line, and livestock enclosures. The water pump in the courtyard was a convenient alternative to lining up at the local water station, but drainage consisted of a narrow channel that ran across the court towards the fresh water source. Rainwater from the roofs and sullied waters from the bathing and laundry wash houses flowed into the same area as the drinking water, putting in jeopardy the clean water used for consumption.

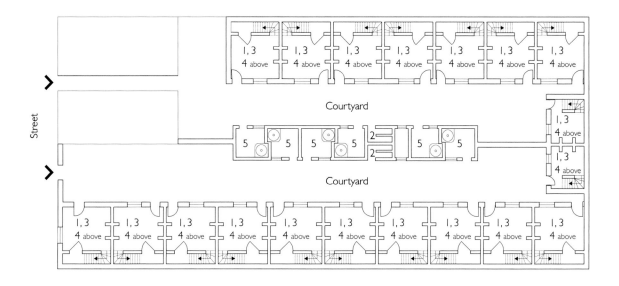

Ground Floor

Two-Storey Back-to-backs

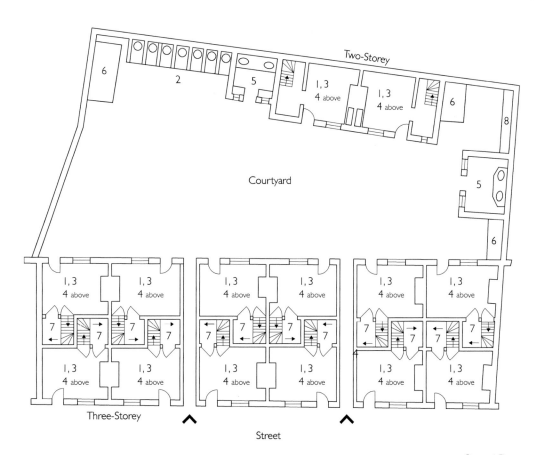

1 Living Room
2 Toilets
3 Kitchen
4 Bedroom
5 Wash House
6 Shed
7 Cellar Access
8 Ash Bins

Ground Floor

Two and Three-Storey Back-to-backs

178–184 Newhall Street, 1904

Court in William Street, 1905

10 Court, Cheapside, 1905

2 Court, Allison Street, 1905

The big yard was also a well-used place for leisure and socialising. The courtyard held a combination of public and private spaces and showed that living in back-to-backs was a very communal and collective understanding and organisation. The big yard was where all residents encountered one another when they went to and from their units, pumped water, did their laundry, and used the wash house and toilets. The courtyard was also a safe place for the resident children to play. Instead of playing outside on the busy streets, the internal courtyard provided a safe outdoor area for the children and the contained space allowed parents and neighbours to keep a close watch. All these activities created a sense of community and security among its residents.

Interiors

The idea of the back-to-backs unit was to offer working-class families in their newly adopted city a similar ideal to what they had in the countryside—a home of their own. Sometimes construed as "urban cottages", the fact the residents had to share sanitary facilities, and the whole family might have shared one bedroom, a sense of individuality was evident in the interiors of the home. Embellishment of the home was a common practice in the back-to-backs. Many families painted, whitewashed, or wallpapered their walls in an effort to make their space appear less utilitarian and more personal and comfortable. All homes were built with the same brick-walled interior with a fireplace connecting a black-leaded range. The range had a fire basket in its centre and served as the heating and cooking source for the home. Above the range was a mantel used to display the family's personal effects—photos, clock, vase, candlesticks, and such ornaments. The wooden front doors were often ill fitting and thin and let in drafts in the colder months. Often a curtain was hung on the inside of the door to keep out the cold in the winter.

Typical Unit Floor Plan Type

The ground floors of back-to-backs could be considered an early form of centre living space. There was not enough floor area to have internal walls to partition into separate areas for different functions. The entire floor was one big room where all family activities took place. It was a common area used for living, eating, and cooking and the upstairs was used for sleeping.

Access Type

Each back-to-backs unit was accessed directly from the street or courtyard and did not conform to any later established access type.

Construction Materials

Back-to-backs were constructed of single wythe brick masonry. Brick was a readily available material and cost effective, and brickwork could be easily and hastily applied without much need for attention. The units had wooden entrance doors and sash windows in wood frames, and the interiors had wood plank floors and painted walls.

Children's home-work, 1908: Making Bundles of Firewood

Home-working, 1908: Pearl Button Carding

Back-to-back Birmingham Reconstruction

Back-to-back Birmingham Reconstruction

SAME
CORPORAT

Fry's Chocolate

ASK
FOR

R. WHITES

LEMONADE
GINGER BEER
SODA WATER
AMERICAN
CREAM SODA
KAOLA &c

HUDSON
SOA

ROYAL
COFFEE

33–35 Cheapside Street frontages, 1904

Owners, Landlords, Developers, Reformers

Britain experienced industrialisation at rapid speed and worker families were arriving into cities for new opportunities just as quickly. Many landowners began to convert their homes into lodging to help fill the housing need, and also to rent out rooms and make a profit. Gardens were paved and built over to form new homes and walls were added in existing homes to partition new units. Such conversions during this time were common. Birmingham was an unincorporated city and had little municipal enforcement to regulate landowners who turned their private property into rental properties. Soon the free market captivated other homeowners and many began to merge or subdivide their land to build rental housing and became landlords. The new business model rewarded landowners with a flush of income, but their unplanned and unmanaged expansion also unknowingly started to negatively reshape the pattern of the city and steeply increase its land values.

Augustus Gough-Calthorpe, 6th Baron Calthorpe

Lord Calthorpe was a well-known landlord in Birmingham. He was a wealthy man who did not live in Birmingham, but purchased vast amounts of land in the city. He developed some of his plots into rental housing stock, which yielded a profit, and thus he repeated the process. Through his broad parcel acquisitions and large sums of return on investment, he upset many locals with his method of business. His critics disapproved of his absentee landlord approach and blamed him for intruding on their city and driving up real estate prices. There were others who were equally dismayed, but placed the fault on people of Birmingham to allow Lord Calthorpe to descend upon and tarnish their city.

Congestion

By the early 1800s, two-thirds of Birmingham's 60,000 inhabitants were living in back-to-backs. Survey maps during this time show Birmingham's city centre clogged with back-to-back developments. Even with so many back-to-backs, the housing units grew congested and dwelling units that were designed to house individuals and small families were instead housing multiple people and large families, and the units intended to house one large family were housing more than one family at a time. Oil lamps and candles, once used without much danger for illumination, now posed a fire hazard in the confined living quarters that were stuffed with people and possessions. The unit's four sides of single wythe brick masonry walls drew up moisture from the lower floors and constantly felt damp, and odours, insects, and vermin eventually crept their way in through cracks and crevices in the walls. The communal areas that were once manageable to maintain and keep tidy were now constantly dirty, dank, and foul smelling.

By 1851, Birmingham's population had swelled to over 520,000 inhabitants. Back-to-back developments were now overpopulated, building and living conditions deteriorated rapidly, and entire neighbourhoods became slum dwellings. Dwelling units were filled many times beyond their planned capacity and cellars that were once used as storage were now used as dwelling units, which were dank places that often flooded when it rained, making them an even more threatening place to reside. Communal facilities designed for a determined number of occupants were overwhelmed. A few hundred people now shared a limited number of sanitary facilities, and toilets regularly overflowed; the local water source became a breeding ground for diseases, and illnesses were rampant. Epidemics of measles, smallpox, typhoid, tuberculosis, and cholera spread through the courts at regular intervals. The overcrowded living quarters and their stresses devastated the health of Birmingham and finally led to the demise of the housing type. The relentless sanitation and health problems that plagued the back-to-backs eventually forced the city to stop their construction. By the 1870s, Birmingham council had banned the construction of its typology and over several more decades, neighbourhoods of courts were demolished to make way for new housing.

Government Departments, Policies, and Regulations

The government recognised the housing problems of overcrowding and unhealthy living standards in back-to-backs and began to enact laws to protect the urban working poor and their families.

The 1855 Nuisance Removal and Disease Prevention Act

After the cholera epidemic had decimated much of the population a few years earlier, the government imposed a law that addressed the unsanitary conditions in overcrowded housing developments. In 1855, the government passed an act to monitor public health and sanitation in housing units. The new law called for city officials to perform house-to-house inspections and fine any units that were found to be in non-compliance with the law.

The 1875 Artisans' and Labourers' Dwelling Improvement Act

The Artisans' and Labourers' Dwelling Improvement Act was created to abolish slum areas and dwellings that were deemed a public health threat. The name of the act was derived from the majority of the occupations of inhabitants living in overcrowded housing buildings. The act granted the right to demolish areas where housing was considered unfit for human habitation, or if poor housing was the cause of poor health. It permitted the sale of slum dwellings and allowed the sites to be redeveloped into new housing construction by local authorities. Under the act, existing and new housing must fulfil basic health and safety requirements. The adoption of the act was not well seized. Local authorities had to purchase the damaged land and property at market rates and pay for the demolition, which made initial costs acutely cost prohibitive.

Present Day

By the 1970s, almost all back-to-backs had been demolished to make way for new housing stock. The National Trust has now saved and restored Birmingham's last surviving nineteenth century back-to-back courtyard. The row of houses now functions as an education centre and museum that commemorates the back-to-backs' importance in history, and offers public tours. A few of the houses also function as an inn and can be reserved for overnight accommodations to learn the full experience of living in a back-to-back.

Lawrence Street

LONDON

Circa 1840 to 1900
London Tenement

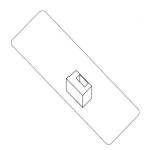

In mid-1800's London, the city encountered an extensive housing shortage. Many migrant workers from proximate towns and countryside descended upon the city for employment opportunities, and in turn, required dwelling. The need for housing was made even more apparent when construction of the London railroads bulldozed streets and forced existing citizens out of their homes. Housing during this time was in short supply and high in demand and accommodations that were available increased rents and their rooms grew crowded. New housing was urgently needed and the city's existing street and block layout restricted the lot and size of new developments. The conditions led to a new type of housing in the city—tenement, multi-storeyed, multi-dwelling unit typology.

The lack of available housing in London, especially for the working poor, was blatant and problematic. The onerous situation evaded the city's attempt to regulate housing to thwart off the crisis, and soon after, charitable organisations became involved in another effort to address and contain the plight. Several philanthropic establishments created model housing and theories designed to house the working poor. Model housing was a physical extension that promoted the doctrine of the charitable organisation. The model house was often in the form of a tenement building that was well built, clean, organised, and comfortable, and the belief was that good homes would cultivate good citizens. In a good home, the working poor would live a civilised life, and in exchange, investors and shareholders of the model housing would see a return from the rent. The hope was also that the model housing would influence other landlords to adopt the same practice and philosophy.

London Tenement Characteristics

A London tenement is a single building five to six storeys in height above a basement. The key characteristics are:

- Built to house the urban working poor in mid-1800s London

- Sturdy masonry construction

- Communal sanitary facilities and kitchens on each floor

- Communal courtyard

- Moderately well lit and ventilated

During this housing shortage, a number of philanthropic establishments initiated model housing catering to the working poor. Model housing consisted of cottages and tenements for families and for single persons. Among the charitable organisations that came to the aid of the people included the General Society for Improving the Dwellings of the Working Classes, Improved Industrial Dwellings Company, Metropolitan Association for Improving the Dwellings of the Industrious Classes, Society for Improving the Condition of the Labouring Classes, and Peabody Donation Fund.

All these organisations shared similar model housing designs and ideals to shelter the working poor. The model housing was all well constructed and was required to be clean and orderly, and the trust was that a good home would improve the life of its occupants. The organisations hired architects to design the model housing and credit was given to their work—unlike in previous times, when the builders were unidentified masonry workers and carpentry tradesmen.

Building Components and Organisation

Layout

London tenement buildings were constructed in brick and had large, sash windows that were found in the existing London street context and neighbouring building façades. The buildings were five to six storeys in height and consisted of a basement, ground floor, dwelling unit floors, indoor sanitary facilities, courtyard, and staircase. A typical dwelling unit had a living area, kitchen, and bedroom and there was access to communal toilets and a wash house on each floor. Units had windows that faced the courtyard or street or both and there was ample daylight and ventilation in every unit. Toilets were often built against an external wall to allow for a window to provide natural light and ventilation.

Staircase

London tenements were built before the invention of the elevator and a wide, communal staircase served as the shared vertical circulation. The staircase was constructed of stone with stone or iron balustrades and connected the residential floors with the ground floor entrance. In the time of a communal staircase as vertical circulation, the lower floors were more desirable and expensive to rent than the top floors. The bottom floors usually housed the middle-income class, while the top floors usually housed the working-class poor. Regardless of the social economic class distinction, the shared staircase served as an informal and important social centre where all residents passed and greeted one another on a regular basis.

Courtyard

A London tenement often featured a communal courtyard. The courtyard was either an enclosed internal space located within the tenement building or it was an external space formed by tenement buildings arranged in a square or rectangle around it. The courtyard was a place of leisure where neighbours were able to socialise with one another and watch their children play. The courtyard was a popular play area for children and a safe alternative to the streets in which to play. The confined space also allowed the children to be easily watched and cared for by parents and neighbours.

Superintendent

A full-time superintendent often lived among the tenants in the same building. The responsibility of the superintendent was to manage and maintain the building and building property and to collect the rent. The presence of a building manager living among the tenants provided a sense of protection for the building and its tenants.

Case Studies

The Model Lodging House for Men

Architect: Henry Roberts
Completed: 1847

The Model Lodging House for Men was built by the Society for Improving the Condition of the Labouring Classes, one of the first philanthropic organisations that provided safe and clean accommodations for urban workers and their families. The Model Lodging House for Men was a five-storey building of load-bearing masonry construction that consisted of a basement with a kitchen and washing facilities, ground floor with a large communal living room, and two floors of dormitories with shared toilets and washhouse on each floor, and a communal staircase. The toilets and washhouses had operable windows to allow for ventilation. The dormitories were partitioned into twenty-six cubicle-like rooms that measured approximately 2.5 metres (9 feet) long and 1.5 metres (5 feet) wide. The windows of the building only faced the street and only half the dormitory cubicles had access to daylight and ventilation.

Model Houses for Families

Architect: Henry Roberts
Completed: 1850

Model Houses for Families was built by the Society for Improving the Condition of the Labouring Classes. Model Houses for Families was five storeys in height with load-bearing masonry construction, and the external façades were of yellow stock brick with rusticated stucco bands. The building consisted of a basement, with 45 dwelling units that overlooked an enclosed communal courtyard and had a wide communal staircase that linked each floor to one another and the street. A typical unit had a living area, kitchen, toilet, and one or two bedrooms and there was a large, shared wash house on each floor. All units had sash windows that faced the street and open gallery to the courtyard, so there was natural daylight and cross-ventilation in every unit. The self-contained units had a toilet, and the size of the units and their facilities were very generous and revolutionary for worker housing at the time. The private unit toilets and communal wash house had operable windows to allow for ventilation. Model Houses for Families became a guide and standard for other tenement buildings to base their design and construction.

The Average London Tenement Buildings

Many London tenement buildings erected during this time period were not as successful as Model Houses for Families. Other tenements aspired to replicate the design ideas and ideals of Model Houses for Families, but many scrimped on design or construction materials which led to their failure. Many of these aspirant tenements had reduced spatial standards, provided smaller unit layouts, narrower corridors and stairs, offered communal toilets, and did not house an on-site superintendent. The smaller units and communal toilets provided savings on construction cost and gains in rentable income as more units could be partitioned and rented out per floor. It was in some of these arrangements that tenements became overcrowded and slowly deteriorated into slum dwellings in certain parts of the city.

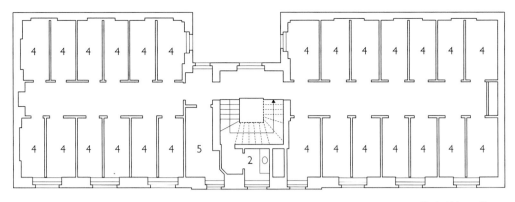

Typical Upper Floors

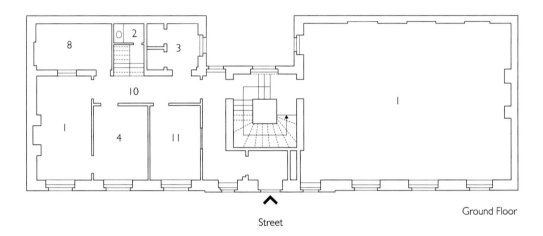

Street

Ground Floor

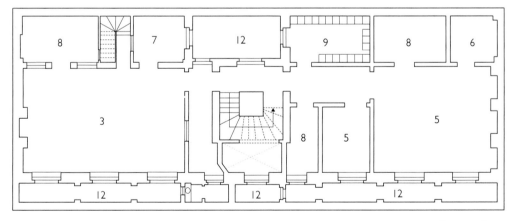

Basement Floor

1 Living Room
2 Toilet
3 Kitchen
4 Dormitory
5 Wash House
6 Drying Room
7 Cleaning Room
8 Storage
9 Pantry
10 Superintendent Unit
11 Office
12 Open Area

Model Lodging House for Men

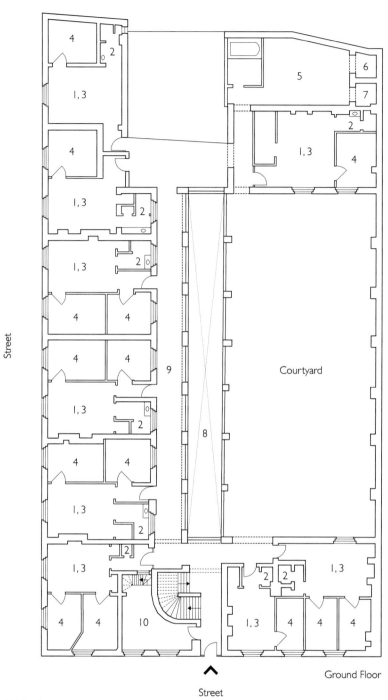

Street

Courtyard

Ground Floor

Street

1 Living Room
2 Toilet
3 Kitchen
4 Bedroom
5 Wash House
6 Coals
7 Dust
8 Sunken Area
9 Open Gallery
10 Superintendent Office, Unit Above

Model Houses for Families

Parnell House - former Model Houses for Families

Parnell House – former Model Houses for Families

Peabody Estates

The Peabody Donation Fund was a philanthropic organisation that was established in 1862 and provided accommodations for the city's working poor. Shortly after the organisation was established, it was renamed the Peabody Trust and the trustees commissioned architect Henry Astley Darbishire to design the tenement estates. Darbishire designed a standard plan that was based on the ideas of Model Houses for Families and the Peabody Trust used the design for more than forty years. The design was a rectangular volume that was four to six storeys in height. Each floor had ten dwelling units and a communal staircase connected all floors.

Darbishire designed all the estates for the Peabody Trust from 1864–1875. Each estate was characterised by its stocky build and austere brick façades. The estates consisted of blocks of buildings arranged around a common courtyard mostly used as a children's play area; each building was four to six storeys in height and housed over one hundred families. The buildings were separated from one another to enable natural daylight and through ventilation even to the lowest floors. Fencing of either woodwork or ironwork separated the buildings from the street and its main gates were locked nightly for the security of its residents.

In each estate's building, there were ten dwelling units per floor. Units ranged from one to four rooms, with living rooms measuring approximately 3.45 × 4 metres (11′4″ × 13′6″), bedrooms at 3 × 4 metres (9′9″ × 13′6″), and ceiling heights at 2.6 metres (8′6″). Each floor had shared sanitary facilities and the centralised location of communal facilities enabled easier inspection and maintenance of the areas. The top floor of the buildings housed communal wash houses and the buildings had garbage chutes that deposited trash directly to the ground level for collection. There was also a coal depository and baby carriage storage area on the ground floor.

Each estate had a resident superintendent and several porters to help manage the building. The responsibility of the superintendent was to review tenant applications, collect rent, keep records of residents, and administer the rules of the Peabody Trust. The residents also had their share of duties and responsibilities. Residents were expected to actively participate in building a safe sense of community and maintaining their home by taking turns sweeping corridors and stairs, cleaning sinks, and every Peabody Trust resident was required to be vaccinated against infectious diseases. The Peabody Trust regularly inspected their buildings for orderliness and cleanliness to ensure that the health of their buildings and tenants was maintained effectively. The routine building management style served the interests of the tenants and was part of the Peabody Trust mission.

The endeavours at housing the working poor were a great success for the Peabody Trust and their estates outperformed all other tenement developments at this time. The estates were held in high regard by local authorities and earned the reputation for good building design, management, and improvement to the health and virtue of its residents and their children. The Peabody Trust estates welcomed a wide range of working poor urban dwellers; among the residents were labourers, porters, coachmen, printers, bookbinders, messengers, hatters, and tailors.

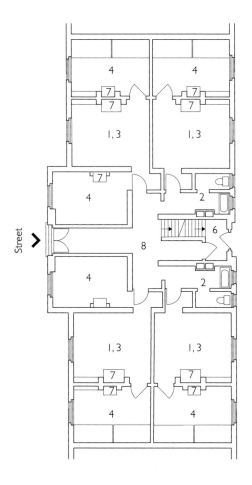

Ground Floor

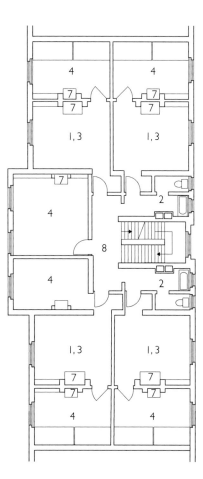

Typical Floors

1 Living Room
2 Bathroom
3 Kitchen
4 Bedroom
6 Cellar Access
7 Fireplace
8 Hallway

Peabody Trust Estate Standard Plan

Islington

Architect: Henry Astley Darbishire
Completed: 1865

The Islington estate consisted of four building blocks, each five storeys in height, arranged around a communal square courtyard. The architectural style was Italianate and the buildings had yellow stock brick façades and slate tiles on the roofs. There were shared laundries on the top floors of the buildings and the property had wrought iron railings that surrounded the estate. In 1866, the Islington estate was praised for its contribution to the good health and well-being of its inhabitants, especially the children, and the building design was used as a standard to plan other Peabody estates, as well as other housing developments throughout the city.

Shadwell

Architect: Henry Astley Darbishire
Completed: 1866

The Shadwell estate was built in three phases and consisted of four large blocks, north, south, east, and west, which formed a communal courtyard for the residents. Each block was six storeys in height, of Italianate architectural style with yellow stock brick façade design and the four blocks housed 195 families.

Lawrence Street

Architect: Henry Astley Darbishire
Completed: 1870

The Lawrence Street estate comprised four blocks and was built closer together than the previous developments. The four blocks formed a communal courtyard for the residents and it was well used by the resident children.

Blackfriars

Architect: Henry Astley Darbishire
Completed: 1871

Blackfriars was a nineteen-block estate and housed 384 dwelling units. In 1871, the *Architectural Journal* praised it for its spacious layout, surrounding trees, and its stronger feeling of home than evident in some of the earlier developments of Darbishire and the Peabody Trust.

Stamford

Architect: Henry Astley Darbishire
Completed: 1875

The Stamford estate comprised of four buildings, was five storeys in height and the buildings were built in the Italianate architectural style with yellow stock brick façade design. It was densely populated and housed 353 dwelling units.

Southwark Street

Architect: Henry Astley Darbishire
Completed: 1876

Southwark Street estate was opened in 1876 and comprised twelve blocks of twenty-two dwelling units in each block. In the 1960s, the estate was renovated and two blocks in the centre were demolished to create a playground for the children residents.

Wild Street

Architect: Henry Astley Darbishire
Completed: 1881

The Wild Street estate was built as part of the citywide effort to clear the area of slums. The Wild Street development comprised thirteen blocks, was six storeys in height and shared the same brick façade design.

Roscoe Street

Architect: Henry Astley Darbishire
Completed: 1883

The Roscoe Street estate was also a response to the city's call to rid the area of slum housing. The development comprised eleven blocks; each building was six-storeys in height, with solid brick façades and the property had wrought iron gates and fences. Each building had a laundry room, but the estate did not have a bath house. There was a coal storage that held up to twenty tonnes of coal and a pram shed that stored thirty-two baby carriages.

Rosendale Road

Architect: Victor Wilkins
Completed: 1902–1908

The Rosendale Road estate was built in the early 1900s and a new architect, Victor Wilkins, succeeded Henry Astley Darbishire as the Peabody Trust architect during this time. The Rosendale Road estate consisted of cottages and tenement building blocks, the buildings resembling the earlier designs of Darbishire except that the brick colour used was red instead of yellow. There was a communal staircase and variety of dwelling unit layouts that comprised studios and one- and two-bedroom arrangements. On each floor of the building were shared toilets and wash houses that had operable windows to allow for ventilation.

Bethnal Green

Architect: W.E. Wallis
Completed: 1910

The Bethnal Green estate was a series of buildings five storeys in height, with solid brick façades and the property had wrought iron gates and fences. The buildings had a communal laundry and bath house, but private toilets for each unit. There was a coal storage that held up to 25 tonnes of coal and a pram shed that stored 14 baby carriages. The units in the estate were larger than in previous developments, with an average living room size of 15 square metres (150 square feet) and average bedroom size of 11 square metres (117 square feet).

Fulham

Architect: Victor Wilkins
Completed: 1912

Fulham estate was opened in 1912 and was comprised 239 dwelling units. In the basement of two estates were social clubs for the residents, where they socialised and played billiards, darts, and cards. The estate also housed a separate bath house and laundry building.

Chelsea Manor Street

Architect: Victor Wilkins
Completed: 1931

Chelsea Manor Street was completed in 1931 and was comprised of eight blocks with 111 flats in each block. The units were self-contained with private toilet and kitchen.

Whitechapel

Southwark

Islington Estate

Wild Street

Shadwell Estate

Roscoe Street

Bethnal Green Estate

Stamford Street

Chelsea Manor

Fulham

Typical Floor Plan Type

The typical floor plan type could be considered a central living space. The living room and kitchen were in the centre of the unit, there was no corridor access, and the bedrooms circulated through the main living space.

Access Type

The access type for most London tenements was horizontal. From the communal staircase, there were long corridors to allow access to each dwelling unit.

Construction Materials

London tenements were constructed of masonry. The buildings were of load-bearing construction, considered well built and fireproof. The floors were built with iron girders and brick arches and there were water and gas pipes throughout the building that was formed of iron. The communal staircase was constructed of stone with stone or iron balustrades. On the exterior, the buildings had brick façades. Many had striated brickwork with stucco or decorative stone banding to interrupt the sameness in the brick pattern that stretched five or six storeys in height. Craftsmanship was valued and care was taken to ensure the buildings were built substantially in order to avoid the necessity of repairs.

Owners, Landlords, Developers, Reformers

George Peabody

George Peabody was a wealthy American businessman who saw the downfall of tenements and wanted to be a positive influence and contributory factor in its betterment. Peabody was an entrepreneur and banker who travelled to London for business, which was at that time one of the centres of international banking and finance, and became enthralled by the city. He decided to establish a permanent residence in the city and, while living among its citizens, he saw great injustice in the way the working poor were housed. He took it upon himself to take action for these people and became a great social reformer, pioneer of many great causes, and philanthropist. In 1862, he started an organisation called the Peabody Donation Fund whose mandate was to provide affordable and decent quality housing to accommodate the urban working poor. In 1862, the organisation was renamed the Peabody Trust and became the most generously endowed and efficiently managed housing association in London at the time.

Octavia Hill

During the same time as Peabody, another citizen who saw social injustice in housing London's labourers was Octavia Hill. She was a social reformer who devoted her life's work to developing social housing to improve the lives of the urban working poor, and she credited her grandfather for her devotion to the cause. Her grandfather, Thomas Southwood Smith, was a leading public health reformer and demonstrated how poor housing conditions and bad sanitation were the greatest threats to life in an industrial city.

Octavia Hill had a specific discontent with housing for the urban working poor; she abhorred the way some landlords routinely took advantage of their tenants and how the tenants were helpless in safeguarding themselves. Hill's solution to lift the injustice and oppression from the working poor was to become a landlord herself. Her aim was to operate a building management strategy that was positive and lawful. She wanted to become a role model landlord who would set an exemplary precedent and to educate and empower her residents to be good tenants, which would hopefully lead to them to be honourable citizens.

Hill pursued investors to help her secure property to manage. She found a financier in John Ruskin, the art critic, patron, and artist, who was impressed with her proposal and invested in her business plan with a five percent annual return on his investment. In 1865, Ruskin helped Hill purchase three run-down cottages of six rooms each in the affluent Marylebone area of London, and both Hill and Ruskin worked together to improve the properties. The cottages were quickly rehabilitated and rented out, and within one year, Hill was able to amass a surplus and Ruskin was able to collect his five percent return on investment. In 1866, Ruskin bought five more houses in the same neighbourhood to be placed under Hill's management. By 1874, Hill, with her vigilant and successful business management performance and achievements, was able to attract new backers, acquired fifteen more housing properties and was landlord to approximately 3,000 tenants. In 1884, Hill was invited to manage a large stock of properties held by the church group in England and Wales, the Ecclesiastical and Church Estates Commissioners for England. She aided them in the improvement of their existing conditions and became the voice for their tenants.

Octavia Hill's management style was personal. She was dedicated and cared for both her buildings and her tenants. She often acted more like a social worker than a landlord, and she believed that the people living in her buildings were equally as important an investment as her properties themselves. Hill maintained close contact with all her tenants and was strongly opposed to impersonal bureaucratic interventions in housing.

A pivotal aspect in Hill's management method was to train and employ tenants to help collect and balance the rent. Some tenants became proficient in managerial skills and were promoted to property managers. The idea to provide tenants with a sense of responsibility, belonging, and vested interested in managing their buildings made her properties a better, cleaner, and safer place in which to reside. Hill created most of the positions for the women in her buildings. Her goal was to encourage and embolden the independence of her female tenants and to provide them with a sense of pride and purpose in their community aside from their domestic lives. Hill also promoted voluntary work within the public. She donated her spare time to tenant associations and children's clubs. Leading by example, Hill's principles were that a person needed to be self-reliant and proactive in bettering themselves, and she firmly believed that people who refuse to exert themselves and rely solely on charity are useless to themselves and to society.

Another important condition Octavia Hill had for her buildings, and for the betterment of her tenants' health, was a need for open spaces. She regarded an area where residents have access to clean air and views for enjoyment a life-enhancing advantage. She demanded these spaces be incorporated in all her buildings and there had to be places to sit, play, stroll and a place comfortable enough to spend a whole day without effort or expense.

In addition to reforming housing standards and improving the lives of those who lived in her buildings, Octavia Hill also actively spoke out for society. She campaigned against building developments on existing woodlands and was one of the first to use the term "green belt" for the protected rural areas surrounding London. She campaigned against construction that would destroy places of natural beauty and historic interests for the nation. In 1894, she helped form a trust called "National Trust for Places of Historic Interest or National Beauty", whose concern was the protection of open spaces and endangered buildings. This became the National Trust, which today owns and protects many areas of outstanding beauty, in addition to a large number of historic properties. In 1865, Octavia Hill founded the Octavia Group.

Charles Booth

Charles Booth was a successful English businessman who later became a philanthropist and social researcher. Booth visited London, from Liverpool, on business trips and eventually made his home in London, where his social circle included Octavia Hill. In London, Booth saw the growing problem of poverty in the city and was openly critical of the government's collection of census on the problem, believed its statistical data were de-emphasised, and argued for its true descriptions.

In the late 1880s, Booth surveyed, analysed, and documented the life of the urban working poor in London. His investigation included housing, education, and occupation, and in 1889 he published his findings in *Life and Labour of the People in London.* The book was a multi-volume edition that featured color-coded maps of London's neighbourhoods indicating levels of poverty and wealth among its inhabitants. His research and maps revealed that 35 percent of the London population was living in inadequate housing and poverty, a figure much higher than the government's census figures. He used his discovery and conclusion to bring about awareness and help improve the lives of the urban working classes.

Architects

Henry Astley Darbishire

The Peabody Trust appointed Henry Astley Darbishire to design many of their estates. Darbishire became known as the Peabody architect and designed some of the earliest and most successful working class tenements for the Peabody Trust. He developed a standard plan that was modelled after the design ideas and ideals of Model Houses for Families, and the Peabody Trust used his design for more than forty years. Darbishire was mostly known for his work with the Peabody Trust, and he designed all their estates up until his death in 1889.

Victor Wilkins

Victor Wilkins was the second architect appointed by the Peabody Trust, succeeding Henry Astley Darbishire after his death. Wilkins was the winner of an architectural competition arranged by the Peabody Trust, and he designed estates for Peabody from the early 1900 for almost forty years.

Congestion

Two neighbourhoods in London that gained notoriety as the worst tenement areas in the city, or rookeries as the most squalid slums were called, were Old Nichol in Bethnal Green, in the East End, and St Giles in Central London.

Old Nichol

Old Nichol was an area of about 30 narrow blocks of dilapidated tenement buildings. It housed around 5,700 inhabitants and had a death rate that was almost double that of neighbouring areas. Overcrowding and inhumane living conditions were largely the cause of its demise, but it was also claimed that its inhabitants "lacked morals". The landlords paid little attention to their tenants or to the decay of their buildings. The rookeries were a profitable property in the city and the landlords capitalised on the despair of their tenants. The Bethnal Green Vestry acted as the local councillors and the men of the church, who had a reputation of being less than honest, had the power to oversee and control the area and its operation. In the 1850s, the Vestry repeatedly obstructed attempts by politicians to have the slum demolished. Their apathy to the blight of the slum added another misfortune for the residents of Old Nichol. By the 1890s, the Vestry had lost its hold and was replaced by the new and ambitious London County Council (LCC). The LCC demolished Old Nichol and rehoused the tenants, and the former absentee landlords tried to claim their share of profits, with the greediest landlords being from the Church of England's Commissioners. In 1900, the area was reshaped into tree-lined avenues. The only people who again did not gain from the transformation were the evicted tenants of Old Nichol. Many were too poor to move elsewhere and so they took up residency in neighbouring areas, which later also turned into slums.

St Giles

The St Giles area of Central London was another area in the city overrun with derelict tenement housing. The area housed 5,000 inhabitants and among the dwellers were alcoholics, drug addicts, prostitutes, and petty thieves. In between many tenements were narrow alleyways that accommodated liquor shops, brothels, and violent fights. The neighbourhood was often deemed too dangerous to be patrolled by police and became a haven for criminals. In the late 1840s, the city began a slum-clearing effort and new infrastructure and transit routes were planned through the neighbourhood. The inhabitants were forced to move and many took up residency in neighbouring areas, which later turned into new slums.

Government Departments, Policies and Regulations

The government recognised the housing problems of overcrowding and unhealthy living standards in tenements and began to establish organisations and laws to protect the urban working poor and their families.

1855: The Metropolitan Board of Works

The Metropolitan Board of Works (MBW) was formed in 1855 and was an appointed government body in London. The mandate of the organisation was to oversee the rapid growth of the city and provide strategic planning for its infrastructure and housing. The MBW attempted to provide model dwelling housing, but was unsuccessful due in part to corruption scandals and distrust amongst its citizens. The organisation ceased its business in 1889.

1855: The Nuisance Removal and Disease Prevention Act

After the cholera epidemic a few years earlier, the government finally feared the disease, how it easily spread in contaminated and overcrowded housing developments, and how it left devastating effects by eradicating the population. In 1855, the government modified and expanded a past act by imposing stricter sanctions to supervise public health and sanitation in this new law. This new act cited that overcrowding in housing was damaging to public health and made house-to-house inspections essential.

1875: The Artisans' and Labourers' Dwelling Improvement Act

The Artisans' and Labourers' Dwelling Improvement Act was created to abolish slum areas and dwellings that were deemed a public health threat. The act's name derived from the majority of the occupations of inhabitants living in overcrowded housing buildings. The act allowed the right to demolish areas where houses were considered unfit for human habitation, or if poor housing was the cause of poor health. It permitted the sale of slum areas and dwellings and enabled the sites to be redevelopment into new housing construction by local authorities. Under this act, existing and new housing must fulfill basic health and safety requirements. However, adoption of this act was passive—local authorities had to purchase the land and damaged property at market rates and pay for its demolition, making its start-up costs acutely expensive.

1889: London County Council

Formed in 1889 and functioning until 1965, LCC was London's top tier of local government. It was the first directly elected strategic local government body for the city and it replaced the traditional structure of administering local affairs through church parishes. The LCC elected its members and the assembly was responsible for transportation, housing, and city planning, and later, education. One of the council's most important roles during its early beginnings was an ambitious plan to redevelop the city starting with the clearing of slum areas and dwellings. In inner London, the council constructed new blocks of housing, and in the city's outskirts they built low-rise cottage estates. Around 9,000 inner city inhabitants that were disrupted by the redevelopment were compensated with temporary housing at the end of an LCC-constructed tramline, which transported the workers into the city core for work. This energetic revitalisation plan for the city raised the construction standards of its buildings and improved the living standards of its inhabitants.

1890: Housing of the Working Classes Branch of the London County Council

A new department was established within the LCC, and this new subsidiary set forth further to improve its housing stock and the living standards of its inhabitants. Their new plan cleared areas deemed unsanitary in inner London, slum dwellings, slaughterhouses, and factories that spewed pollutants, and built more new housing with healthy construction practices.

Present Day

Many of the tenement buildings from the 1800s have lasted for centuries and can be found in use as housing in London today. The Model House for Families still operates as housing. The building was acquired by Peabody in 1965 and has since been renamed Parnell House. Parnell House operates as rental housing, is managed by Peabody, and in 1974 was designated a heritage building. Many Peabody Trust estates have been modernised and still function as rental housing stock. Some have expanded to include more blocks and many have been designated heritage buildings. Today, the organisation is in existence and known as Peabody. Peabody continues to honour George Peabody's aim in providing people with access to affordable and clean housing in London. The organisation now owns and operates close to 30,000 dwelling units across London and offers a variety of community support for its residents.

The legacy of Octavia Hill now exists in a not-for-profit organisation called the Octavia Group. The group comprises of four subsidiaries, Octavia Housing, Octavia Living, Octavia Support, and Octavia Foundation. Octavia Housing provides affordable housing and manages around 4,700 properties in London, including original properties Octavia Hill supervised. In keeping with Hill's goals, residents in Octavia Housing are encouraged to participate in tending to the property or the business side of the property management. Octavia Living develops housing for the open market and assists people in all financial circumstances with help to attain home ownership. Octavia Support offers housing and services with different levels of care to seniors with complex needs, and Octavia Foundation is a charity that lends support to people affected by unemployment, ill health, social isolation, or low income. All four groups keep the spirit of Octavia Hill and help people create better lives for themselves and their communities.

Some of the tenement buildings are on the United Kingdom's Statutory List of Buildings of Special Architectural or Historic Interest and part of the National Inventory of Architectural Heritage. Parnell House is a listed heritage building in the London Borough of Camden. The building is a surviving example of successful urban dwelling units that provided accommodation for the working poor, and offers annual public tours into some of its dwelling units for visitors to experience themselves.

Rue Soufflot, c.1853–70

PARIS

Circa 1850 to 1870
Haussmann Apartment

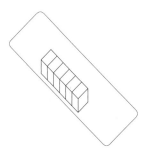

The city of Paris experienced an unprecedented population growth during the mid-1800s. With the Industrial Revolution, rail transport allowed an immense volume of migrant workers from nearby suburbs and villages to inundate the city and look for employment opportunities in its new industries. Between the city's population censuses taken in 1801 and 1851, the population of Paris doubled. In 1801, there were about 500,000 inhabitants, and then, in 1851, there were more than one million inhabitants in the city. The city's roughly 35 square kilometres (13 square miles) area now supported almost 30,000 people per square kilometre (80,000 people per square mile) which placed a strain on its streets, infrastructure, and especially on its housing stock.

The years 1852 to 1870 in France were known as the Second French Empire. During these eighteen years, when Napoleon III ruled the country, the layout and organisation of Paris remained mostly unchanged since the fifteenth century. He saw this as a need and opportunity to renew Paris and he marshalled one of the world's largest and most aggressive urban renewal projects. Napoleon III hired Baron Georges Eugene Haussmann, a public administrator, not an architect or urban planner, to undertake and oversee the extensive reconstruction and transformation project. Haussmann razed the city, tore down old medieval neighbourhoods and hundreds of old buildings, redesigned and rebuilt new infrastructure, monuments, and buildings, and, more specifically, created the iconic Haussmann apartment housing blocks.

The remaking of Paris was solely the vision of two men, Napoleon III and Baron Haussmann, but the design and skill was solely of one, Haussmann. Napoleon and Haussmann worked together to map out and mark up their aspirations for their city. They both envisioned an orderly, geometric city grid layout and used the Seine river as a natural geographical boundary, to divide old medieval neighbourhoods into districts, or *arrondissements*. They annexed nearby suburbs to enlarge the city, and from there, with Paris doubled in size, they reconceived and rebuilt the city. Napoleon III and Haussmann prioritised their wants and the first item on their agenda was to extend, widen, and beautify avenues and boulevards, illuminate city streets with gas lights, followed by new infrastructure for water, sewer, and gas networks, then building monuments and new public edifices, and finally multi-unit residential architecture to accommodate the crowded population. The renovation of Paris would make Paris a modern and beautiful city, changing its shape and perception.

In 1853, Haussmann began the "Renovation of Paris". Alongside the long list of plans for this major transformation, one other essential idea was to connect all the *arrondissements* together to make Paris look and feel like one unified city. To achieve the concept, Haussmann employed tens of thousands of labourers who worked the city into a geometric grid according to his plans. Haussmann carved out large arteries of avenues and boulevards, and shaped streets to run both east and west, and north and south. He ran all routes through the districts, connected them together, and radiated major avenues from the city centre to each *arrondissement*'s central points. Haussmann made all the avenues look alike by requiring buildings, including residential buildings, to be similar in height, style, and colour, and he lined the avenues with rows of leafy trees. It was here that the city began to develop an urban design aesthetic and identity, which reinforced his idea of one unified city.

With the new generous and vegetated streetscapes and improved infrastructure, the city inhabitant's previous health ailments, crowding stresses, and traffic congestion began to improve greatly. In balance with the expanded streets, there were also increases in residential building height. The medieval housing types were four to six, on average five storeys in height, half-timbered houses, supported on stone ground floors in crowded narrow streets, had a shop or workshop at street level and living quarters above. Among the city's newly designed character, a newer type of residential architecture was also introduced. In Haussmann's new residential building scheme, he attached an extra storey to the former housing stock skyline and this new, on average six-storey housing block, traced along the avenues. The additional height increased the amount of living space within the new city limits, alleviated overcrowding, and bettered public hygiene and sanitation. This new housing type is affectionately known as the Haussmann Apartment.

Haussmann Apartment Characteristics

The Haussmann apartment form is six storeys in height with a 45-degree sloped mansard roof. The key characteristics are:

- Building conforms to city's street pattern, orientation, height, style and colour

- Each block forms a unified whole

- Neoclassical style clad with cream-colored stone

- Shop on the street level

- Flat façades that are plain or elaborately detailed, with or without balconies

The Haussmann Apartment was known by a few different names. It was also referred to as Paris apartment, apartment house, maison flats, French flats, *immeuble* or a *maison-à-loyer*. Regardless of its name, it is a multi-unit rental residential building, five- to seven-, on average, six-storey building, built in a Neoclassical style and clad in cream-colored Lutetian limestone, also known as "Paris stone". The Haussmann Apartments were designed in blocks because Haussmann saw the street block holistically and as an entire architectural body. He treated buildings not as individual objects, but as elements in an integrated urban landscape. By designing the buildings in blocks, Haussmann also created the illusion of a larger building mass, and also by doing so, created a uniform, harmonious, and strong street façade presence. An emphasis on the horizontal can be seen in the façade, which followed the horizontal of the streets, adding to the symmetry and geometric unity that Haussmann set forth for the new Paris to sustain.

In the previous century, housing in Paris featured tall and narrow buildings that were four to six storeys in height, framed in wood, had wooden walls and floors, and rested on stone ground floors. The ground floor housed a shop and the shopkeeper lived above the shop. The floors above the shopkeeper were living units for other families and the top floor, the attic floor, was used for storage. By the 1850s, the size of the medieval residential building could not sufficiently accommodate the growing population and its demand on housing. After centuries of a narrow housing style, Haussmann adopted a wider approach and in his redesign, his residential buildings were one storey taller and wider than their predecessor.

Haussmann conceived of the idea for uniform residential architecture to line the streets, but it was the work of many different architects who actually designed the multitude of residential buildings and blocks.

Le Boulevard de Capucines, Okänd, 1890

Though Haussmann did not design the buildings himself, the name Haussmann Apartment was termed because the unified vision was his and the design had its origins in Haussmann's earlier architectural work, in his monuments and public buildings. These residential buildings were an integral presence along the lush avenues and boulevards, and they were an intrinsic aspect in Haussmann's renovation of Paris.

The Haussmann Apartment was designed for and inhabited by the residents of Paris. Most Parisians, regardless of their economic status, lived in Haussmann Apartment buildings. At the street level of each building were rows of orderly shops and a covered main entrance—*porte cochère*— for inhabitants and carriages. Above the shops was a rhythm of perfectly aligned windows, and sometimes balconies, and the windows were all set into matching cream-coloured stone façades. The top row differed in that it had dormer windows set into a dark-coloured slate or zinc-clad mansard roof. Haussmann's attention was on the horizontal, both in the façade with the horizontal lines of stonework and the balconies, and also spatially; Haussmann chose to centralise his residents horizontally rather than vertically, to maximise liveable space.

Building Components and Organisation

Layout

All Haussmann Apartments followed a standard spatial arrangement. The building was organised into three components: base, main body, and crown. The base contained the vaulted cellar, the ground floor, sometimes a mezzanine *entresol*, an arched main entrance (*porte cochère*), and communal courtyard. The cellar was used for shop storage and if the building had central heating, the coal-burning hearths. The ground floor housed a shop and shopkeeper's quarters, or if there was an *entresol*, that was additional storage for the shop, or used as shopkeeper's quarters, and a covered *porte cochère* entrance for residents and their horse carriages with access to the back courtyard and horse stables. The main body was the residential floors and consisted of first, second, and third floors. The first floor, if the building did not have an elevator, was the *étage noble*, the most desired and expensive floor to rent. The *étage noble* had the tallest floor–ceiling height, close to the street, which during this time was the life of the city, and was up only one flight of stairs. The owner, landlord, or principal high-paying tenant occupied the floor. If the building had an elevator, then the second floor became the *étage noble* with the taller floor–ceiling height and was the more desired and expensive to rent. The crown consisted of the fourth and attic floors. The fourth floor had the lowest ceilings in the building, and was the least expensive to rent, and the attic was used for resident storage and domestic help quarters.

Main Entrance

The main entrance, the *porte cochère*, was connected to the main vestibule and main staircase, the *grand éscalier*, and these three spaces were considered semi-public areas for both the building and the street. The arched *porte cochère* was lit by gas lighting and provided shelter when entering and exiting carriages from the street. It also allowed for access into the back courtyard and stables, and though it was closed off at night with an iron gate, it was paved in the same stone as the public street, and was seen as a continuation of the street. The unheated main vestibule and *grand éscalier* were located directly off the main entrance and, unless the weather was very inhospitable, the doors always remained open.

These interconnected areas created a place to socialise with neighbourhood acquaintances, building neighbours, concierge, trades, and domestic help.

Staircase

The main staircase, the *grand éscalier*, was located directly off the main entrance. With or without elevators in the building, the main communal staircase connected the residential floors with the ground floor vestibule. The *grand éscalier* was constructed of stone and had woodwork detailing. The stair was wide enough to fit two people comfortably and served as an informal and important social centre where all the building residents passed and greeted one another on a regular basis. Apart from the main staircase, there were usually one or two other smaller staircases in the building. The narrower, secondary staircases were located toward the back of the building and were used by tradesmen and domestic help.

Façades

Most of the façades of Haussmann's residential buildings were designed in the Neoclassical architecture style. Haussmann perceived that the experience of neatly aligned rows of a repetitive housing type in the same architectural fashion would help strengthen his look and feel of a unified Paris. The use of the same type of façade enabled the cost for the buildings to be more economical to construct and the buildings would appear "classical". The façades all had the same Lutetian limestone and mansard roof, but the use of balconies and how elaborate the balconies were detailed, differed between the different types of Haussmann Apartment buildings.

The façades were all faced in Lutetian limestone, a cream-coloured limestone that ranges in hue from light yellow to warm grey and is native to Paris. The stone had been used in building construction since ancient Roman times (Lutetia was the Latin name for Paris). It was a local, economical, and sustainable building material at the time and Haussmann used it extensively for much of his renovation of Paris. The façade embodied rows of windows and that reduced the amount of stone required to clad the entire face.

Roofs

The mansard roof, also known as a French roof, topped most of the Haussmann residential buildings. This type of roof, named after the French architect François Mansart who popularised it in his buildings in the early 1600s, has a distinct character of four, two-tiered, tall, and steeply sloping sides with dormer windows on the lower tier. The steep slope profile, which extended within 45 degrees from the cornice of the roof, allowed daylight to reach the sidewalks below and the interior of the mansard roof provided a usable, yet low, floor–ceiling space and enabled the creation of a habitable attic space.

Un locataire qui doit trois termes.

Un locataire qui doit trois termes, Locataires et
Propriétaires

Un locataire qui paye exactement son terme

Un locataire qui paye exactement son terme, Locataires
et Propriétaires

Tableau de Paris, Paris, 1852

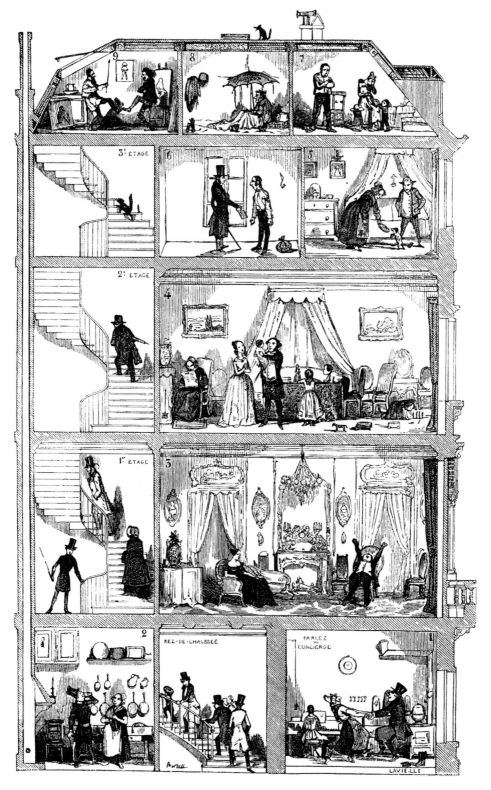

Tableau de Paris, Paris, 1852

PARIS: HAUSSMANN APARTMENT **67**

Types of Haussmann Apartment

Though the Haussmann residential buildings were very similar in building organisation, material and construction, they did vary slightly in design to reflect or attract the different socio-economic class of people living in them. Though the Haussmann Apartments predominately housed the Parisian middle class, the buildings were differentiated by the detailing to their façades and were categorised into 1st, 2nd, and 3rd class buildings.

1st Class

The 1st class Haussmann Apartment primarily housed the upper-middle class. These buildings had ornate adornments of sculptured friezes, embellished columns, and elaborate ironwork balconies and the residential floors were designed to house one family per floor. The base organisation remained typical: at the ground floor were shops, shopkeeper's quarters, *porte cochère*, and communal courtyard. The main body organisation still housed the first floor with the owner or landlord resident. The second floor, *étage noble*, was the tallest of all the residential floors and was more desirable and expensive to rent. It was separated by two levels from the ground floor, had better views, more privacy and fresh air and natural light, and had a detailed wrought iron balcony and elaborate cut stonework around the windows. It was not uncommon to see a balcony on the third and fourth floors, but with less decorative detailing than the second floor. The attic floor in the crown had a similar style balcony to the third and fourth floors and was the width of the building, and held resident storage and domestic help quarters. It was customary to provide two domestic help bedrooms for each apartment unit, and the service staircases linked the attic space to the kitchens of the apartment units below.

The spatial organisation of these dwelling unit layouts was well defined, traditional, formal, and generous. These dwelling units had clearly arranged and distinct zones, such as social, service, and personal zones. The building's grand staircase or elevator had direct access to the unit's front entrance, where it was illuminated with gas lighting. There was a formal entrance area and hallway to receive guests; several rooms to entertain and socialise; a dining room; a kitchen with running water, hooded wood or coal stove, ice chest, cupboards, and utensil rack, where domestic help prepared food and where they would access through its adjacent narrow back staircase; four to five bedrooms; toilet rooms; and there were generously proportioned windows in all four orientations throughout the unit for natural daylight and cross-ventilation.

2nd Class

The 2nd class Haussmann Apartment primarily housed the middle class. These building façades were less ornate, but had balconies and the residential floors had two to four units per floor, designed to house two to four families on each floor. The base organisation remained similar to 1st class. At the ground floor were shops, shopkeeper's quarters, *porte cochère*, and communal courtyard. The main body organisation housed the first floor with the owner or landlord resident. The second floor, *étage noble*, was the tallest of the residential floors, more desirable and expensive to rent, and had a wrought iron balcony and stonework around the windows. The third and fourth floors often had a balcony, but with less decorative detailing than the second floor. The attic floor in the crown had a similar style balcony to the third and fourth floors and was the width of the building. The attic comprised a combination of resident storage, servant quarters, and rentable dwelling units. In the main body, on the residential floors, the dwelling units that faced the street were more expensive to rent than those that overlooked the courtyard.

The layout of each dwelling unit was comfortable and less formal. The building's grand staircase, series of staircases, or elevator opened onto a shared corridor that was lit with gas lighting, and each dwelling unit was accessed from there. In each unit, there was a small formal entrance to receive guests; a larger room to entertain; dining room; kitchen; two to three bedrooms; a toilet room; and generously proportioned windows that faced two orientations throughout the unit, for natural daylight and cross-ventilation.

3rd Class

The 3rd class Haussmann Apartment primarily housed the lower-middle class. These buildings often did not have balconies or stonework, were smaller than the 1st and 2nd class buildings, and had two to three units per floor, designed to house individuals or one small family per floor. The base organisation housed ground floor shops, shopkeeper's quarters, and *porte cochère*. The main body organisation housed the first floor, *bel étage*, with a taller floor–ceiling height and was occupied by the owner or landlord. The second to attic floors were residential, the attic being divided into numerous dwelling units. The attics had the lowest ceiling heights and were the least expensive to rent in the building. Usually artists, craftsmen, and the working poor occupied these units.

The layout of each dwelling unit was adequate. The building's grand staircase or elevator opened onto a shared corridor that was lit with gas, from where each dwelling unit was accessed. In each unit there was a corridor entrance, a larger room to entertain, kitchen, one or two bedrooms, and toilet room. It had generously proportioned windows that faced two orientations, one of which faced a small internal courtyard, for natural daylight and cross-ventilation.

Modern Conveniences

In the previous period of housing, infrastructure for pipes, shafts, running water, and sanitary facilities were already in place but during the Second French Empire, modern amenities and mechanical conveniences were introduced. Heating a home was a necessity, and during this time central heating was popularised. The fireplace was still a common source of heating, but now it played a less significant role. The fireplace could almost be considered to have evolved into a highly ornate piece of furnishing in the grand salon. Traditional design and materials used to construct the fireplaces were replaced with cut stone to imitate and replicate the Neoclassical combination of pilasters and entablatures of the external façade. The firebox was also lined in cut stone, the opening was trimmed in metal, and the dampers were controlled with chain and counterweights.

At this time, in the kitchen, the stove evolved into another enhancement—a heavy, freestanding unit made of cast-iron. The stationary appliance was heated by coal, and upon which water was boiled and food cooked either on burners or in its oven, and this became the centrepiece in a Haussmann Apartment kitchen.

Central heating was the major modern convenience during the Second French Empire. Central heating throughout a building was incorporated into many Haussmann Apartments and this greatly improved comfort within the home. In buildings with central heating, a coal-burning hearth would be installed in the cellar level and large clay pipes connected the central hearth to vents hidden throughout floors and

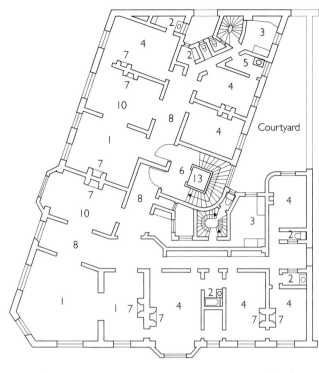

Typical Floors

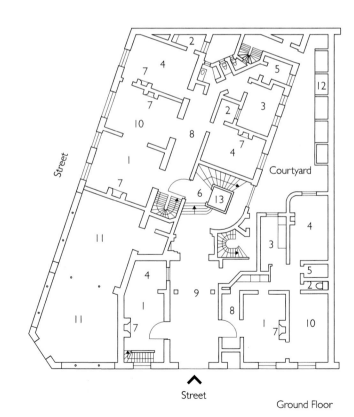

Street

1 Living Room
2 Toilet
3 Kitchen
4 Bedroom
5 Bathroom
6 Main Staircase/Elevator
7 Fireplace
8 Foyer
9 Main Entrance
10 Dining Room
11 Shop
12 Bicycle Storage
13 Elevator

Courtyard

Street

Ground Floor

1st Class Maison à Loyer

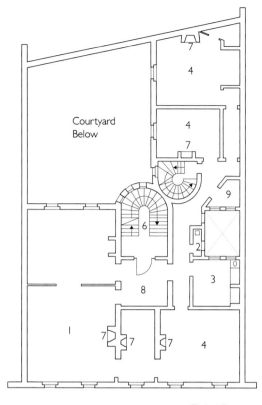

Typical Floors

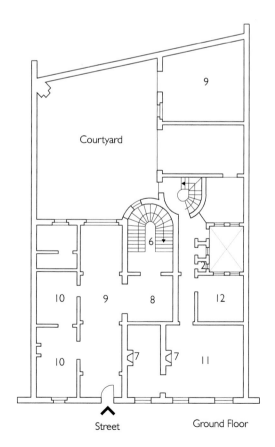

1 Living Room
2 Toilet
3 Kitchen
4 Bedroom
5 Bathroom
6 Main Staircase
7 Fireplace
8 Foyer
9 Main Entrance
10 Stables and Coach House
10 Caretaker Office and Unit
11 Shop
12 Shop Office

Street   Ground Floor

2nd Class Maison à Loyer

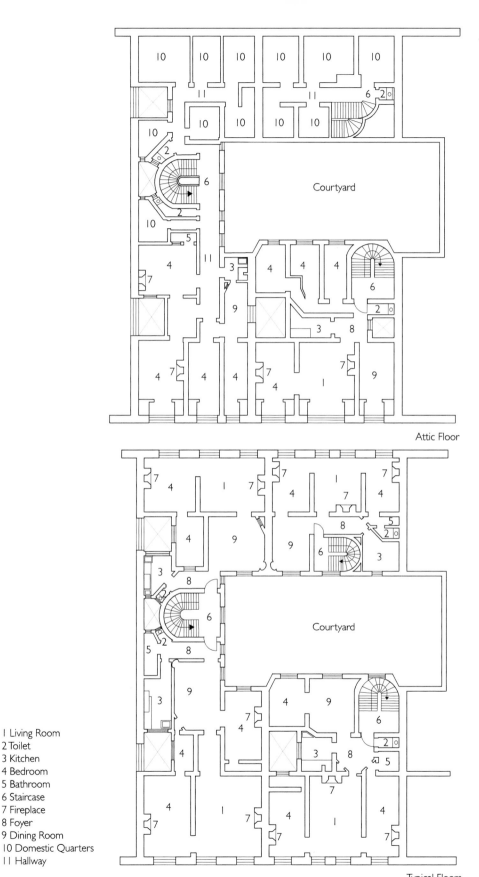

Courtyard

Attic Floor

Courtyard

1 Living Room
2 Toilet
3 Kitchen
4 Bedroom
5 Bathroom
6 Staircase
7 Fireplace
8 Foyer
9 Dining Room
10 Domestic Quarters
11 Hallway

Typical Floors

2nd Class Maison à Loyer

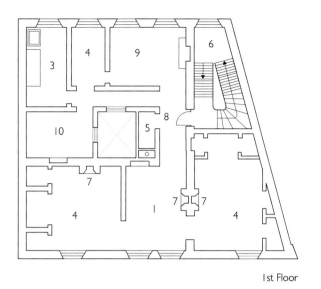

1st Floor

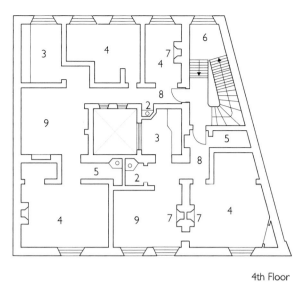

4th Floor

Street

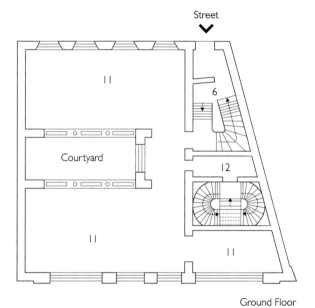

Ground Floor

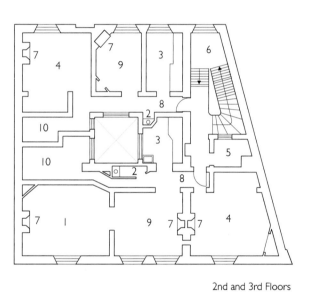

2nd and 3rd Floors

1 Living Room
2 Toilet
3 Kitchen
4 Bedroom
5 Bathroom
6 Main Staircase
7 Fireplace
8 Foyer
9 Dining Room
10 Domestic Quarters
11 Shop
12 Storage

3rd Class Maison à Loyer

Boulevard Saint Germain, c.1853–70

Rue de Rennes

Boulevard Malesherbes

Boulevard Haussmann (du Fabourg St Honoré)

Boulevard St. Germain c.1853–70

Boulevard du Palais, c.1853–70

partition walls in each individual dwelling unit. The heating permeated only the grand salons and dining rooms in the residential units. Sometimes only the *étage noble* was heated. The heating worked as hot air rose and moved through the pipes, and to help drive the air, outflow vents were installed near the ceiling to increase its flow. These vents are visible on the external façade in the form of a small ornamental cast-iron grate above windows, and made known visibly if the building had central heating.

The invention of the elevator, and its debut in residential buildings, changed the hierarchy of the apartment floors. During the Second French Empire, the hydraulic elevator slowly started to be incorporated into residential building design. The hydraulic elevator was powered by water pressure. Apartment buildings with an elevator connected into the city's infrastructure and used its non-potable water to operate the elevator. In the Haussmann apartments that had an elevator, the *étage noble* was no longer seen as the most desirable floor on which to live. As the elevator became more commonplace, the top floors became more popular for their views, sunlight and privacy.

Typical Unit Floor Plan Type

The typical Haussmann Apartment unit floor plan was separate rooms, all with clearly defined and formally arranged functions to separate private family areas and public guest areas within the home.

Access Type

The access for Haussmann Apartments was vertical. There was a common staircase or elevator in its core for circulation.

Construction Materials

The Haussmann Apartments were built of load-bearing stone. The tradition of wood and plaster architecture and construction ceased with the availability and ease of use of stone. The use of stone became widespread after the invention of hydraulic cement, which replaced lime for heavy construction during the Second French Empire. The combination of stone and cement created a much stronger and secure connection and buildings now became more structurally sound.

Mechanical stone cutting was a momentous benefit during the Second French Empire. With the aid of a mechanical tool, stone now could be cut to precise sizes and angles, and it became remarkably easier to dress a wall surely and quickly. As stone was becoming more efficient to work with, more decorative elements and stone patterning began to emerge in the architectural façade design as well.

The exteriors of the buildings were kept consistent with Lutetian limestone façades and mansard roofs. The use of the same materials meant that the buildings could be constructed more quickly and efficiently because labourers had a set repetitive routine that did not require much skill. The more detailed

Attic — Crown

4th Floor

3rd Floor — Main Body

2nd Floor

1st Floor/
Bel Étage

Base

Ground Floor

Main Entrance

Elevation - 2nd Class Maison à Loyer

architectural features that adorned the buildings, such as the iron and cast iron work for balconies and railings, were also time efficient and cost effective in that they were mass-produced. The rise of industries during the Second French Empire advanced construction with the availability and affordability of industrially produced building elements. Many of these industries were the support behind the aesthetic identity of the buildings in Haussmann's renovation of Paris. Iron was one material that most strongly marked the architecture of the industrial era in Paris, and it found its way into Parisian apartment buildings at an affordable cost.

The interiors were built of stone. The main staircase, *grand éscalier*, was constructed of stone and had woodwork detailing. In the individual dwelling units, the heavy masonry construction kept out any sounds, smells, and pests from neighbouring units. Many of the building had typical internal finishes of herringbone parquet wood flooring, carved wood doors, plaster walls with ornate mouldings and trims, and marble fireplaces, all reflecting the classical elegance of their external façades.

Developers

Baron Georges Eugene Haussmann

The vision, design, and skill for the remaking of Paris can be credited to Baron Georges Eugene Haussmann. In the eighteen years during which Haussmann modernised the city, whole neighbourhoods were demolished and more than 350,000 inhabitants were uprooted from their homes. The ambitious restructuring of Paris disrupted and displaced many lives, but the city experienced tremendous advancement in living, health and safety conditions and standards, and employment rates and opportunities were at an all-time high. With new tree-lined streets and open spaces, substantial housing, and fitting infrastructure, Paris became a much easier and safer city to manoeuvre and there was less sense of overcrowding and its burdening demands on the city. Baron Georges Eugene Haussmann's impact to monumentalise buildings refashioned Paris into a modern and picturesque city.

Haussmann and his vision for Paris made multi-unit living comfortable and widely acceptable. By the end of the nineteenth century, Haussmann Apartments evolved into sophisticated urban multi-storeyed buildings and became highly desired and valuable. With their striking street façade appearance along tree-lined avenues, grand boulevards and promenades, generous spatial standards, and mechanical conveniences such as central heating systems and elevators, these new apartments became an attractive and stylish housing lifestyle for most Parisians across socio-economic classes. More than 100,000 dwelling units were built during this time, and long before modern debates on urban density, Haussmann left a strong predilection and legacy for a convenient and compact city, and Haussmann's Paris became a portrait of style. His grand vision put the city through an excruciating, yet profound advancement and made Paris into a leader in planned city making and design.

Architects

The Second French Empire was also a promising time for architects. The large number of architects employed and working on city projects, and the abundant amount of architecture projects in the city, were at their peak in this time period more than in any previous periods in France's history. There was also a new method of working for architects during this time. Prior to the Haussmann renovation, many architects had wealthy private clients and built mostly large, single-family homes for them. Now architects were working on large-scale projects, many were public buildings, and many proposals without a single client in mind, such as residential housing, and architects had to adjust to this type of work process. Large architectural practices were established to compete and accept new business, and these offices employed many other junior architects and trades to join their offices. Large property companies that developed land also formed around this time and many became closely associated with the larger architectural practices.

The plentiful reduplication of the Haussmann Apartment design created plenty of employment for architects. The construction of *maison-à-loyer* guaranteed plentiful and lucrative work. Since the projects were marked by similarity and unity, there were many tasks and jobs that required little to no knowledge of design or construction. The majority of work mostly followed and implemented Haussmann's preconceived and strictly regulated aesthetic, and so, low-level skilled workers were suitable for projects and could also earn a decent living. The Haussmann renovation of Paris employed a vast and anonymous class of tradesmen and technicians who also made an important contribution to the city's transformation.

Although there were many *maison-à-loyer* projects, there were some architects who chose not to work on residential housing and instead focus on new areas of architecture that presented themselves during this time. The renovation of Paris provided new circumstances for a diverse range of employment opportunities and that enabled architects to engage work differently. Architects now were not limited to design, but could specialise in obtaining and expediting building permits, navigating bureaucracy, and advising and consulting for other architects.

Haussmannisation

The Haussmann renovation of Paris engaged and involved numerous people: architects, developers, tradesmen, policy makers, government officials, and reformers, but the one person who could be credited for this significant effect was Baron Georges Eugene Haussmann. The terminology Haussmannisation was used as a noun and chronicled the creative destruction of an entity for the greater part of the whole. The term was ubiquitous and often applied to describe Haussmann's major upheaval to modernise Paris.

Government Departments, Policies, and Regulations

1850: The Melun Law

The Melun Law of 1850 was one of the first public health measures to regulate the internal conditions of private dwellings in France. The law, presented by Viscount Andre de Melun and named after him, introduced a series of design standard requirements, such as the need to provide an adequate amount of natural air and light into a unit, to aid in the health buildings for habitation. The law was optional and not enforced, but was used by Haussmann in his renovation for Paris.

1851: Paris Commission on Unhealthful Dwellings

In 1851, the municipal government created the Paris Commission on Unhealthful Dwellings. The commission was made up of members that included a doctor, an architect, and different representatives from the various government agencies. The function of the commission was to visit neighbourhoods and residential buildings that had been reported as unsanitary, investigate and identify the causes, and immediately set in motion a way to rectify the issue. The commission issued notices to building owners or landlords to amend any problems and set and enforced fines to ensure the problems were corrected.

1859: New Building Regulations

The New Building Regulations of 1859 had only one purpose, and that was to increase the height of the existing medieval housing stock by one storey so residential blocks could be more densely occupied.

Present Day

The enormous and ambitious programme known as "Haussmann's Renovation of Paris" or "Haussmann Plan" is still the design that prevails in central Paris today, and the Haussmann Apartment is one of its most recognisable building styles. Haussmann Apartments remain largely the same in appearance and use as in the nineteenth century. Residents of Haussmann Apartment buildings are responsible for its maintenance and occasionally receive assistance from the city. In the 1970s and 1980s, the buildings across the city underwent widespread external cleaning and restoration. The building interiors have been modernised with elevators and dwelling unit interiors have been renovated. Most interiors have kept the original finishes of herringbone parquet wood flooring, carved wood doors, plaster walls with ornate mouldings and trims, and marble fireplaces, but partition walls from the previously separated room layouts have been removed and rooms opened up. Haussmann Apartments are located in prime real estate areas in central Paris, and individual dwelling units are available to inhabit as rental or ownership property and are highly coveted real estate.

Mott Street, New York, N.Y.

NEW YORK

Circa 1880 to 1930
New York Tenement

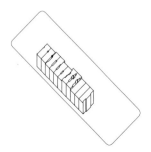

The population of New York grew rapidly in the late 1800s. A large flow of European immigrants arrived in the city to seek better opportunities in America, and New York served as an immigration landing port to enter the country. While some immigrants continued through and moved on to other parts of the United States, many decided to make New York their home, and of those, many settled in the Lower Manhattan area of the city. The Lower Manhattan neighbourhood was situated close to manufacturing plants, harbour docks, slaughterhouses, and other industries that required manual labour, and the factories provided employment for many workers in the area.

The New York tenement housing typology emerged in Lower Manhattan during this time. The building type housed the city's working poor and helped accommodate new immigrant workers and their families. The tenement was constructed quickly and in great succession to keep pace with the new growth of recent arrivals in the Lower Manhattan neighbourhoods. In the mid-1800s there were approximately 15,000 tenement buildings in the city and, by the early 1900s, there were more than 80,000 buildings.

By the late 1800s, New York had evolved into a dense metropolis with many different versions of compact housing developments that reflected its density and identity. The tenement buildings in Lower Manhattan served the city's need for densification and contributed to its rich history in housing. During this time, the dominant characteristics of the city's culture of housing began to arise—New York became a city not of houses, but of housing, and a large proportion of its inhabitants lived in a form of multi-unit dwelling that was unique in the nation.

New York Tenement Characteristics

A New York tenement is a type of row house development five to six storeys in height. The key characteristics are:

- Economical housing solution to accommodate urban working poor

- Building attached to both sides of neighbouring tenement buildings

- Lot size usually 25 feet (7.6 metres) wide by 100 feet (30.5 metres) deep

- Four apartments on each floor

- Central shared staircase

- Communal sanitary facilities

New York tenement buildings housed many of the city's working poor, and with the arrival of the immigrants, the housing type provided affordable and convenient dwellings to the newcomers. The two areas in Lower Manhattan where tenements and urban poor coexisted in abundance were Lower East Side and East Village. These two neighbourhoods and their tenement buildings became home to the majority of the new European settlers.

In Lower Manhattan, and other areas on the island of Manhattan, construction developments fitted within a street grid that was subdivided into lot sizes 25 feet (7.6 metres) wide by 100 feet (30.5 metres) long. The system was established to perceptively plan for density on the island, and tenement buildings efficiently conformed within the system. The tenement building was designed with wood joists that spanned the 25-foot (7.6 metre) width and eliminated the need for columns. Early tenement buildings occupied half the lot size and the remainder provided a courtyard at the back of the building. Eventually landlords realised it was more profitable to build more dwelling units to rent, and later tenement buildings took up almost all of the lot size.

Types of Tenements

The proportions and designs of tenement buildings varied slightly throughout the years. Policies and regulations to govern construction and the health and life safety of the inhabitants were created and amended over time, but the lot size did not differ. During the tenement evolution, the width and length of the housing type stayed within the lot size boundaries and the height of five to six storeys remained unchanged. Though sanitary conditions were improved with each new design, garbage remained disposed of in boxes located at the front of each building. The garbage receptacles often overflowed and the annoyance led the tenants to throw their debris into the air shafts, where the waste could not be collected and was left to decay. Soon after, the windows in the air shafts could no longer be opened to emit fresh air and many tenement buildings deteriorated and became unsanitary buildings in which to live.

The architects of many tenement buildings were often unknown, never credited or recorded. Many of the men who designed or built tenements were the new European immigrants, who had either trained as builders or studied architecture in Europe before immigrating to the United States.

Back-to-backs

Back-to-back tenements were a row of dwelling units that were constructed back to back from one another. The units were six storeys in height and organised along two narrow alleys. The back of one house adjoined the back of another and was attached on either side, except for the end units. Windows for natural daylight and air in each dwelling units were limited to the front. There was no cross-ventilation in the units.

Railroad

Railroad tenements were long and rectangular with a series of narrow dwelling units organised in a line, reminiscent of railroad cars. Before 1850, railroad tenements occupied half the lot with the remaining half used as a communal yard. Around 1850, some tenements featured a separate building at the back of the lot that reduced the size of the yard. The additional building increased dwelling units and landlords were able to rent more units and collect more rent. After 1850, the annexed portion was united with the main building and the entire tenement occupied three-quarters of the lot, with the remaining quarter used as a communal yard.

Air-shaft

Air-shaft tenements were constructed after the Second Tenement House Act around 1880. The centre of the floor plan was recessed to allow for windows to provide natural daylight and ventilation. In the

1879 designs, the indentation allowed for two small, square windows. From 1880 to 1887, the plans allowed for three windows that were wider and rectangular shaped. Shortly after 1887, the openings grew wider and were increased to five windows.

Dumbbell

The dumbbell tenement was named after its shape in plan. In 1879, the magazine *The Plumber and Sanitary Engineer* sponsored a competition and the winning entry was the dumbbell scheme, named for its resemblance to a dumbbell. James Ware designed the dumbbell tenement, the plan for which had a larger central opening for more windows to allow in natural daylight and air. The building footprint fitted within the standard lot size, but the building covered approximately 90 percent of the lot and left 10 percent for a communal yard. The new design appealed to tenement owners for its healthy environment and increased rentable area for improved profitability.

Building Components and Organisation

Layout

New York tenement buildings were five to six storeys in height and consisted of a basement, ground floor with one or two shops, residential floors, communal staircase, and yard. There were four dwelling units per floor and a typical unit had a living area, kitchen, and one or two bedrooms. Ground or lower floor dwelling units were noisier than the upper floors, but had the advantage of fewer stairs to climb. The upper floor units were generally the quietest, but had the most stairs to climb. Earlier units had windows that faced the street or yard, and later units had additional windows that faced an internal airshaft. Toilets in early tenements had shared outdoor facilities, but in later tenements, were located indoors, on each floor, and against an external wall to allow for a window to provide natural daylight and ventilation.

Shops

New York tenements had one or two ground floor retail shops that served the residents and the community. The continuous rows of shops at the pedestrian level created a strong urban character and street presence in the neighbourhoods.

Staircase

New York tenements had narrow staircase that served as the shared vertical circulation. The staircase was constructed of wood and connected the residential floors with the ground floor entrance. The staircase served as an informal and important social centre where all residents passed and greeted one another on a regular basis.

Hallway

Early tenements did not have windows in the centre of the floor plan and the hallways were quite dark. Later tenements had air shafts that enabled the installation of windows to provide a source of natural daylight and air. It was much later that lighting was required in the hallways and gas lighting was installed.

Yard

Most New York tenements had a small communal yard. In earlier tenements, the yard was where the water pump and communal outdoor toilets were located and where resident children played. In later years, cold-water plumbing and toilets were installed indoors and the yard became a larger play area for children. Throughout the years, residents used the yard to hang their laundry to dry.

Rooftop

The rooftop of a New York tenement was flat, not inhabitable, but was often used in the summer as a place to sleep. Some dwelling units did not have enough windows for cross-ventilation and the rooftop provided a good escape from the stale air and heat inside the units.

Fire Escape

In later tenement buildings, fire escapes were a mandatory addition to provide a secondary means of egress. Fire escapes were affixed to the building façades and were not inhabitable. Many tenants used the structure as balconies and some residents slept on the fire escape in the summer months.

Interiors

New York tenement interiors consisted of three or four rooms. There was a parlour, kitchen, and one or two bedrooms. In units that housed larger families, the parlour and kitchen were often used as additional sleeping space. In units with a kitchen sink, the basin was used to wash dishes, clothes, and the residents. Each tenement dwelling unit had one or two fireplaces that were used as a source for cooking and heating. The fireplace was either wood or coal burning and had a mantel that stored cooking spices and the family's personal effects, photos, clock, vase, candlesticks, and such ornaments. In later tenements, some units had wood or coal-burning stoves. Embellishment of the home was a common practice and many families painted or wallpapered their walls, placed carpets over the wood flooring, hung lace curtains on the window and photos on the walls in an effort to make their space feel more personal and comfortable. Internal walls, openings, and doors were not closely constructed and ventilation was poor, which led to problems with vermin, smells, and odours.

Superintendent

Seldom was there a full-time attendant living in New York tenements among the residents. In some tenements, a housekeeper collected the rent and looked in on the building to sweep the stairs, hallways, and sidewalk. The tenements with housekeepers were often better kept than those that did not have frequent managerial staff on site. The tenements that had no regular management staff inspection were often overcrowded and mistreated.

100 feet (30.5 metres)

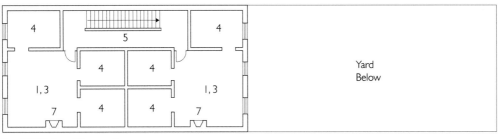

25 feet (7.6 metres)

Pre-1850 Railroad Tenement

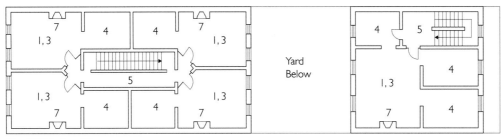

25 feet (7.6 metres)

Circa 1850 Railroad Tenement

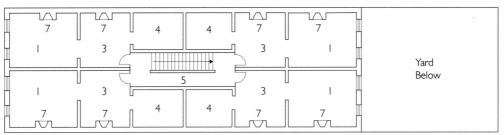

25 feet (7.6 metres)

Post-1850 Railroad Tenement

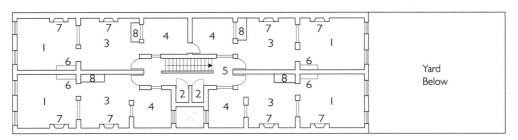

25 feet (7.6 metres)

Circa 1905 Railroad Tenement

1 Parlour
2 Toilet
3 Kitchen
4 Bedroom
5 Hallway
6 Closet
7 Fireplace
8 Rack
9 Fire Escape

100 feet (30.5 metres)

25 feet (7.6 metres)

1879 Air-shaft Tenement

1880-1887 Air-shaft Tenement

1880-1887 Air-shaft Tenement

1894 Dumbbell Tenement

Yard Below

Typical Floors

Tenement Evolution

Mulberry St., New York, N.Y., c. 1900

Case Studies

Gotham Court

Architect: Silas Wood
Completed: 1850

Gotham Court was located in the Lower East Side. The development consisted of two rows of six back-to-back tenements, six storeys in height, and oriented parallel to two narrow alleyways. Each back-to-back tenement contained two dwelling units that measured fourteen feet (4.2 metres) wide and ten feet (3 metres) long. The dwelling units had two rooms, a main room and a bedroom. The main room was used for cooking, eating, and leisure, and the bedroom was where the family slept. The back wall abutted the back of the other tenement and there were two windows in the front that faced an alleyway. The only source of natural daylight and air was from the front of the unit, and there was no cross-ventilation. A continuous cellar extended underneath the alleyways and housed the toilets and sinks. There were small ceiling grates embedded in the alleyway pavement to provide daylight and ventilation to the cellars. The first two tenements that faced onto the street were reserved for shops that mostly served the tenement inhabitants.

Gotham Court was designed to house 140 families. By 1879, the number of inhabitants had grown to 240 families and single dwelling units began to house more than one household. Up to five families crowded into some units and the congestion forced others to make their home in the cellars below. The development deteriorated and became congested, filthy, and riddled with disease and crime. The overcrowding, neglect, decay, and lawlessness turned Gotham Court into a slum and it became a favourite problem for social and housing reformers to want to fix. In 1895, the outcry by the social and housing activists was heeded and Gotham Court was demolished.

97 Orchard Street

Architect: Unknown
Completed: 1863

Orchard Street spans eight city blocks in the Lower East Side. 97 Orchard Street was a five-storey, railroad tenement building that housed four dwelling units per floor. The tenement had a below grade level that was accessible from the street and was designed to accommodate two shops. There were four shops in total, two on the ground floor and two below grade. The shops provided provisions for the inhabitants and commercial rental income for the landlord. The 20 dwelling units were three-room units designed to accommodate 20 families and were not self-contained. Communal toilets were located in the rear yard. Lucas Glockner was the owner, builder, and landlord of the building. He was a German immigrant and lived in the tenement with his family.

A communal, wood staircase that did not have window openings to allow natural daylight and air linked each floor. A typical dwelling unit was approximately 325 square feet (30 square metres) and had three rooms. The front room was the largest and known as the parlour, and the other two rooms were used

Alley playground: children play with barrels under the washing hung between tenements in Gotham Court, Cherry Street, c.1890

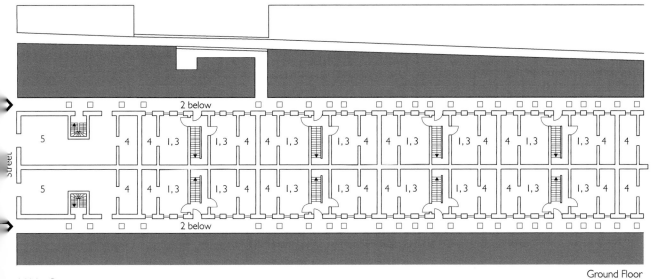

Ground Floor

1 Living Room
2 Toilet
3 Kitchen
4 Bedroom
5 Shop

Gotham Court

as the kitchen and bedroom. The parlour was located either at the front and faced the street, or at the rear of the building and faced the yard. The parlour was the only room in the unit to have windows for natural daylight and ventilation and had a fireplace for source of heat for warmth and cooking. The kitchen and bedroom did not have natural daylight or air and often a single family of seven people or more occupied one unit.

97 Orchard Street had two fire escapes, one in the front of the building and another at its rear. The fire escapes were iron and affixed on the external façades of the building. 97 Orchard Street was built before New York passed the tenement laws that required the installation of fire escapes, but Glockner cared about the safety of his tenants and his own family and provided additional means of egress in his building in case of an emergency.

Lucas Glockner was a responsible landlord who cared for 97 Orchard Street and its residents. The building, its maintenance, and the building residents were a good example of a successful and healthy New York tenement at the time. Orchard was kept in a state of good repair and though the tenant population increased steadily over the years, from about 70 people in 1863 to slightly over 100 in 1901, the tenants remained respectful towards each other and their living environment.

The Average New York Tenement

The majority of New York tenements erected during this time were five- to six-storey brick buildings and many tenements were not as successful as 97 Orchard Street. With the continuous arrival of immigrants in Lower Manhattan, many developers saw a business opportunity to build large numbers of tenements and rent the dwelling units for profit. Many tenements were built hastily, and construction materials and details were often compromised to save on costs. The low-cost construction measures coupled with absentee landlords eventually led to the decline of many tenement buildings and to the health of its residents. While tenement buildings were designed and suited to be cheap places to live, not all tenements were in squalid or crime-infested conditions as portrayed by some social reformers. Tenements were home to the city's working poor and new immigrants with young families. The occupations of many residents were in industry and though life in a tenement was hard, residents had a strong sense of community pride and streets in tenement neighbourhoods had a lively atmosphere.

Typical Unit Floor Plan Type

The New York tenement floor plan type could be considered as central living space in tenements built before 1850 and corridor type in the majority of tenements built after 1850. In tenements built before 1850, the main room was the central living space and the bedrooms were accessed through the main room. In tenements built after 1850, the parlour was the largest room and located at the end of the unit. The parlour, kitchen, and bedrooms were aligned and all rooms were connected through a corridor.

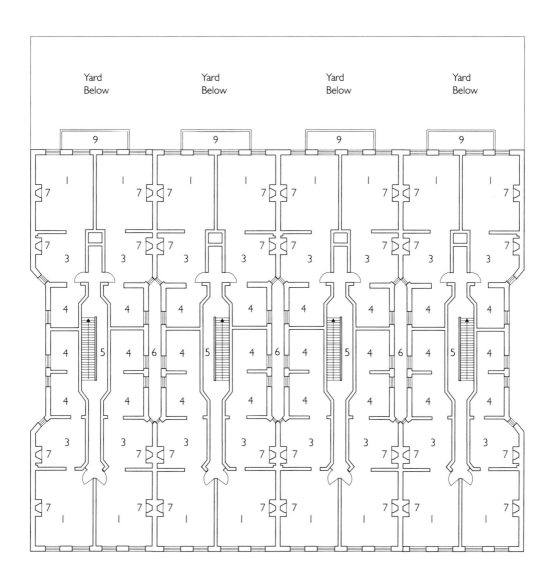

1 Parlour
2 Toilet
3 Kitchen
4 Bedroom
5 Hallway
6 Air Shaft
7 Fireplace
8 Rack
9 Fire Escape

Air-shaft Tenements

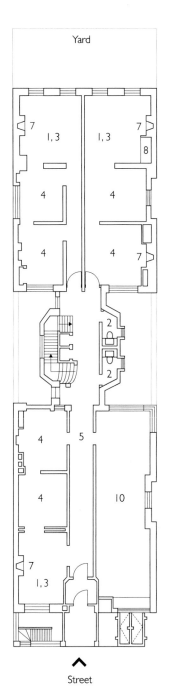

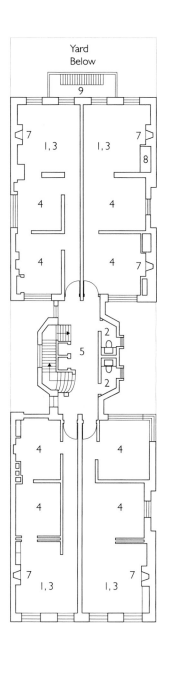

Yard

Yard
Below

9

Street

1st Floor

Typical Floors

1 Parlour
2 Toilet
3 Kitchen
4 Bedroom
5 Hallway
6 Closet
7 Fireplace
8 Rack
9 Fire Escape
10 Shop

Dumbbell Tenement

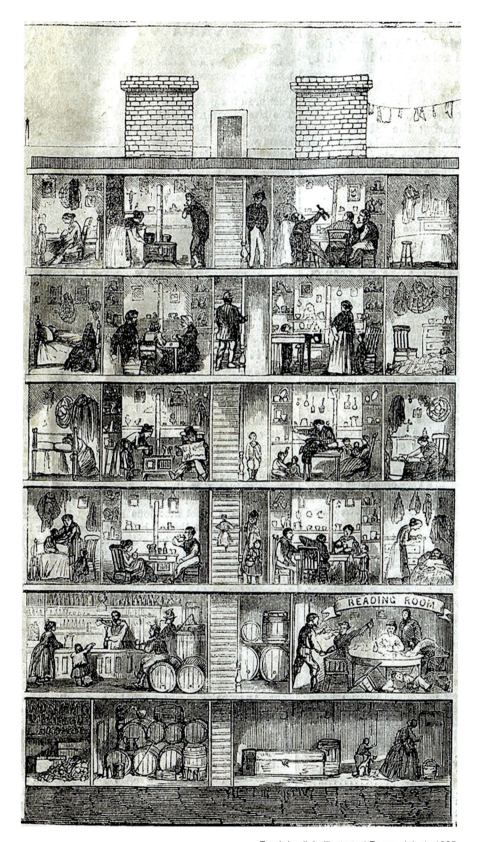

Frank Leslie's Illustrated Paper, July 1, 1865

"Knee-pants" at forty-five cents a dozen – a Ludlow Street sweater's shop

Room in a tenement, 1910

Mott Street, New York, N.Y., c.1905

The Ghetto, New York, N.Y., 1900–1915

Life on the Lower East Side, corner of Pitt and Rivington Streets, New York, N.Y.

Italian Neighborhood with Street Market, Mulberry Street, New York, N.Y., 1900–1915

Lower East Side Street Scene, New York, N.Y.

Sunday Morning at Orchard and Rivington, New York, N.Y., 1915

Access Type

The access type for New York tenements was vertical. All dwelling unit entrances were grouped in the centre of the building floor plan, around the communal staircase, and all the units were accessed a few steps from the staircase.

Construction Materials

New York tenements were unreinforced brick masonry and wood construction. The building was two brick walls of single wythe, load-bearing brick that ran parallel to the lot and abutted against its neighbouring buildings. Wood joists spanned the width and were twelve or sixteen inches (30 or 40 centimetres) thick. The building rested on a stone foundation that was two feet (0.6 metres) thick and supported the five- to six-storey building. Many buildings were often hastily constructed and used inferior building materials and practices. The single-wythe brick construction did not insulate well against cold weather and was susceptible to decay and erosion.

Owners, Landlords, Developers, Reformers

Landlords

Many New York landlords bought up city blocks to develop rows of tenement housing for the purpose of a housing rental business. Very few landlords lived among their tenants and even fewer knew or cared about their tenants, how they lived, or in what condition their buildings were. Many landlords were merely focused on the accumulation of tenants and in the collection of rent. By the late 1800s, many tenements were overcrowded and in various states of disrepair. During this time, many landlords prospered in the housing rental business and the unscrupulous practice became a common and lucrative housing enterprise.

Reformers

Jacob Riis

During this time, Jacob Riis, a photojournalist and Danish immigrant to New York City, brought attention to the dire tenement situation and actuated government response. Riis photo-documented the dilapidated tenement conditions and the impoverished tenement dwellers and their lives in the tenement buildings. He exposed the perilous and unsanitary living conditions of the tenements in the Lower East Side, and in 1890 published a book of his records called *How the Other Half Lives: Studies among the Tenements of New York*. His book highlighted the urban blight and raised awareness with upper- and middle-class societies. More importantly, his investigation alerted legislative authorities and began another closer examination into housing reform.

From Jacob Riis' reports, the state and federal governments realised a need to standardise tenement buildings. By the mid-1890s, the two levels of government responded with their own investigation

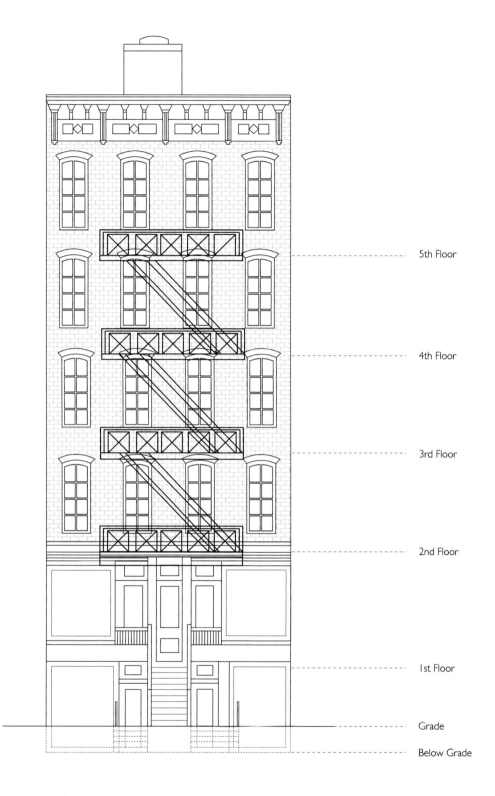

5th Floor

4th Floor

3rd Floor

2nd Floor

1st Floor

Grade

Below Grade

Elevation

and mandate and conducted two major studies relating to tenements. In 1894, the New York State legislature established the Tenement House Committee, which led another study, and in 1895, the federal government set forth another extensive examination. Both inquiries used statistics to analyse the tenements, and the 1894 report revealed that over one-half of the New York population lived in squalid tenements.

Like Jacob Riis, the Tenement House Committee documented their findings with photographs to show the situation of the tenement residents and the way they inhabited the buildings. The exercise was to learn and determine how to better the design and construction of future tenement housing and the living standards for its inhabitants. The study was not limited to how new regulations could positively affect one building, but rather how appropriate implementations could favourably influence entire tenement neighbourhoods. One progressive recommendation from the committee was to develop rapid transit, specifically subways, as quickly as possible to alleviate overcrowding in the tenement districts.

Another investigation made by the Tenement House Committee was to record all the events that resulted with the tenement housing in Europe. Even though Europe had enacted its first tenement law about 40 years earlier, it was through the Tenement House Committee inquiry that the conditions in Europe were made known to America. It was through this finding that the federal government concluded that tenement housing needed to be officially and properly constituted.

Nelson Derby and Edward T. Potter

Alongside government agencies, two architects, Nelson Derby and Edward T. Potter, led a housing reform. These architects proposed extensive methods to better design tenement housing to improve i ts living conditions and thwart its problems and stigma. In 1877, Derby wrote a proposal to use four, 25 feet (7.6 metres) wide by 100 feet (30.5 metres) long lots to plan a new living layout around an internal courtyard to improve air circulation and quality. In 1878 and 1879, Potter published an analysis to reorganise the New York City grid system to unlock land lot sizes, and in 1888, he proposed widening the tenement lot size to 37 feet 6 inches (11.4 metres) wide by 100 feet (30.5 metres) long lot. In 1901, the propositions put forth by the architects proved beneficial. The Tenement House Act (The New Law) was created and the legislature required that every new tenement building be built with outward-facing windows in every room, an open courtyard, indoor toilets, fire escapes, and garbage removal. This was a great victory.

Congestion

New York tenements were notorious for being overcrowded and poorly kept buildings. With the large number of people living in tight quarters, illness and hazards often broke out. Diseases, such as yellow fever, smallpox, tuberculosis, and cholera, and hazards such as fires were frequent and led to the decline of many buildings and blocks.

Yard of Tenement, New York, N.Y., 1900–1910

A scene in the Ghetto, Hester Street, c.1902

Government Departments, Policies, and Regulations

Before 1860, city surveyors and fire wardens enforced building laws and standards. In the 1860s, a centralised department was created and new legislation was created to address the design, health, and safety of tenement buildings and its occupants. Over the years, reforms to encourage better tenement construction and maintenance were created, adopted or amended for improvement.

1862: Department of Survey and Inspection of Buildings

In 1862, the Department of Survey and Inspection of Buildings was established. The department was responsible for the examination of both pre-construction building plans and inhabited buildings to ensure that the design, health, and safety of the tenement were up to code for the protection of the building and its residents.

1867: First Tenement House Act

In 1867, the New York Board of Health introduced the First Tenement House Act. The Act required that all new tenement developments had to install fire escapes as a mean of emergency exit and that each room had a window to allow for light and air. The window could open to the exterior or to an internal corridor. The Act banned the construction of poorly lit and unventilated buildings, and the statute was seen as a great improvement.

1879: Second Tenement House Act

In 1879, the New York Board of Health established the Second Tenement House Act. The Second Tenement House Act revised the First Tenement House Act in that each room was to have a window that opened onto a source of natural daylight and fresh air, and not an internal corridor.

1901: Tenement House Act (The New Law)

The Tenement House Act of 1901 was a major revision to the previous housing acts. The New Law required that rooms in existing tenements with no windows had to be outfitted with an opening of a minimum of 15 square feet (1.4 square metres) into a ventilated room. New tenement developments were required to be built with windows in every room that faced a natural daylight and fresh air source, have an open yard, indoor toilets, fire escapes, and garbage removal. The 1901 Tenement House Act set new standards for housing and created a new government department. The Tenement House Department was established out of the New Law and was responsible for the implementation of the new legislation.

Present Day

Rows and blocks of New York tenements remain visible and in use as housing in Lower East Side and East Village. The presence of its former Jewish, Italian, Polish, Russian, Ukrainian, German, and Irish immigrants lives on in the form of delis, bakeries, and restaurants in the two neighbourhoods. Tenements are now completely renovated and modernised with hot water, indoor plumbing, and full bathrooms and kitchens, but remain walk-ups with garbage disposal out front. Some dwelling units have been converted to market ownership and equity co-op housing, while many remain rental-housing stock.

97 Orchard Street and its inhabitants have been documented in books and is now part of the Tenement Museum. The building has housed approximately 7,000 people from 26 countries throughout its years, and about 1,400 of the residents are recorded by name. The Tenement Museum is located in the Lower East Side and preserves, interprets, and honours the history and stories of the thousands of immigrants who settled in Lower Manhattan. The museum occupies a storefront on Orchard Street and offers public tours of their restored tenement buildings and units, and the neighbourhood.

New York tenement buildings in Lower Manhattan are a sought-after housing stock to reside in. The Lower East Side and East Village have gentrified over the years and evolved into a popular area of quaint shops, cafés, and restaurants. The rich history and charm of the buildings and neighbourhoods attract many admirers. The positive attention has given tenements a new appreciation and lease on life, and makes the buildings desirable places to live.

Hong Kong c.1940

HONG KONG

Circa 1840 to 1960
Hong Kong *Tong Lau*

Tong lau is a housing typology that is found predominately in South China and Southeast Asia in cities such as Hong Kong, Macau, and Singapore. This chapter focuses on the Hong Kong *tong lau* that was predominate in Hong Kong from circa 1840 to 1960. *Tong lau* translates to "Chinese building" in Cantonese, and the term was used to differentiate between a style of housing that was zoned for Chinese or Westerner residents. Commonly, a *tong lau* was a building that was three to five storeys in height and where the ground floor accommodated a small shop and the upper floors were residences. It was built in continuous rows along a street and had uniform façades. With shops on the ground floor, *tong lau* buildings were also known as "shophouses" and had become a generic terminology that was widely used to describe Hong Kong's once abundant urban shophouse buildings.

The Hong Kong *tong lau* provided cost-effective housing and commercial trading space. The building functioned as a residence, showroom, and warehouse and its architectural style was derived from many influences. *Tong lau* buildings displayed the traditional architectural styles of South China and Southeast Asia through their use of materials and construction and featured European, or "Western-style", elements.

At the beginning of the 1840s, *tong lau* were a common type of residence. Up until circa 1850, the majority of Hong Kong *tong lau* developments were a solution to accommodate the high ratio of migrants during and after the Pacific War. In Hong Kong, the *tong lau* typology had been associated with tenement housing. Though during this time, the *tong lau* still housed a shop on the ground floor, but the upper floors were subdivided into smaller units for renting to multiple households in response to a shortage of affordable housing for workers.

Hong Kong *Tong Lau* Characteristics

A Hong Kong *tong lau* is a single building three to five storeys in height and the ground floor accommodates a shop. The key characteristics are:

- Usually built in continuous blocks with long, narrow units
- Built in rows of two to four buildings attached along streets with uniform façades
- Three to five storeys high with balconies or verandahs facing the street
- Load-bearing walls with timber floors
- Main entrances directly off streets

Historical Context

The Victorian Era Early *Tong Lau*: Circa 1840–1900

In 1842, under the Treaty of Nanking, Hong Kong became a British colony. Hong Kong was acquired by Britain mainly for trade purposes. With the region being located on the South China Sea, Britain made good use of Hong Kong's geography and quickly developed it into a hub for commerce and industry.

As a result of colonisation and trade development, the population of Hong Kong grew. Before the colonial period, Hong Kong was sparsely populated with around 7,000 native inhabitants who mainly lived along the coast and further inland. Shortly after colonisation, the Hong Kong population and the distribution of the population shifted. By 1845, the population of Hong Kong had grown to approximately 100,000 inhabitants, most of whom were living on the mainland of Hong Kong. This growth forced the development of denser, multi-unit housing living, and the *tong lau* housing typology emerged.

For a brief period in the 1840s, *tong lau* were known as common residences where a family, usually the shopkeeper, owned their *tong lau* and the extended family lived together. Each family unit would occupy a different floor, but all families would share the kitchen and living space. By the 1850s, the typology became known as tenement housing when it functioned as a housing response to Hong Kong's population increase during the trade agreements between China and foreign powers. During this time, a large number of mainland Chinese migrated out of China for better livelihoods. Hong Kong was seen as a politically and economically stable place to take up residence, and the demand for housing became critical.

When the British took over Hong Kong, they decided to set up their military facilities and government offices in central Hong Kong and the area soon attracted both Westerners and Chinese to work and live. Shortly after the British were established in the neighbourhood, the area was designated for Westerners and "Western buildings" only, which meant only buildings with standardised space and sanitary requirements, and the Chinese residents were relocated to areas zoned for Chinese and "Chinese buildings" only. In the early 1850s, a portion of the Chinese zoned area was used as tenement housing to accommodate the newly migrated Chinese settlers in *tong lau* buildings. The area, called Tai Ping Shan, became Hong Kong's first "Chinese town" and the earliest form of *tong lau* housing was built there. Tai Ping Shan was roughly 75,000 square metres (800,000 square feet) in area and supported an estimated 200,000 Chinese settlers in Hong Kong.

During this early tenement phase of *tong lau* construction, Hong Kong was newly established under British rule and there was no specific planning policy or building regulations for Chinese buildings. Although the architecture of early Hong Kong *tong lau* buildings was very similar to those in South China and Southeast Asia, there were subtle, yet noticeable, differences. The Hong Kong *tong lau* had a European, or "Western" influence that was evident throughout their decorative elements, such as ornate stonework and wrought iron detailing. Due to Hong Kong's rugged geography, high land prices, and expenditure required to level sites for building, there was an economical necessity of space and the Hong Kong *tong lau* buildings were more compact than their neighbouring counterparts.

Hong Kong *tong lau* were first constructed back-to-back; two buildings abutted, with a shared back wall and windows on flat façades that faced the street. The buildings were mostly of two to four storeys and each storey was approximately four metres (13 feet) in height and five metres (16 feet) in width. The wood used for construction was Chinese fir, and the load-bearing walls were vernacular Chinese grey brick and lime mortar. The brick surface was made smooth with traditional Chinese construction techniques and the roof was tiled with unglazed semicircular clay tiles laid with overlapping ends. Often, the eave tiles were decorative and glazed. The buildings were constructed in continuous rows facing the street and the façades were uniform in design. In later construction, a back alley separated *tong lau* buildings. The alley design was deemed more sanitary as the alley provided natural daylight and air.

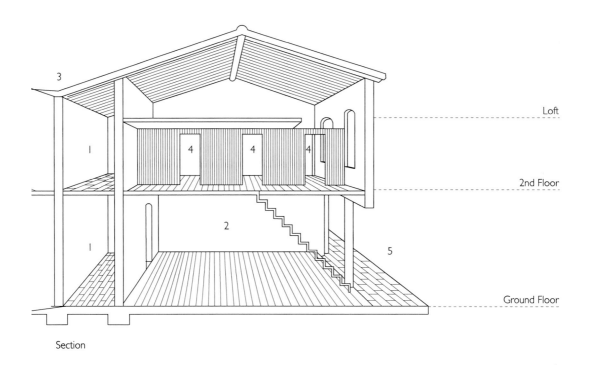

3

Loft

1

4   4   4

2nd Floor

1

2

5

Ground Floor

Section

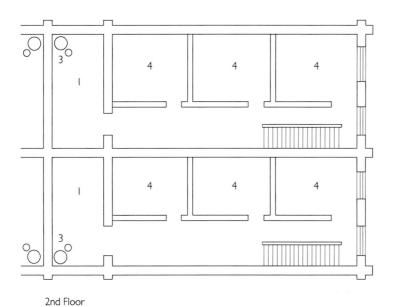

3

1   4   4   4

1   4   4   4

3

2nd Floor

1 Cookhouse
2 Shop
3 Smoke Hole
4 Partitioned Rooms
5 Street

Tai Ping Shan circa 1880

Tai Ping Shan, Chinese Town

Each *tong lau* had a ground floor shop and the upper floors were residential. In the residential portion, each floor was one undivided room but subdivided by wood partitions into several spaces to house different families. The area of each floor was about 50 square metres (530 square feet) and each floor was divided into three, 9.5-square metre (100-square feet) cubicle-like rooms separated by wood partitions. At the ceiling, the partitions were finished with wire mesh that allowed in light and air. Only the cubicle that faced the street received direct light and air. The cubicles were often furnished with bunk beds, and life inside each cubicle was crowded.

There was a communal kitchen at the back of each floor, and a long and narrow wooden straight-run staircase connected the floors. Windows were at the front of the building and provided little natural daylight or ventilation. The two rooms that were situated in the centre of each floor did not receive any natural daylight or ventilation. It was also common that livestock, such as chickens and pigs, were kept in the *tong lau*. Overall, the living conditions within the earliest *tong lau* tenement buildings were overcrowded. The *tong lau* during this time lacked indoor toilet and sanitation facilities and used shared outdoor public latrines and washhouses.

With such overcrowding in the buildings and again within the cubicles, most inhabitants used their homes for sleeping and the rest of their time was spent in the city. The inhabitants of Hong Kong were very much part of the city and contributed to its energetic street life. With convenient, abundant, and affordable eateries, places to socialise, and areas for recreation that were available all hours of the day and night, civic amenities outside the home afforded people the luxury of giving little concern to housing. With a rich and fulfilling city life, there was little incentive for the people of Hong Kong to object to their housing stock.

By 1881, more than 160,000 people lived in Hong Kong and more than 90 percent of these were Chinese. Throughout this time, *tong lau* developments continued to be built, and the expense and difficulty of new construction on high-premium real estate encouraged developers to fully impose on any land to which they could purchase and develop. *Tong lau* housing was one of the foundations of Hong Kong life for the working class, and its architecture was an expression of its past before colonialism.

A New Era: Circa 1900–1935

In 1894, a bubonic plague outbreak in Hong Kong killed more than 2,000 people—mostly those living in close quarters in *tong lau* housing. In 1903, the Public Health and Buildings Ordinance was passed to improve the health and living conditions of *tong lau* housing. Under this enactment, newly built *tong lau* housing had light wells, was limited to four storeys in height to allow light to permeate to the lower floors, window sizes increased, and the depth of rooms from windows was shortened to allow for better natural daylight and ventilation. Frontage was reduced to 4.75 metres (15 feet) to ensure sufficient open space between each building, and a small courtyard space was provided at the rear of the building. At the rear of the building was a 2-metre (6-feet) laneway that eliminated adjoining back-to-back construction of *tong lau* buildings. Chinese grey brick and lime mortar was still the principal building material, but clay roof tiles were replaced with concrete flat roofs.

By 1931, the population had reached 841,000 and the need for housing reached another crisis level. In some areas there were, on average, close to 2,300 persons per hectare (930 persons per acre) and more housing was built. In this second period of *tong lau* design, the most evident update was a reinforced concrete external space that replaced the flat façade of its predecessor. The debut of the external space, either as a verandah or cantilevered and recessed balconies, increased natural daylight and ventilation through the *tong lau* floor plates, improved the health and living conditions of its inhabitants, and fulfilled an essential requirement of the 1903 Public Health Ordinance. The revised and improved *tong lau* layout was better than its previous design, but eventually became crowded and lacked in-house sanitary facilities.

The Inter-War Years (Pacific War World War II): Circa 1935–1940

In 1935, another government Housing Commission was set up to review the persistent problem of overcrowding. A further report was catalogued and Hong Kong passed its first building ordinance, entitled Building Ordinance 1935. The regulation requested more natural daylight and ventilation and reduced *tong lau* developments to three storeys, with stricter governance over natural daylight and ventilation. Now every floor plate and staircase was also accessible by light and air, windows were required in the kitchen area for cross-ventilation, and in-house sanitary facilities were introduced. During the time, the principal building material was changed to reinforced concrete and the internal staircase was formed in concrete and designed to be a compact, half-turn stair layout.

The most evident design update in this period of *tong lau* housing was a half-turn stair that received natural daylight and air at the front of the building. The replacement of the long and narrow staircase by a shorter and more efficient half-turn stair allowed for a more useful area space per floor. The half-turn stair was located at the front of the building to house a naturally daylit and ventilated stairwell on the façade. Windows were installed at the rear of the building, with the existing external space for either a verandah or cantilevered or recessed balcony; more daylight and air could then circulate into the living space. During this period, these changes improved the living standards of the tenants living in *tong lau* buildings.

Post-War Period of Transition: Circa 1940–1960

From 1945–1951, Hong Kong experienced another sudden surge in inhabitants. During this six-year span, with mass arrival of Chinese refugees entering the city to escape war and political unrest in Mainland China, the population rose to 2.1 million. During this wave of population influx, the newly displaced were housed in *tong lau* buildings. During this time, there were no new developments of *tong lau*. The typology had been recognised and experienced from the previous period, Hong Kong was well established, living standards were better, residents had higher purchasing power to afford better housing, and former *tong lau* tenants vacated and made way for new immigrants. During this phase, very few new *tong lau* buildings were built and the few that were constructed were modernised. Wooden staircases were replaced with terrazzo staircases and wooden windows with metal windows; floors were divided into rooms, and kitchens and bathrooms were shared among the tenants on each floor.

During this time, some long-term *tong lau* inhabitants purchased buildings and returned these to single-family use for themselves and rented out portions of their floors to residential or commercial tenants to generate additional income. The ground floor remained a shop and was rented out for retail use, but either the first floor was partitioned with glass walls and leased to small businesses, or the whole floor

Hong Kong c. 1940

Hong Kong c. 1940

View of Queens Road, Victoria, c.1890

Queens Road on Chinese New Year's Day, Hong Kong

A Typical Street in Hong Kong

Wellington Street, c.1800

was rented out to a residential tenant, and the owner family would live on the upper floors. On the owner's floor was an area or an entire floor used for socializing, cooking, and eating, and a separate area or the floor above for sleeping.

As Hong Kong evolved into a dense urban centre and its population increased rapidly, traditional housing made way for newer types to keep up with the population growth and housing need. From the 1960s, many *tong lau* developments were demolished to make way for residential high-rise towers.

Types of *Tong Lau*

The following five types of *tong lau* in Hong Kong are representative of the styles that can be found in the city. This is not an exhaustive list of examples of Hong Kong *tong lau* designs—buildings can be comprised of a mixture of elements from each of the types.

Flat Façade (Victorian Era Early Years: Circa 1840–1900)

The flat façade type of *tong lau* was constructed of load-bearing brick party walls with Chinese fir wood beams and floors. The style of *tong lau* had a flat façade and was a precursor to the *tong lau* buildings with verandahs and balconies. The kitchen occupied half the width of the back of the building.

Verandah (New Era: Circa 1900–1935)

Verandah types of *tong lau* were constructed of load-bearing brick party walls with Chinese fir wood beams, and the floors and had a deep-set verandah as an external space. The tenants would use the verandah as outdoor leisure space, but in the earlier years of this typology, tenants used the space to dry their laundry, keep livestock, and grow vegetables. The verandah was approximately 1.8 metres (6 feet deep), supported by brick columns that projected over the entire width of the building and formed an arcade for the ground floor shop. Many of the balustrade designs were influenced by European architecture, with heavy Neoclassical features. In later years, the verandah was windowed off to create an enclosed internal space, and from the exterior the *tong lau* resembled the flat façade type of *tong lau* building from an earlier period.

Cantilevered Balcony (New Era: Circa 1900–1935)

Cantilevered balcony *tong lau* housing was constructed of load-bearing brick party walls with Chinese fir wood beams and floors, and were usually four storeys in height and built along narrow side streets. The building site did not have sufficient depth to construct a verandah, but enabled the creation of narrow cantilevered balconies. These balconies were constructed of reinforced concrete, supported by suspended wrought-iron posts, had decorative wrought iron balustrades, and were about 61 centimetres (2 feet) deep. Despite a thin and confined balcony, the building managed to provide an external space for laundry, and additional usable space, and there were often light wells incorporated into the floor plans.

Recessed Balcony (New Era: Circa 1900–1935)

Tong lau with recessed balconies were constructed of load-bearing brick party walls with Chinese fir wood beams and floors. The façades of these buildings were recessed inward to form a balcony about 61 centimetres (2 feet) in depth. Light wells in this type of *tong lau* were rare, but some had windows in the kitchen.

Façade Stairwell for Half-turn Staircase (Inter-War Years: Circa 1935–1940)

The structure of this type of *tong lau* changed during this time period, with the later use of reinforced concrete. There was a half-turn staircase facing the street that complied with the new requirement under Buildings Ordinance 1935—for staircases on every floor to allow more natural daylight and air. The building's frontage width was increased to accommodate the stairwell design, there were windows in the kitchen, and sanitary fittings were introduced.

Building Components and Organisation

Staircase

A communal staircase served as the vertical circulation. In earlier *tong lau* buildings, the staircase was long, narrow and constructed of wood. In later buildings, the staircase was formed from concrete, and in all buildings the staircase connected the residential floors with the ground floor entrance. In the time of communal staircases as vertical circulation, the lower floors were more desirable and expensive to rent than the top floors. The shared staircase served as an informal social centre where all residents passed and greeted one another on a regular basis.

Shop

Tong lau buildings had a shop on the ground floor that served the residents and the community. The rows of shops at pedestrian level created a strong urban character and street presence in the neighbourhood.

Kitchen

In multi-tenant *tong lau* buildings, kitchens were located at the back of each floor. In single-family housing, kitchens were located at the back of one floor, usually the second floor. Kitchens consisted of a heat source fuelled by wood or coal for cooking and there were windows for exhaust and ventilation. The walls and floors were often tiled to allow for easier maintenance.

Cubicles

In multi-tenant *tong lau* buildings, residential floors were subdivided to accommodate multiple tenants and families. The area of each floor was about 50 square metres (530 square feet) and each floor was subdivided into three, 9.5-square metre (100-square feet) cubicle-like rooms separated by wood partitions. At the ceiling of each partition was wire mesh that allowed in light and air. Only the cubicle that faced the street received direct daylight and air. The cubicles were often furnished with bunk beds and life inside each cubicle was crowded.

Rooftops

The rooftops of *tong lau* buildings were not habitable, but often used as a place to sleep in warmer weather. There was insufficient cross-ventilation inside the building and the air on the residential floors, especially in the cubicles, was still and stale. The rooftop was flat and was sometimes used as an area for the resident children to play. Kite flying was a favourite rooftop children's pastime.

Typical Unit Floor Plan Type

The early 1840s single-family *tong lau* housing could be considered the corridor unit floor plan type, and for later tenement use *tong lau*, the unit floor plan type could be considered central living.

Access Type

The access type in *tong lau* buildings was vertical. First and second period *tong lau* building designs had a long and narrow straight-run staircase, and third period had a half-turn staircase, all of which allowed for direct access to the units. All residents used the staircase. The narrow width of the stair required neighbours to brush by one another, and the stair thus was a place where neighbours shared visual and physical contact with each other.

Construction Materials

Floors

Some of the finishing flooring for ground floor shops had unglazed red tiles, but the earthen floor was often left exposed. The residential floors upstairs consisted of planks of Chinese fir wood whose length determined the width of their spans. Wood lengths were usually between 3.5 and 4.5 metres (12–15 feet) long, and the material length and usage resulted in a long and narrow building. In much *tong lau* housing constructed in the inter-war years, tile replaced wood as the finishing flooring for the upper residential floors. A tiled floor was easier to maintain and provided cooling relief in the summer when people slept on bamboo mats laid on the floor.

Walls

Walls were constructed of traditional Chinese grey brick and lime mortar, which was soft and porous. Unlike the "Western buildings" that had standardised space and sanitary requirements, "Chinese buildings" used inferior building materials and specifications. Granite from local quarries was often used in the ground floor shop for door jambs and lintels. The walls were usually plastered, but sometimes left with exposed brick that was made smooth with traditional Chinese construction techniques.

Roofs

The roofs of *tong lau* buildings were tiled with unglazed semicircular clay tiles set with overlapping ends. The eave tiles were frequently decorative and glazed. Later-period *tong lau* constructions had flat concrete roofs.

Doors

The entrance doors of earlier *tong lau* buildings were made of heavy wood, but in the later periods were constructed of heavy metal. Current, existing *tong lau* entrance doors are metal, with slots cut into the front to receive mail delivery.

Owners, Landlords, Developers, Reformers

Reformers

Osbert Chadwick

By 1881, Hong Kong was acutely unhygienic and the British government enlisted the expert advice of Osbert Chadwick, a sanitary engineer, to assess the situation. Chadwick confirmed that the living standards in *tong lau* were severely congested and poor, and living in such confined spaces with little to no access to natural daylight and fresh air was detrimental to the health of its inhabitants. Chadwick proposed a number of improvements to the design of the housing and its streets, and the government set out and brought about Chadwick's recommendations by improving water supplies and drainage systems and constructing new animal depots, slaughterhouses, and latrines.

Even with Chadwick and the government's best intentions and efforts, Hong Kong succumbed to the bubonic plague and many inhabitants lost their lives in the epidemic. The greatest numbers of victims were Chinese, and the area that was worst hit was the *tong lau* neighbourhood of Tai Ping Shan. Following this catastrophe, Chadwick was commissioned by the government to produce further investigations on Hong Kong's sanitary requirements. In 1903, Chadwick's findings and recommendations were chronicled in the form of Public Health and Buildings Ordinance 1903. Under that code, Chadwick set out minimum standards of habitable floor area, minimum sizes for windows to allow adequate daylight and air, and height and depth of buildings.

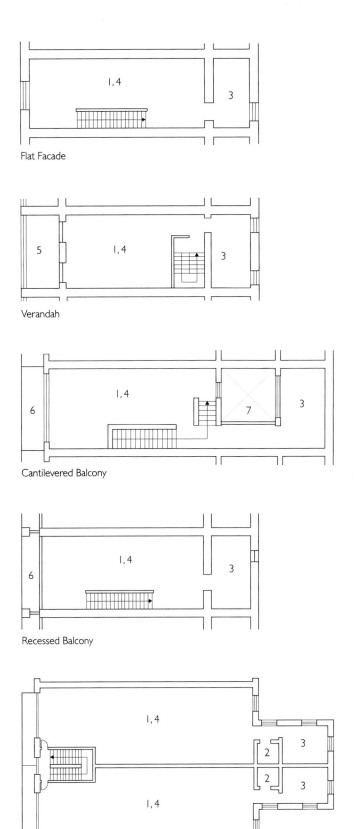

Flat Facade

Verandah

Cantilevered Balcony

Recessed Balcony

Facade Stairwell for Half-turn Staircase

1 Living Room
2 Toilet
3 Kitchen
4 Bedroom
5 Verandah
6 Balcony
7 Light Well

Typical Floors

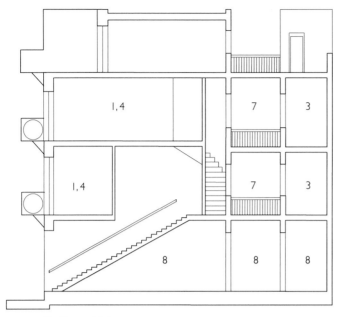

Cantilevered Balcony

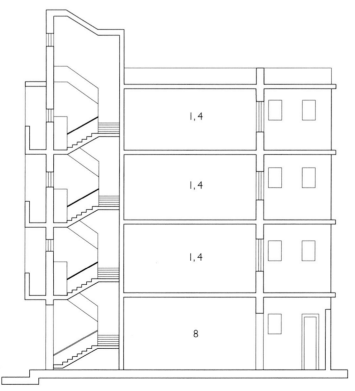

Facade Stairwell for Half-turn Staircase

1 Living Room
2 Toilet
3 Kitchen
4 Bedroom
5 Verandah
6 Balcony
7 Light Well
8 Shop

Sections

Verandah – 60–66 Johnston Road

Cantilever Balcony (Blue House) – 72 Stone Nullah Lane

Half-turn Staircase – 29–31 Bridges Street

Cantilever Balcony – 1–11 Mallory Street

Recessed Balcony – 35 Bonham Road

Flat Façade – 6–8 Hing Wan Street

Government Departments, Policies, and Regulations

1856: Building and Nuisances Ordinance

In 1856, Hong Kong inherited its first buildings ordinance passed down by the British government. This first ordinance primarily dealt with Western housing and had little to do with Chinese buildings. It was much later that Hong Kong received enactments that pertained directly to Chinese buildings and to buildings in areas of the city where non-Western people lived.

1903: Public Health and Buildings Ordinance

The early authorities in Hong Kong imposed little statutory control on the architecture of Chinese buildings. In the early 1900s, however, Hong Kong was facing severe public health issues among its population. Since the outbreak of bubonic plague in 1894, the Hong Kong government had considered a series of radical reforms that included the demolition of the *tong lau* district of Tai Ping Shan, where the disease outbreak was first established, killing hundreds of people, but realised that more prudent plans and concerted efforts were needed to combat matters in the longer term. In 1903, the government engaged Osbert Chadwick, a sanitary engineer, to assess the situation and help put in place its first comprehensive set of enforceable building regulations under the Public Health and Buildings Ordinance 1903.

The ordinance tried to curb overcrowding by defining a ratio of inhabitants to inhabitable floor space, and by creating unobstructed access to internal air space. Other governances included the provision of open space and a laneway of at least 6 feet (1.8 metres) behind the buildings; limiting new *tong lau* building height to four storeys, to ensure that surrounding streets would receive adequate natural daylight and ventilation; prohibiting the keeping of cattle on the premises; lengthening staircases so they were not perilously steep, to compensate for floor space gains; establishing a defined minimum window size to allow for fresh air; and the introduction of light wells. For the calculation defining a non-overcrowded living condition, the authorities recommended one adult for every 50 square feet (4.65 square metres) of inhabitable floor space.

1935: Buildings Ordinance

The Buildings Ordinance 1935 represented the last building edict to be issued in Hong Kong before the Pacific War (World War II). It was important because it was the final set of lawful governance for the architecture of *tong lau* and it formed the basis for all future building regulations to follow. The building regulations under this ordinance were essentially a continuation of those introduced in Public Health and Buildings Ordinance 1903, but with more rigorous rules. The amended ordinance made for tighter restrictions for control over building height, acceptable types of building materials, proper construction methods, minimum size of openings, need for cross-ventilation in habitable spaces, and approval and filing of building plans were mandated.

Present Day

Since 1960, *tong lau* development and construction have declined markedly and many buildings have been demolished. Today, the surviving *tong lau* buildings are experiencing a renewed appreciation. There is an active community that values the *tong lau* as an important part of Hong Kong's cultural heritage, and wants to conserve its architectural identity. A growing number among the younger generation, especially architecture and urban planning students and enthusiasts, are calling for cultural awareness and environmental sustainability in their society. The current planning system in Hong Kong does not have policies to address heritage conservation and redevelopment. Private citizens and organisations, such as the Hong Kong Housing Society (HKHS) and Urban Renewal Authority (URA), have become involved and are preserving, restoring, and converting the buildings. Many existing *tong lau* buildings have been modernised with elevators, some buildings have been returned to multi-dwelling units or single-family housing, while others have been renovated for commercial use, such as art galleries, tea shops, restaurants, and boutique hotels.

More recent times have seen the advent of "archi-tourists", both locally and internationally, in search of the few remaining *tong lau* houses. The Blue House on Nullah Road has become an iconic and popular photo destination. The building is actively used as housing and there is a sign at its entrance, written in both Chinese and English, cautioning people to respect the privacy of the residents and that the building is not open to the public. Wing Lee Street is one of the last streets lined entirely by *tong lau* buildings from the 1950s. In 2003 the buildings were scheduled to be demolished, but due to public protest they have been preserved, restored, and remain as housing with ground floor shops. Public education on heritage preservation has become an active endeavour in Hong Kong, and efforts have been made to promote public awareness through information centres, galleries, and heritage and architectural walking tours.

IBA 84/87, Block 70 – Fraenkelufer and Admiralstrasse

BERLIN

Circa 1920, 1950 and 1980
Perimeter Block, Linear Block, and Block-Edge

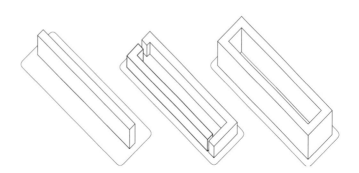

In Berlin, block housing was an early housing form that eventually evolved into a typology synonymous with the city. The three types of block housing most visible in the city are perimeter block, linear block, and block-edge. There were three distinct periods in Berlin's housing and urban planning history that used the block-housing types: Berlin Housing Estates in the 1920s, and two international building exhibitions, *Internationale Bauausstellung* (IBA) in 1957 and IBA 1987. The three developments can be regarded not only as projects, but also as manifestos. The government, architects, and urban planners addressed and responded to the social issues of the times, introduced new ideals and developed and constructed theories and designs into pragmatic dwelling solutions.

The Berlin Housing Estates development and the IBA 1957 and IBA 1987 exhibitions were extraordinary precedents for mass housing concepts and construction in the twentieth century. The Germans viewed mass housing projects that were well designed, realised, and received as the epitome of communal organisation, and that a successful development was a step towards a better community, city, and nation. The projects from the three movements attested to the innovative housing policies and were commendable examples of the building reform movements that improved housing for the masses through novel approaches in town planning, architecture, and landscaping. The developments opened up discussions on societal and housing policies and actions, and the architects shaped and influenced housing ideas and designs in Germany and other parts of the Western world.

Perimeter Block Characteristics

Perimeter block building type is a single development that occupies a city block. The key characteristics are:

- Corresponds to individually developed parcels of land
- Building form conforms to the street pattern, height, depth, and other zoning regulations in the city
- Buildings can be single entity or fragmented and divided up by recessed openings or reveals
- Usually has two orientations: street and courtyard
- Courtyards are semi-private green spaces designated for use by residents of the building
- Ground floors can be zoned for retail

Linear Block Characteristics

The linear block building type is linear in shape and stands free from adjacent buildings. The key characteristics are:

- Not necessarily informed by aspects of the specific block
- Building appears as autonomous object
- Multi-layered volume, whose presence can structure an entire urban area
- Usually cost-effective concrete slab building construction

- Comprises a large number of dwelling units

- Usually stacked and systematic floor plans

- Units are arranged along a single or double-loaded internal access corridor

- Units usually face one orientation

Block-Edge Characteristics

The block-edge building type is a single development that completes one portion of an existing urban block or defines formerly undeveloped block edges. It shares the same characteristics as the perimeter block typology.

Historical Context

Between the late 1800s and early 1900s, Berlin built many city blocks of tenement housing, *Mietskaserne*, to accommodate the sudden surge in population. Like any other urban and industrial city during this time, migrant workers from nearby communities besieged Berlin to seek employment opportunities in the city's new industries. In 1920, the Greater Berlin Act amalgamated the city's neighbouring boroughs and created Greater Berlin. With this enactment, the population of Berlin doubled immediately, from about 2 million to nearly 4 million inhabitants, the city's area increased to over 870 square kilometres (335 square miles), and the demand for additional housing rapidly presented itself.

The architecture of the *Mietskaserne*, tenement housing, was very distinct. The buildings were five storeys in height, multi-unit, constructed from heavy masonry, utilitarian in design, devoid of embellishment, built around communal courtyards at the back, and sat squarely on the city's blocks. Its solid street presence occupied large areas of the city and its uniform façades were repeated along in block after city block. From an aerial view, the *Mietskaserne* looked like massive extruded square blocks with a central void. The housing type comprised and supplied the bulk of the city's housing stock and accommodated the great majority of the population, many of whom were newly arrived working-class labourers. The housing type was not unique to Berlin, and was developed in other German cities during this time, but the sheer number of *Mietskaserne* in Berlin was overwhelmingly disproportionate to the other cities. The name *Mietskaserne* is a German term that translates to rental barracks. The derisive name compared the characteristics of the building to living in a military barracks, and the term was viewed as demeaning to its inhabitants. A more neutral term for the housing was *das Berliner mietshaus*, which translates as the Berlin rental house. Regardless of its name, it could be argued that this strong typology set a precedent for block housing in Berlin.

In the 1900s, there were three urban renewal events that played important roles in the building of Berlin, and these all included housing: the government-initiated Berlin Housing Estates in 1920, and the exhibitions of IBA 1957 and IBA 1984/87. These three showcased advanced city planning and building ideas and projects, and best addressed Berlin's reformed housing development and design. The projects in each design period included a combination of civic buildings and residential housing, and the housing designs presented were comprised of different housing typologies. However, there were three noticeable housing types that reappeared: perimeter block, linear block, and block-edge.

Circa 1920 Berlin Housing Estates

The years after the First World War were distressing for Berlin. Many of its buildings had been destroyed by warfare and the city experienced a housing crisis. During this time, the politically left-leaning Weimar Republic took office and Berlin was transformed into a hub of improvement, optimism, and activism. The Weimar Republic created a new way of life; the Weimar culture encouraged and enabled a radical and experimental shift in the arts and architecture that was unwelcome and curtailed by the previous regime. The Weimar period was also a vibrant age in the history of Berlin. The burst of exploratory arts was closely associated with social democratic ideals and values. Also, during this period, the establishment of Greater Berlin made Berlin the third largest city in the world, after New York and London, and helped the city gain widespread prominence for its forward-thinking attitude in the disciplines of politics, arts, humanities, and social sciences.

During the Weimar Republic, Berlin produced illustrious architects and architecture. In the 1920s, the city's most influential figures in Modern architecture—Mies van der Rohe, Walter Gropius, Bruno Taut, Martin Wagner, and Hans Scharoun, to name a few—established their careers and reputations during this time. Many of these esteemed architects responded to Berlin's post-war housing needs and helped fix the situation with a massive housing development known as the Berlin Housing Estates.

The most severe post-war housing shortage was between the years 1919 and 1923. Nearly 100,000 dwelling units needed to be built to accommodate all those whose lives had been disrupted by the war and for the newly unemployed and wounded soldiers returning home, but fewer than 9,000 dwelling units were built. Between 1924 and 1930, approximately 135,000 new dwelling units were constructed. The Berlin Housing Estates was a large housing complex developed on parcels of Berlin's newly united boroughs. The Estates addressed the new housing focus and was largely funded by the Weimar Republic and then by trade unions, cooperatives, and municipal and charitable housing associations. The development was conceived as a chance to alleviate the overcrowded and unsanitary conditions in the tenement worker housing, which had been exacerbated by the war, and better the lives of the labouring classes. The key elements for the new and reformed housing vision involved building independent communities away from the congested city centre, supportive environments for fulfilling work and neighbourly exchange, and that afforded a pleasurable gardening pastime. The ambitions were reminiscent of the garden city movement, and part of the main goal of the new housing initiative was to provide equal housing opportunities and standards to all citizens regardless of their economic status.

The estates were envisioned as a modern community of planned housing that promoted neighbourly interaction, which would lead to a sense of belonging and community. The government's overall goal was to provide the common citizen with a decent place to live, and in a healthy, natural environment with all the comforts of city living. The developments were also a larger social experiment in housing to educate the inhabitants, or citizens in general, that life was better lived together in a communal partnership rather than individually, and was labelled "the people's apartment", *die Volkswohnung*.

The Berlin Housing Estates project was led mostly by Bruno Taut, then Martin Wagner and Hans Scharoun, and in collaboration with many of their architect and landscape contemporaries. The development was made up of six large housing estates spread over an extensive area of land. Each estate was divided into smaller sections, each containing different residential buildings, and a different architect designed each building. Each estate and building style exemplified the new Weimar culture of a radical and experimental shift in architectural design, responded to the city's housing emergency, and embodied new and improved housing design innovations, solutions, and policies. The buildings applied the latest in engineering techniques that enabled the mass production of steel, glass, and concrete, and each dwelling unit had modern amenities and conveniences such as private bathrooms, modern kitchens, and access to outdoor spaces.

Bruno Taut was the chief planner and consultant architect who guided and managed most of the overall planning of the six housing estates. From Taut's master plan, different architects laid out each housing estate, and within each housing estate different architects designed each individual building. The architectural style differed from estate to estate and from building to building, but the majority of the multi-dwelling unit block housing looked modern in style. Most buildings, with their plain and simple forms and flat roofs, evoke the manner of the Bauhaus. The Bauhaus motto of "form follows function" was closely exercised and very evident in the planning of the estates. The housing typologies differed from one estate to another, and from one building to another building, but the two noticeable types that frequently reappeared were perimeter block and linear block. The housing estates were: Falkenberg Garden City, by Bruno Taut and Heinrich Tessenow, in 1913; Schillerpark Estate, by Bruno Taut and Hans Hoffman, in 1924; Britz Residential Estate (Horseshoe Estate), by Bruno Taut and Martin Wagner, in 1925; Carl Legien Estate, by Bruno Taut and Franz Hillinger, in 1928; White City, by Otto Rudolf Salvisberg, Bruno Ahrends, and Wilhelm Büning, in 1929; and Siemensstadt Estate ("Ring" Estate), by Otto Bartning, Fred Forbat, Walter Gropius, Hugo Häring, Paul-Rudolf Henning, and Hans Scharoun, in 1929.

"Sun, Air, and House for All!"

The architects of Berlin Housing Estates re-evaluated what it meant to live in a healthy environment. They deduced that residing within close access to open green space, fresh air, and sunshine made for better and happier living. An exhibition, entitled Sonne, Luft und Haus für Alle! was held and it was all about the possibilities for leisure in the big city. Soon after, the catchphrase "Sun, Air, and House for All" was adopted and put into practice, and Le Corbusier's *The Athens Charter* and the gardens cities movement was implemented on the estates. Bruno Taut befriended Ebenezer Howard in England in early 1900 and became intrigued with Howard's Garden City ideas of planned communities surrounded by green space. Taut became a loyal supporter and follower of the Garden City movement. He was a firm believer in the idea that housing should be self-sufficient, free-standing communities and that a house and its surrounding environment should be a place that makes its residents happy and fulfilled, and these beliefs were brought to his planning and design for the Berlin Housing Estates.

Berlin Housing Estates Components and Organisation

Green Space

The estates were influenced by the Garden City movement and were designed within large green spaces. All dwelling units had access to vegetation, gardens, and outdoor areas. Units within the blocks had private balconies and units on the ground floor had private gardens. Green space was an integral part of the design of the estates and further instilled the idea of an idyllic garden city. Generous green spaces were designed throughout the estates as open, centralised parks and as green buffers between housing blocks.

Architectural Details

Attention was paid to the architectural details in all of the housing developments. Design elements such as cornices, entrance details, balconies, windows, doors, porches, brickwork, and patterns revealed each architect's individual style. The design and materials for the detailing were considered costly then, but were durable and required little maintenance.

Colour

The estate architects experimented with colour in all the housing developments. The use of colour was a move away from the oppressive brick of the old Berlin blocks. Colour combinations of black, white, blue, green, red, yellow, and terracotta were expressed on doors, window frames, and even entire façades. The use of colour was an essential part of the belief that housing surrounded by a cheerful environment would make the residents happy and fulfilled.

Kitchens

The kitchens on the estates were developed by the housing association GEHAG, and were known as the GEHAG kitchen. The GEHAG kitchen was an efficient and scientific kitchen for its time, using materials that were easy to clean and keep hygienic. The kitchens were divided on an asymmetrical, horizontal layout for ease of user workflow, allowing for airflow and ventilation from cooking smells and food storage. The kitchen had a dual-flame gas cooking range, a basin sink with a drain, pantry under the kitchen window to keep food cool, and ventilated and extra cupboards for storage. The kitchen range and sinks were of stainless steel, the wall behind the range was tiled, and the countertops and cupboard doors were of hard plastic laminate for durability and ease of maintenance. The layout and materials were sophisticated for the time.

Dwelling Units

Units in the estates were developed by GEHAG and based on the innovative approach and methods of Alexander Klein. An average apartment was one-and-a-half bedrooms (the half-room accommodated a single bed) and measured 43 square metres (460 square feet). GEHAG found that the most efficient and comfortable unit floor plan dimensions were approximately 6 metres (19 feet) wide by 9 metres (29 feet) long, with a balcony 1.5 metres (5 feet) deep. The living rooms were 16.58 square metres (178 square feet), the principal bedrooms were 11.84 square metres (127 square feet), the kitchens were 8.32 square metres (90 square feet), the half-bedrooms were 3.15 square metres (34 square feet), the foyers were 3.11 square metres (33 square feet), and the balconies were 5 square metres (54 square feet). The measurements were derived from studies and considered to be ergonomic for the user.

Interiors

The use of strong colours carried into the interiors. Rooms were painted in shades of red, yellow, blue, green, grey, and white; floorboards were painted dark red and grey, and multi-coloured wall paint or tiles were used in the bathrooms, kitchens, hallways, and staircases.

Case Studies: The Estates

Britz Residential Estate (Horseshoe Estate)

Architects: Bruno Taut and Martin Wagner
Construction Period: 1925–1930

The Britz Residential Estate, known by its more informal name, Horseshoe Estate, was the first residential estate in Germany after the war that fulfilled the vision of reformed housing. It was thought to be experimental and a model construction site for the public sector. The estate's nickname stemmed from its horseshoe shape of dwelling units that enclosed a large patch of communal green space at its centre, and it became the symbol of the social democratic ambition to create housing that offered easy access to light, air, sun, and green space. The Horseshoe Estate was evocative of a large city perimeter block housing with a communal courtyard, and the dwellings provided clean and comfortable living accommodations that would appeal to a majority of the population. The estate contained close to 2,000 dwelling units of varying sizes and layouts, from one- to three-bedroom units to accommodate families with children, and housed over 5,000 people.

The Horseshoe Estate was built on a generous site covering approximately 30 hectares (74 acres) and was constructed over six phases. The strong horseshoe form dominated the landscape and political motivation was the rationale behind its peculiar arrangement. Alongside the state, the Horseshoe Estate was funded in part by cooperative and trade union companies. Their aim was to be, and to provide, a better housing alternative than those provided by the private enterprises, and the architecture represented the cooperative view of collectively and solidarity. The overall design and organisation was built for, and with, the working class in mind and was celebrated for being efficient, functional, and enjoyable. The Horseshoe Estate was considered a major achievement and success in its duty and function.

Branching out from the horseshoe shape was a mix of single-family townhouses and multi-dwelling unit linear block buildings that sat together and were aligned neatly in rows. The presence of the rows of linear blocks with their flat roofs can be seen from afar and stretched to the boundaries of the entire estate area. Narrow residential streets fan out from the horseshoe form, providing access and service to the townhouses and linear block housing.

Colour was used and celebrated as an element of design and each section, row, or cluster of buildings was colour-coded in a spectrum of strong colours—red, yellow, white, or blue—for visual identity and way finding. For Taut, the use of colour was an inexpensive way to help foster vitality and diversity among the inhabitants. The most striking colours were those painted on entrance doors. A different mix of colours, patterns, and textures gave the otherwise utilitarian entranceway, and recurring types of construction, a cheerful and individual character.

Some of the linear block buildings had private balconies or terraces, but all dwelling units had easy access to ample daylight, air, sun, and green space. The linear blocks ran parallel to tree-lined footpaths that led to the large communal, landscaped green space at the centre of the horseshoe-shaped complex, also referred to as the big outdoor living room, that sat in close proximity. The shared outdoor living environment was an important design element for Taut and Wagner. They wanted to create a space that visually enforced and maintained the idea of moral social housing and enhanced the happiness and lifestyle of its inhabitants. The outdoor living room was completed with a grass lawn, trees, plants, a pond, and places to socialise and relax.

The estate held communal spaces for the residents to use and interact if they so wished. There were designated areas for a social gathering space, to hang clothes to dry, a children's playground, event space, place to clean large household equipment, to repair small machinery, for basic wood working, and an area of uniformly designed and distributed waste receptacles for garbage disposal. The spaces were connected by a network of footpaths and serviced the needs of the residents in an exemplary manner.

Carl Legien Estate

Architects: Bruno Taut and Franz Hillinger
Construction Period: 1928–1930

Bruno Taut found planning of the Carl Legien Estate his most challenging to date. Named after Carl Legien, a trade union leader who died in 1920, the estate was located close to Berlin's city centre, and needed to conform to the city's existing inner city streets and spatial organisation. With this in mind, Taut was confined to strict city guidelines and was not able to fully apply the garden city ideas to the Carl Legien Estate as he was able to with his two previous estate designs. However, like his two predecessors, Taut was able to utilise modern building materials and innovations to efficiently realise a cost-effective mass residential housing construction project. The housing estate contained just over 1,000 dwelling units, the majority of which were one- and two-and-a-half-bedroom layouts.

Taut disliked and dismissed the idea that the Carl Legien Estate had to conform to the city's prescribed rigidity of blocks and streets. Instead, he devised a design solution that still provided the estate's inhabitants and dwelling units with the same open and easy access to ample daylight, air, sun, and green space. To achieve this, Taut divided the estate's one large block into six smaller blocks. In each smaller block he placed five-storey, multi-dwelling unit buildings that faced onto a landscaped green space. The majority of the five-storey buildings were U-shaped, space-enclosing structures, but the northeastern block was a perimeter block type which was also the only building that had ground floor commercial spaces intended to serve the residents; the southeastern block was a linear block. There was no evidence to suggest a reason for the difference in the two end typologies.

Horseshoe Estate

Horseshoe Estate

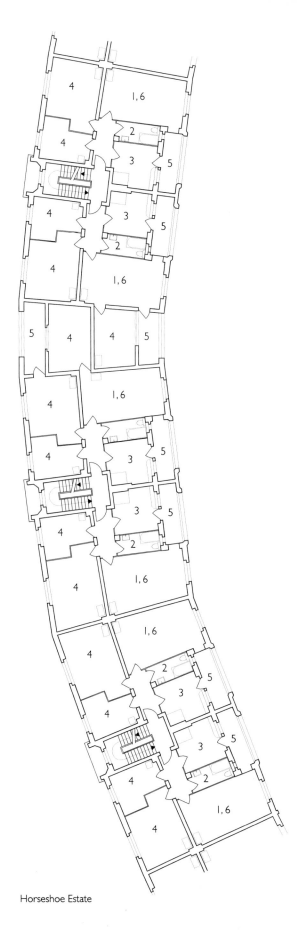

1 Living Room
2 Bathroom
3 Kitchen
4 Bedroom
5 Balcony
6 Dining Room

Typical Floors

Horseshoe Estate

Horseshoe Estate Bedroom Restored

GEHAG Kitchen

Horseshoe Estate

Horseshoe Estate

The communal landscaped green spaces in all six smaller blocks were the feature attraction for each block, and for the estate as a whole. It visually and physically provided lots of green space and a sense of openness and spaciousness. To further enhance the experience for the residents, the corner balconies were rounded to draw attention to the gardens, and the linear blocks were used widthwise to optimise the availability of light, sun, and garden views to the units; living rooms, bedrooms, and balconies faced the gardens, and bathrooms and kitchens faced the streets. To ensure this design method stayed consistent for all dwelling units, the buildings were mirrored to face the garden and repeated across the blocks.

Colour was also used and celebrated as an element of design in this estate. The building façades that faced the streets were painted yellow to make the narrow streets appear brighter and wider, and the landscaped green open spaces were planted with different varieties of colourful vegetation that added to the estate's bright and cheery atmosphere. On a site that Bruno Taut once thought was unworkable, he managed to successfully create a feeling of spaciousness among social housing buildings enclosed by open green space in the middle of the city.

White City

Architects: Otto Rudolf Salvisberg, Bruno Ahrends, and Wilhelm Büning
Construction Period: 1929–1931

White City was the fifth estate to be constructed, and housed just over 1,000 dwelling units of mostly one- and two-bedroom layouts. Similar to the previous descriptions and design principles of The Horseshoe and Carl Legien Estates, White City was made up of mostly multi-storey, multi-dwelling unit linear block housing that provided ample light, air, and sunshine, nestling among landscaped green spaces. However, unlike the previous estates' use of colours, all the buildings in White City were painted bright white and that was how the estate's name was generated. With its clean lines, geometric building forms with smooth plaster finish, and colour scheme reminiscent of newness, cleanliness, and hygiene, White City was a symbol for modern residential estate construction and it inspired other all-white building structures around the world. White City also experimented with its ground floor development. It was the first estate to provide expanded amenities and services to its residents. The estate contained a medical office, kindergarten, school, sports facilities, and shops, which were extremely uncommon for the time, and it emphasised and reinstated the message that White City represented social housing for the people.

Carl Legien

Carl Legien

Siemensstadt Estate ("Ring" Estate)

Architects: Otto Bartning, Fred Forbat, Walter Gropius, Hugo Häring, Paul-Rudolf Henning, and Hans Scharoun
Construction Period: 1929–1931

Siemensstadt Estate was the last of the six estates that made up the Berlin Housing Estates, and was planned by Hans Scharoun. Many of the architects were members of an architectural organisation known as "Der Ring", and the estate was often known as the "Ring" Estate. The estate was actually named after the local Siemens electrical factory and was used as worker housing for its many employees. Unlike the previous five estates that were funded by the state and planned in garden city fashion, the Siemensstadt Estate was financed by private companies and was denser in design. It was an efficient, economical, and modern dormitory-style settlement for a large number of workers and their families.

The estate housed just over 1,000 dwelling units, the majority of which were one- and two-and-a-half-bedroom-size apartments. The housing typology was made up mostly of linear blocks, each five storeys high, and different architects were each assigned an area on the site to develop. Though all the forms were of similar typology, some buildings looked utilitarian, like Gropius'; some looked organic, like Häring's curved balconies; and some were colourful and appeared angular, like Scharoun's contribution.

The linear blocks were arranged in parallel rows with a north–south orientation to ensure maximum light, air, and sunshine reached the units. The building height and spacing were denser than those of the previous estates, but careful attention was paid not to repeat the oppressive density of the earlier *Mietskaserne* housing form. The spaces between the buildings were green spaces and deep balconies, which acted as an extension of the units' living rooms, overlooking those areas. A promenade was designed to accommodate a children's playground, a playschool, and quiet seating areas. There was a "green centre" where green spaces between the linear blocks led into a large open garden for communal use by the inhabitants. The majority of colours used in this estate were earth-toned and natural in appearance. There were uses of yellow-brown brick, beige plaster, white paint around window frames, and dark brown paint on entrance doors. The colours helped create a warm and comforting atmosphere.

Plan Type

There were numerous and different floor plan layouts throughout block housing on the estates. The types ranged from one- to two-and-a-half-bedroom units with square areas ranging from 50 to 70 square metres (530 to 750 square feet). However, most of the unit floor plan types were separated rooms. An average apartment was one-and-a-half bedrooms and measured 43 square metres (460 square feet). GEHAG derived the layout and dimensions from studies and found the measurements to be efficient and comfortable for the inhabitants.

Siemensstadt Exhibition

Siemensstadt-Hugo Häring at Goebelstrasse

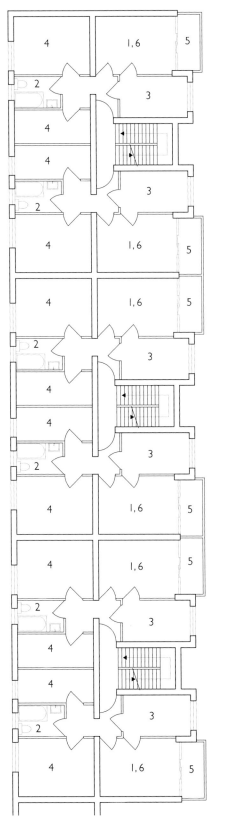

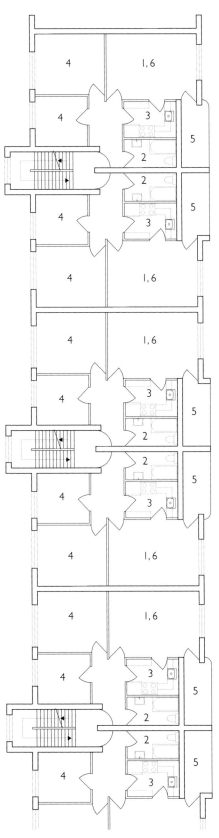

Typical Floors
Walter Gropius

Typical Floors
Fred Forbat

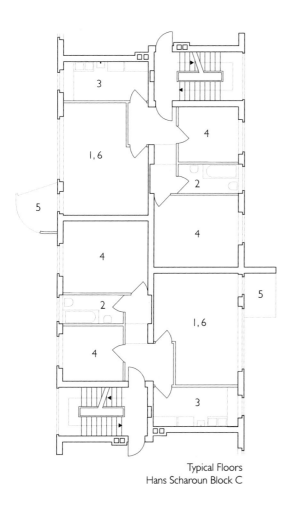

Typical Floors
Hans Scharoun Block C

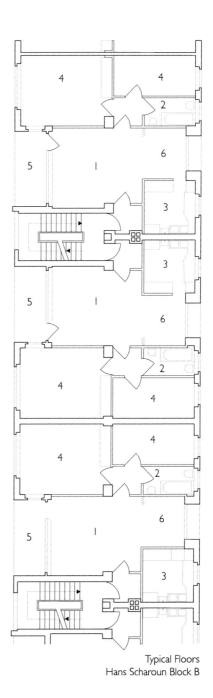

Typical Floors
Hans Scharoun Block B

1 Living Room
2 Bathroom
3 Kitchen
4 Bedroom
5 Balcony
6 Dining Room

Siemensstadt Estate

Siemensstadt-Hans Scharoun at Jungfernheideweg

Siemensstadt-Fred Forbat at Geisslerpfad

Siemensstadt Façade-Fred Forbat at Geisslerpfad

Siemensstadt-Fred Forbat at Geisslerpfad, Balconies, Block 6, West Side

Siemensstadt-Fred Forbat at Geisslerpfad, Balconies, Block 6, West Side

Siemensstadt-Hugo Häring at Goebelstrasse

Siemensstadt-Hugo Häring at Goebelstrasse

Access Type

The Berlin Housing Estates were comprised of numerous and different types of layout. The access in the Horseshoe, Carl Legien, White City and Siemensstadt Estates shared a vertical, central stair circulation with dwelling unit entrances directly off the landing of the stairs. The central staircase reaffirmed that the housing was built as a social model to freely share opinions and beliefs and that it was a place to live and be intellectually and socially receptive, a common utopian ideal at the time.

Construction Materials

Bruno Taut and Martin Wagner streamlined construction methods to keep costs affordable. The use of modern construction equipment and machinery, such as rail-mounted trucks and bucket-wheel excavators, coupled with the modern, clean, and efficient design of the estates and conventional measurements and standard sizes of components, contributed to an economical model for the design and development of mass housing. The block housing buildings on the estates were made of brick. The exteriors were covered with a mineral-dyed plastering mortar that either had a colour tinted into it or the façades were later painted. The windows were double-glazed glass, the flat roofs were held by steel beams set into the external masonry walls, and the storeys all sat above a basement. The internal walls were lightweight and prefabricated, the hallway and living room floors were wood, and the kitchen and bathroom floors were either terrazzo or magnesite.

Internationale Bauausstellung (IBA) Housing Exhibitions

The *Internationale Bauausstellung* (IBA) is an international building exhibition held in Germany, showcasing the country's innovative research and design in architecture, engineering, and urban planning. The IBA exhibitions in 1957 and 1984/87 were held in Berlin, and in both exhibitions the housing proposals were built throughout the city. The actual construction of the buildings for the exhibition allowed visitors to view and experience exemplary housing projects and, after the exhibit, enabled some to live in a model of housing history.

IBA '57: Interbau Berlin, "The City of Tomorrow"

In the final years of the Second World War, many buildings were badly damaged, if not completely destroyed, in the city of Berlin. The city was eager to start anew and held an international building exhibition, IBA, that was funded by the State of Berlin and the Federal Republic of Germany. IBA '57 was held in 1957 in Hansaviertel, a central district of Berlin, and the exhibition was known as Interbau Berlin, "The City of Tomorrow". Interbau Berlin focused on housing development, although it included some institutional projects and was an enthusiastic programme aimed at rebuilding and rejuvenating the Hansaviertel area of the city.

The Hansaviertel site for Interbau Berlin was an area of 25 hectares (62 acres) centrally located in Berlin that had been heavily bombed in the Second World War. The site was chosen for its circumstances, but also for political reasons. Hansaviertel was situated in West Berlin, close to the East Berlin border, and had a commuter train that carried thousands of East Berliners past the site daily. The exhibition was used as a means to display West Berlin's post-war economic development and progressiveness, contrasting with the situation in East Berlin. The restructuring of Hansaviertel was completed in 1961, and a total of 48 buildings comprising 1,300 dwelling units were realised. The housing proposals for Interbau Berlin were primarily social housing, and a total of 56 prominent architects from 14 countries presented their experimental and forward-thinking proposals for varying multi-unit housing typologies that fitted the purpose and the exhibition theme. The public embraced and praised the work, but many urban planners felt the exhibition lacked a clear and strong urban design concept. Many urban designers criticised the exhibition as a collection of fanciful buildings designed by famous architects; and the fact that the buildings were named as objects added to the sentiment.

Interbau Berlin provided an optimistic approach to the future of housing and proposed to better the lifestyle of the people. New furnishings, materials, and appliances were introduced and model dwelling units were displayed with furniture, curtains, carpets, and washing machines to advertise a modern lifestyle. The exhibition offered and emphasised ideas of greater leisure time, spaces for physical activities, and homes with a strong connection to community and family. The overall planning of the site recalled ideas of ample light, air, sunshine, and green space. Buildings were spaced far enough apart to allow for spacious landscaped areas for residents to have more time to enjoy physical activities and live with a secure sense of community.

Many renowned local and international architects designed objects for Interbau '57:

- Object 1: Klaus Mueller-Rehm and Gerhard Siegmann, Germany
- Object 3: Alexander Klein, Israel
- Object 4: Hans Mueller, Germany
- Object 5: Guenther Gottwald, Germany
- Object 6: Günther Wilhelm, Germany
- Object 7: Walter Gropius, USA and Wils Ebert, Germany
- Object 8: Pierre Vago, France
- Object 9: Wassili Luckhardt and Hubert Hoffmann, Germany
- Object 10: Paul Schneider-Esleben, Germany
- Object 11: Ernst Zinsser and Hansrudolf Plarre, Germany
- Object 12: Luciano Baldessari, Italy
- Object 13: Egon Eiermann, Germany
- Object 14: Oscar Niemeyer Filho, Brazil
- Object 15: Fritz Jaenecke and Sten Samuelson, Sweden
- Object 16: Alvar Aalto, Finland
- Object 17: Willy Kreuer, Germany
- Object 18: Gustav Hassenpflug, Germany
- Object 19: Hans Schwippert, Germany
- Object 20: Raymond Lopez and Eugène Beaudouin, France
- Object 21: J.H. van den Broek and J.B. Bakema, The Netherlands
- Object 22: Ludwig Lemmer, Germany
- Object 23: Werner Düttmann, Germany
- Object 24: Bruno Grimmek, Germany
- Object 25: Paul G.R. Baumgarten, Germany
- Object 26: Max Taut, Germany
- Object 27: Kay Fisker, Denmark
- Object 28: Otto H. Senn, Switzerland
- Object 29: Manfred Fuchs, Germany
- Object 30: Berhard Pfau, Germany
- Object 32: Franz Heinrich Sobotka and Gustav Mueller, Germany
- Object 33: F.R.S. Yorke, UK
- Object 34: Franz Schuster, Austria
- Object 35: Godbar Nissen, Germany
- Object 36: Berhard Hermkes, Germany
- Object 38: Hans Scharoun, Germany

- Object 39: Eduard Ludwig, Germany
- Object 40: Arne Jacobsen, Denmark
- Object 41: Gerhard Weber, Germany
- Object 42: Alois Giefer and Hermann Maeckler, Germany
- Object 43: Johannes Krahn, Germany
- Object 44: Sep Ruf, Germany
- Object 45: Wolf von Möllendorff and Sergius Ruegenberg, Germany
- Object 46: Josef Lehmbrock, Germany
- Object 47: Werner Fausser, Germany
- Object 48: Guenter Hönow, Germany
- Le Corbusier, Unite d'Habitation outside Hansa district, France
- Hugh A. Stubbins, Congress Hall outside Hansa district, USA

Hansaviertel IBA 1957, Members of the Japanese Upper House Visit the Berlin Pavilion,
Dr. Karl Mahler Explains a Model

Case Studies: The Objects

Object 5

Architect: Professor Günther Gottwald, Berlin

A linear block building located at 13–17 Klopstockstrasse was four storeys in height, approximately 55 metres (180 feet) long by 13 metres (42 feet) wide, and sat on an east–west orientation on the site. It comprised 32 dwelling units that ranged in size from studios to two-bedrooms units, 40 square metres (430 square feet) and 70 square metres (753 square feet), respectively. The units' living rooms opened onto a south-facing balcony that spanned the entire width of the unit, and provided the unit with plenty of natural light, air, and sunshine. The internal walls were of wood construction with sound insulation between them for noise absorption and reduction within each unit. The external façade was painted white and the south façade had thin, vertical concrete screens that were arranged in an alternating pattern, to shade parts of the balconies.

Object 8

Architect: Pierre Vago, Paris

A linear block building located at 14–18 Klopstockstrasse was nine storeys in height, approximately 64 metres (200 feet) long by 12.5 metres (41 feet) wide, and sat on a north–south orientation on the site. The building housed 59 dwelling units that ranged in size from studios to three-bedrooms units, 50 square metres (530 square feet) to 118 square metres (1,270 square feet) respectively. The units' living rooms opened onto a west-facing balcony. The basement level had storage rooms and a communal laundry room for the residents, and there was a partially covered outdoor green space that was used as a children's playground. The external east façade had a square grid pattern painted grey, white, and yellow, and the west façade had painted metal guardrails for the balconies.

Object 9

Architects: Professor Wassili Luckhardt and Baurat Hubert Hoffmann, Berlin

A linear block building located at 19–23 Klopstockstrasse was four storeys in height, approximately 65 metres (210 feet) long by 10 metres (32 feet) wide, and sat on an east–west orientation on the site. The building housed 28 dwelling units that ranged in size from studios to two-bedroom units, with the majority having two bedrooms, 30 square metres (320 square feet) to 94 square metres (1,000 square feet) respectively. The units' living rooms opened onto a south-facing balcony that spanned the entire width of the unit, and provided the unit with plenty of natural light, air and sunshine. The internal walls were plaster-covered cinder block. The basement level had storage rooms and a communal laundry room for the residents. The external east and west façades were covered in square concrete panels and the balconies on the south side had red-painted metal guardrails.

Object 13

Architect: Egon Eiermann, Karlsruhe

A linear block building located at 2–4 Bartningallee was eight storeys in height, approximately 63 metres (200 feet) long by 16 metres (52 feet) wide, and sat on a north–south orientation on the site. The building housed 96 dwelling units that comprised one- and two-bedroom units, at 36 square metres (380 square feet) and 50 square metres (530 square feet) respectively. The units' living rooms opened onto an east-facing balcony. The ground floor had a communal laundry room for the residents. The external façades were unfinished concrete and the east façade had a concrete frame around each balcony that formed a grid, and there were transparent glass guardrails for the balconies.

Object 14

Architect: Oscar Niemeyer Soares Filho, Brasilia

A linear block building located at 4–14 Altonaer Strasse was seven storeys in height, approximately 75 metres (250 feet) long by 15 metres (50 feet) wide, and sat on a north–south orientation on the site. The building housed 78 dwelling units that comprised studios and two-bedrooms units, with the majority two bedrooms, 44 square metres (470 square feet) to 78 square metres (830 square feet) respectively. The units' living rooms opened onto a west-facing balcony that spanned the entire width of the unit. The basement level had storage rooms and car parking and the top floor accommodated the communal laundry room for the residents. The entire building was raised on V-shaped concrete supports, the external north and south façades were clad in smooth concrete, the east façade had horizontal windows with a band of green spanning the entire width of the façade, and the west façade had balconies with horizontal metal guardrails.

Object 15

Architects: Fritz Jaenecke and Sten Samuelson, Malmö, Sweden

A linear block building located at 3–9 Altonaer Strasse was ten storeys in height, approximately 35 metres (114 feet) long by 11 metres (36 feet) wide, and sat on an east–west orientation on the site. The building housed 68 two-bedroom dwelling units, each of 115 square metres (1,200 square feet). The units' living rooms opened onto a south-facing balcony that spanned the entire width of the unit, and provided the unit with plenty of natural light, air and sunshine. The units had radiant floor heating and garbage chutes beside the elevator core. The ground floor was used commercially and accommodated stores and offices. The external east and west façades were concrete, the north façade was a continuous corridor open to the outdoors, and the south façade featured balconies with linear orange guardrails.

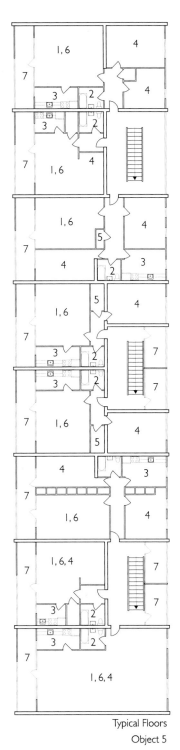

Typical Floors

Object 5

Floors 1, 3, 4, 6 and 7

Object 8

Floors 2 and 5

Object 8

1 Living Room
2 Bathroom
3 Kitchen
4 Bedroom
5 Storage
6 Dining Room
7 Balcony
8 Study
9 Elevator

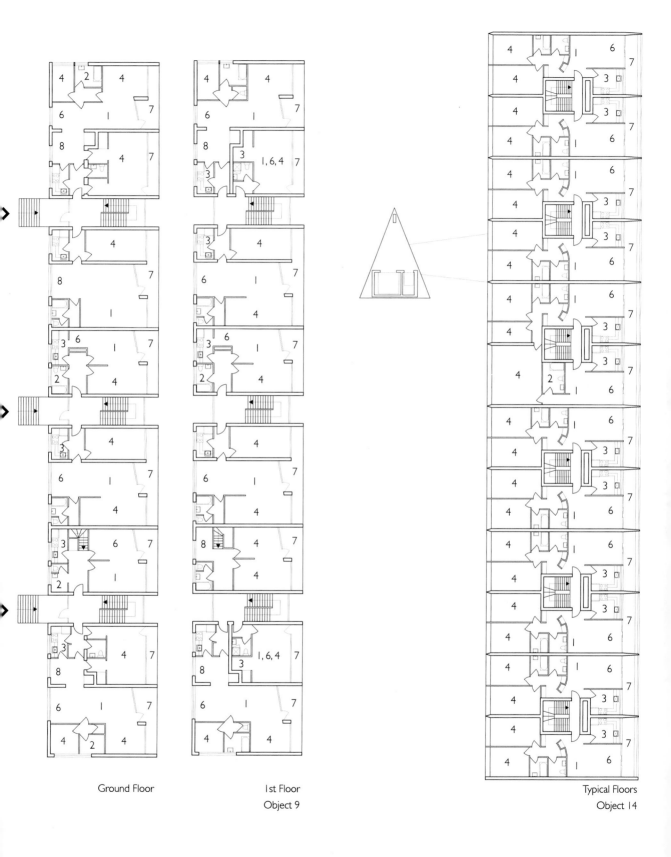

Ground Floor

1st Floor
Object 9

Typical Floors
Object 14

Hansaviertel IBA 1957, Object 5

Hansaviertel IBA 1957, Object 8

Hansaviertel IBA 1957, Object 9

Hansaviertel IBA 1957, Object 14

Hansaviertel IBA 1957, Left: Object 8, Right: Object 15

Hansaviertel IBA 1957, Left: Object 7, Middle: Object 8, Right: Object 15

Interbau House Architekt Pierre Vago, 1957

Wohnung Interbau Architekt Guenther Gottwald, 1957

Hansaviertel IBA 1957, Object 7

Typical Unit Floor Plan Type

The six linear block floor plans were all separated rooms. Every room in the unit were treated as its own individual room with access doors to access. There were conscious efforts to plan varied floor plan types to accommodate different types of inhabitant, and layouts ranged from studios to three-bedroom units.

Access Type

The six linear block housing typologies in Hansaviertel were all vertical access. All the buildings shared the same vertical, central stair and elevator circulation with entrances to dwelling units directly off the landing of the stairs or vestibule of the elevator. All buildings over five storeys at Hansaviertel had vertical access by both stair and elevator.

Construction Materials

The six linear block housing projects were concrete structures. Concrete was used for external walls and roofs and internal building forms. Building performance and comfort for the residents were important, and research was carried out into sound and thermal properties to strengthen the thermal and acoustic performance of the buildings. Innovative technologies, such as thicker insulating materials, thermal barriers, barrier coatings, insulated aluminium window units, and heated floors and ceilings were integrated into many of the buildings to protect the well-being of the building and its inhabitants. Heating for all six linear block buildings was provided by a central heating system on the property. All buildings connected into this system and had heat and hot water directly supplied on site. Buildings were also outfitted with on-site call systems and community communication antennae. The interiors of the units were fitted out with modern appliances, custom-integrated furnishings designed by the architects, or mass-produced modular furniture by other designers. Kitchens had built-in upper and lower cabinets made of steel and finished in enamel, storage spaces, and new stoves and refrigerators. There was also adequate storage space for linens, clothing, and larger items such as luggage and skis. The social housing approach, where equal opportunity and standards were to be provided to all citizens regardless of their economic status, was translated in IBA '57 into the interiors as well.

IBA '84/87: "The Inner City as a Place to Live"

In the mid-1970s, Berlin was threatened with a reduction in employment prospects, population, and morale. The city was outdated and neglected and was in desperate need of rejuvenation to reclaim it as a vigorous place in which to live. In 1979, IBA launched another large-scale construction exhibition in Berlin. Like Interbau Berlin, the State of Berlin and Federal Republic of Germany funded the exhibition and the focus of IBA '84/87 was on the urban revitalisation of West Berlin. The theme of the exhibition was "The Inner City as a Place to Live", and it set out to prove how an endangered city could be rescued and refashioned, and why it was necessary to reintegrate active residential living back into the social, functional, and formal organisation of the city. IBA '84/87 arose from a desperate need to revitalise the city, and the theme promoted an optimistic view of the economical, social, political, and technical circumstances and expectations of living in the city.

The exhibition was divided into two categories: new urban construction and urban renewal. The project sites were spread out across the inner city, and due to the size of the exhibition site and scope of the works, the exhibition started in 1979 and ended in 1987. It was known as IBA '84/87, and the completion date was purposely planned to coincide and commemorate the 750th anniversary of the founding of Berlin. The scope and scale of IBA '84/87 was extensive and projects spanned the entire core of Berlin. There were six development areas: Tegel, Prager Platz, Southern Tiergarten, Southern Friedrichstadt, Luisenstadt, and South East 36. The new urban construction projects were mostly concentrated in the neighbourhoods of Tegel, Prager Platz, Southern Tiergarten and Southern Friedrichstadt, and the urban renewal projects were in the older areas of Luisenstadt and South East 36. It was considered the most ambitious project in the world and it showcased works by more than 200 international architects.

IBA '84/87 moved away from the ideas of Interbau Berlin and instead concentrated on the needs of the existing city in a site-specific and meaningful manner. The new projects were developed within the old city blocks, which helped close the gaps left over from the wars and reinstate the former block identity of the early 1900s. The projects were associated and named in blocks to further instill the idea of a re-established block formation. Alongside the many new residential projects, IBA '84/87 built many new institutional, educational, recreational, and commercial buildings and public parks, and renovated and rehabilitated many existing buildings. IBA '84/87 did not specify an architecture style, only that all buildings be of high-quality construction and energy efficient, but despite the many international architects and different project types, postmodernism dominated the exhibition. For residential architecture, the buildings were a variety of experiments that accommodated many different user groups. There was housing for special social groups, introduction of living/working spaces, and flexible floor plans for future adaptability. When completed, the IBA '84/87 exhibition created approximately 2,500 new dwelling units and renovated around 7,000 existing units. IBA '84/87 bettered the lives of many and improved the city core greatly.

More than 200 renowned local and international architects were invited to participate in IBA '84/87, including the following.

- Block 1: Hans Christian Müller, Oswald Mathias Ungers, Horst Baumeister, and Bernd Richter

- Block 2: Myra Warhaftig, Zaha Hadid, Christine Jachmann, Friedrich Karl Borck, Mattias Boye, Dietrich Schaefer, Jan Rove, Rolf Rave, Dietmar Grötzebach, Günter Plessow, Reinhold Ehlers, Christoph Langhof, Thomas M. Hänni, and Herbert Meerstein

- Block 4: Christian Koch, Lutz Borchers, Elia Zenghelis, Rem Koolhaas, Matthias Sauerbruch, Alex Wall, Oriol Bohigas, Josep Martorell, David Mackay, Peter Faller, Christian Muschalek, Hermann Schröder, Jean Flammang, Burkhard Grashorn, Aldo Licker, Herbert Pfeiffer, Christoff Ellermann, Joachim Schürmann, Margot Schürmann, Fin Bartels, and Christoph-Schmidt-Ott

- Block 5: Peter Eisenman, Hans Kammerer, Walter Belz, and Klaus Kucher

- Block 7: Gernot Nalbach, Johanne Nalbach, Georg Kohlmaier, Barna von Sartory, Peter Brinkert, Günter Zamp Kelp, Laurids Ortner, Manfred Ortner, Klaus Effenberger, and Josef Paul Kleihues

- Block 9: Dietrich von Beulwitz, Pietro Derossi, Heinz-Jürgen Drews, Antonio Armesto, Yago Bonet, J. Francisco Chico, Antonio Ferrer, Carlos Marti, Xavier Monteys, Santiago Padres, Salvador Tarrago, J. Carlos Theilacker, Santiago Vela, and Jochen Brandi

- Block 10: Aldo Rossi, Gianni Braghieri, Dietmar Grötzebach, Günter Plessow, Reinhold Ehlers, and Raimund Abraham

- Block 11: Bruno Reichlin, Fabio Reinhart, Raimund Abraham, John Hejduk, and Moritz Müller

- Block 14: Wolfgang Scharlach and Rainer Wischhusen

- Block 19: Jasper Halfmann, Clod Zilich, and Helge Bofinger

- Block 20: Abram Mott, Harald Schöning, Jan Bassenge, Kay Puhan-Schulz, Johannes Heinrich, Walter Schreiber, Felix Thoma, Ralf D. Dähne, Helge Dahl, Jan Rave, Rolf Rave, Hansjürg Zeitler, Helmut Bier, Hans Korn, John Hejduk, and Moritz Müller

- Block 24: Heinz-Jürgen Drews

- Blocks 28/31: Rob Krier, Barbara Benzmüller, Wolfgang Wörner, Dietrich Bangert, Bernd Jansen, Stefan Scholz, Axel Schultes, Andreas Brandt, Thomas Heiss, Axel Liepe, Hartmut Steigelmann, Joachim Ganz, Walter Rolfes, Urs Müller, Thomas Rhode, Eckhard Feddersen, Wolfgang von Herder, Jasper Haffmann, and Clod Zillich

- Blocks 26/30: Herman Hertzberger

- Block 33: Hans Kollhoff, Arthur Ovaska, Werner Kreis, Ulrich Schaad, Peter Schaad, Horst Hielscher, Georg-Peter Mügge, Franz Claudius Demblin, Jochem Jourdan, Bernhard Müller, Sven Albrecht, John Eisler, Emil Prkryl, Jiri Suchomel, Hans Kollhoff, Arthur Ovaska, Arata Isozaki, Dieter Frowein, and Gerhard Spangenberg

- Block 70: Hinrich Ballerand Inken Baller

- Block 121: Alvaro Siza

- Block 234: Mario Botta

- Block 622: Douglas Clelland, Mario Maedebach, Werner Redeleit, Joachim Schmidt, Gino Valle, Mario Broggi, Michael Burckhardt, Jasper Halfmann, Clod Zillich, Christoph Langhof, Thomas Hänni, and Herbert Meerstein

Case Studies: The Blocks

Block 1: Wohnblock Köthener Strasse

Architect: Oswald Mathias Ungers

A perimeter block typology located at 35–37 Köthener Strasse, the concept of Wohnblock Köthener Strasse was to better assimilate the neighbourhood's existing commercial program with inner city living. The new urban construction brick building was five storeys in height with a flat roof and a partial basement for parking. The building opened on to the street on four sides and allowed light, air and sightlines to pass through the building. A grid of punched windows with soundproof glazing was present on all façades and dwelling units faced both the street and the large communal green space in their internal court. There was extensive landscaping and a green roof. The building housed close to 50 family-oriented dwelling units, the floor plans varied in size, and each unit had vertical access in each of its four corners.

Block 7: Condominium Mendelsohn-Bartholdy Park, Schöneberger Strasse

Architects: Haus-Rucker-Co., Günter Zamp Kelp, Laudris Ortner, and Manfred Ortner

A block-edge typology located at 9–12 Schöneberger Strasse, the project has a clean façade that aligns with the adjacent buildings. The building completes the existing neighbourhood street block and engages the historical architecture context. The concrete building is five storeys in height with a solar roof for passive energy conservation. The neighbourhood is family-oriented with a large park and child-care facilities. The street is a leafy tree-lined street and the building engages the vegetation with terrace gardens that face the streets, and an internal green space. In keeping with the commercial amenities in the neighbourhood, the building has ground floor shops and offices. The typical upper floors house residential units with a large percentage of two-bedroom dwelling units.

Block 7: Wohnungsbauten Hafenplatz, Schöneberger Strasse

Architects: Georg Kohlmaier and Barna von Sartory

A block-edge typology located at Schöneberger Strasse, the five-storey, brick building houses 43 units with private balconies and was designed to be energy-efficient. The use of brick was an acknowledgement to the office and factory buildings that formerly stood there, and the flat arch shape follows the edge of the historic block. The building has four vertical access points that service two to three units each. Most of the units are two-bedroom and some are two-storey units.

Stresemann Strasse

Block 1

Bernburger Strasse

Köthener Strasse

Dessauer Strasse

Schöneberger Strasse

Block 7

Hafenplatz

☐ Existing Building Blocks   ☐ New IBA '84/87 Building Blocks   ■ New IBA '84/87 Building Blocks - Case Studies

Partial IBA '84/87 Buildings Site Plan

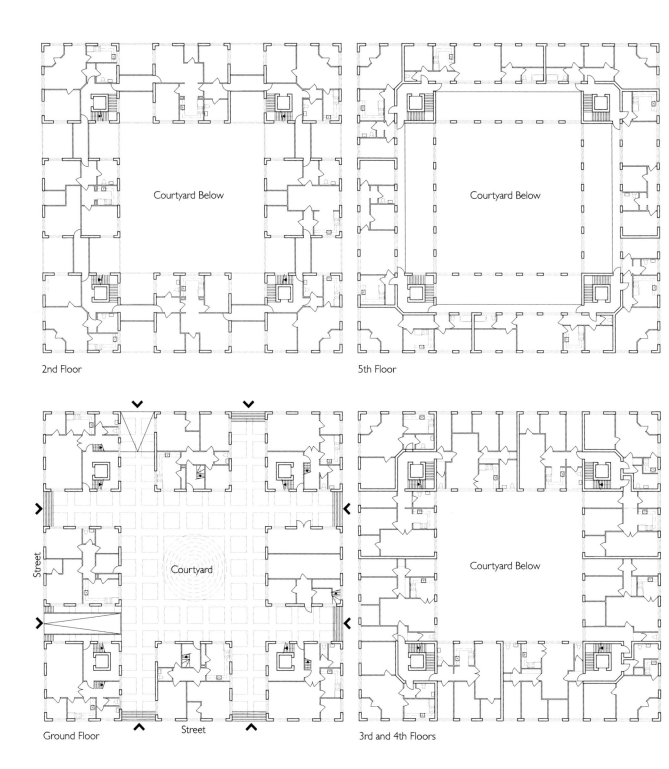

2nd Floor

5th Floor

Courtyard Below

Courtyard Below

Street

Courtyard

Street

Ground Floor

Street

Courtyard Below

3rd and 4th Floors

Block 1 - Wohnblock Köthener Strasse

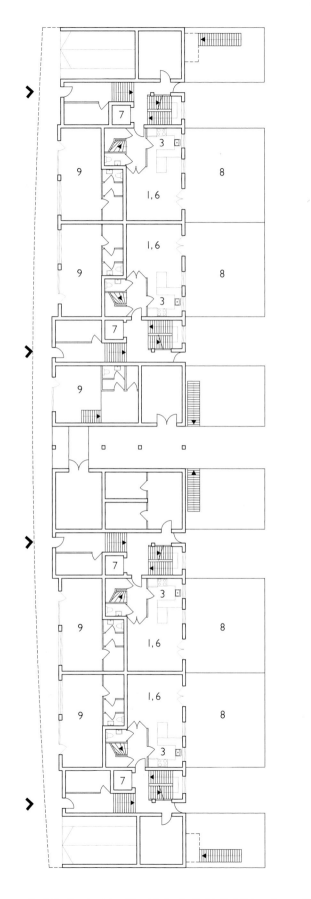
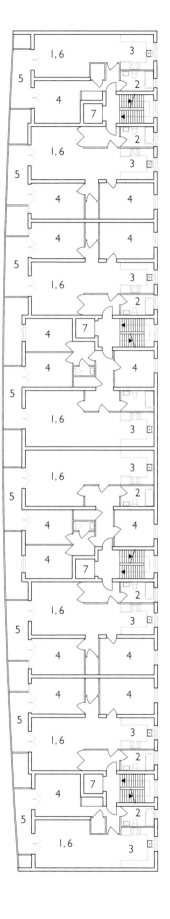

Block 7 - Condominium Mendelsohn-Bartholdy Park, Schoneberger Strasse

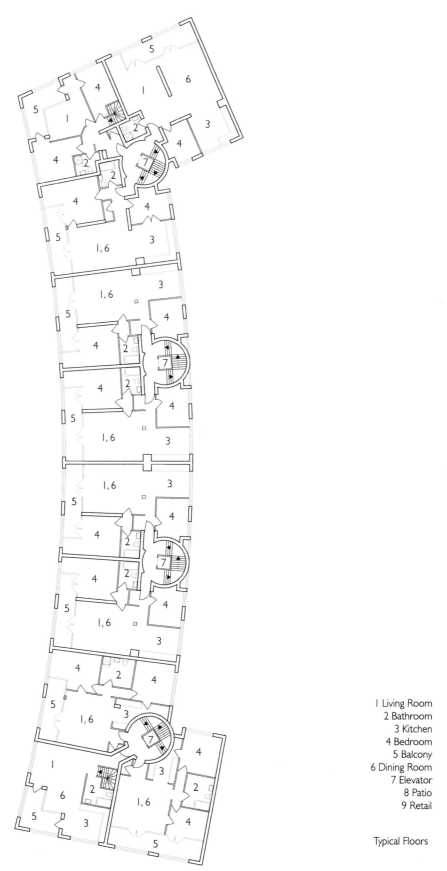

1 Living Room
2 Bathroom
3 Kitchen
4 Bedroom
5 Balcony
6 Dining Room
7 Elevator
8 Patio
9 Retail

Typical Floors

Block 7 - Hafenplatz 1-2, Dessauer Strasse 22a, Schöneberger Strasse 13a

Block 7 – Condominium Mendelsohn-Bartholdy Park, Schöneberger Strasse

Block 7 – Hafenplatz 1–2, Dessauer Strasse 22a, Schöneberger Strasse 13a

Block 28 – Ritterstrasse-Nord

Block 28 – Ritterstrasse-Nord

Block 28: Ritterstrasse-Nord

Architect: Rob Krier

A perimeter block typology located on a large urban site at Lindenstrasse and Oranienstrasse, this new urban construction comprises two 6-storey buildings that make up one broader perimeter block. Rob Krier conceived of and developed the master plan and many architects contributed to the buildings that completed the block project. The building was state-subsidised housing and there are approximately 180 dwelling units that range in size from studios to four bedrooms. All units have access to their own outdoor space by terrace, balcony, porch, or garden. Alongside the private green spaces, the block housing encloses two landscaped internal communal courtyards. The construction material is brick, with uniform punched windows on all façades, and the buildings have flat roofs. The ground floor accommodates commercial space and below grade is car parking for approximately 100 vehicles.

Block 70: Fraenkelufer and Admiralstrasse

Architects: Hinrich Baller and Inken Baller

Located in the block at Fraenkelufer and Admiralstrasse, the project comprises four buildings that were a restoration of a partially destroyed perimeter building block. The existing block had three vacant voids, street numbers 28, 38, and 44, and a courtyard. Baller and Baller designed three buildings to fill in the street façade and another building in the courtyard. Of the three buildings that completed the street edge, two buildings acted as "gateways" or "gatehouses" into an internal courtyard and the third was a corner building that redefined the intersection of Fraenkelufer and Admiralstrasse. The building in the courtyard was built against the side of an existing building and faced the inside of the communal courtyard garden. The buildings align with the existing mass and height of the existing six-storey block, and the concrete façades are articulated in a German Expressionism style in colours of pink, blue, and yellow with white upturned and pointed balconies and eaves. A total of 87 new dwelling units were created and, in addition, approximately 200 units within the existing block were renovated. The units in the new buildings had non-right angled, even curved, internal walls and housed one- and two-bedroom units with vertical access. There was emphasis placed on greenery and alongside the garden, lush plant life was incorporated into the balconies as hanging gardens.

Block 121: Schlesische Strasse

Architect: Alvaro Siza

A block-edge typology located at 1–9 Schlesische Strasse, the project fills the corner of a block that was destroyed during the Second World War. The building is seven storeys in height and is a mixed-use development that is stylistically consistent with many other buildings in the neighbourhood. The project is social housing with a combination of dwelling units, artist studios, a school, and a day-care centre, and at the rear is a courtyard. The corner façade and roofline are slightly curved and gently bulge out from the surrounding blocks. The exterior is a uniform grey colour with a rigid grid of windows that reflect the pattern of the adjacent buildings.

Block 70 – Fraenkelufer and Admiralstrasse

Block 70 – Fraenkelufer and Admiralstrasse

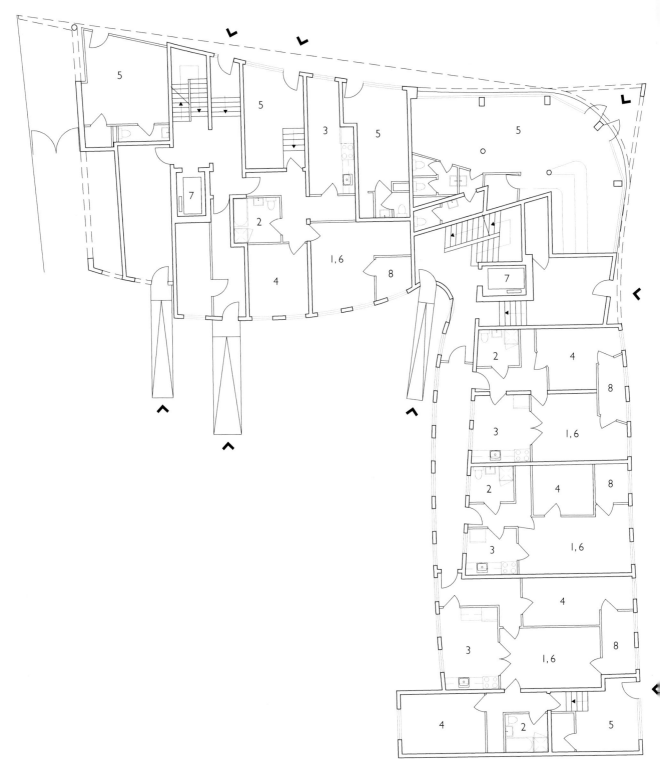

5

5

3

5

5

7

2

1, 6

8

7

4

2

4

8

3

1, 6

2

4

8

3

1, 6

4

8

3

1, 6

4

2

5

Ground Floor

1 Living Room
2 Bathroom
3 Kitchen
4 Bedroom
5 Retail
6 Dining Room
7 Elevator
8 Study

Typical Floors

Block 121 - Schlesische Strasse 1-9

Block 121 – Schlesische Strasse 1–9

Block 121 – Schlesische Strasse 1–9, Interior

Block 121 – Schlesische Strasse 1–9, Interior

Typical Unit Floor Plan Type

The typical unit floor plans for all four buildings could be considered as separated rooms. The rooms in each unit were treated as its own individual room with doors to access it, with the exception that the living and dining rooms were combined. Floor plans varied to accommodate different types of inhabitant, and layouts ranged from studios to three-bedroom units.

Access Type

Perimeter Blocks 1 and 28 and block-edge Block 7 featured vertical access. The buildings had a central stair and elevator circulation with entrances to dwelling units directly off the landing of the stairs or vestibule of the elevator. Block-edge typology Block 121 had horizontal access. The units there shared a central stair and elevator circulation off the building, and a corridor from that connected the units.

Construction Materials

All new buildings in IBA '84/87 were designed with high-quality construction and as energy-efficient. Novel ecological materials and techniques, such as green roofs and façades, were introduced and applied to some buildings.

Owners, Landlords, Developers, Reformers

Circa 1920s Berlin Housing Estates

Martin Wagner
Martin Wagner was an architect, urban planner, political organiser, and social reformer. He served as the chief city planner for Berlin and was a founder of GEHAG. Wagner was a principal planner in the Berlin Housing Estates and was responsible for the development of many modern housing projects in Berlin.

GEHAG
The Social Democratic Weimar Republic and free trade unions established GEHAG GmbH (Gemein-nützigen Heimstätten, Spar- und Bau-Aktiengesellschaft) in 1924. GEHAG was part of a network of charitable housing organisations initiated by Martin Wagner. It was a not-for-profit social building and housing construction company, and was the main developer of the Berlin Housing Estates.

Alexander Klein

Alexander Klein was the first architect in Germany to publicise his research and study on dwelling units. He analysed and designed plans for small dwelling units and presented his work at the International Congress for Housing and Planning in Paris in 1928. His work garnered praise from architects and urban planners in Germany and abroad, and his principles were applied to many projects. Klein divided dwelling factors into four important categories: the general grouping of rooms; sizes, proportions, and connection of rooms; orientation of the units; and the design and furnishing of the interiors. The idea behind these categories was to help organise the functions of the spaces and group similar rooms together within the unit for layout and user efficiency and comfort.

IBA '57: Interbau Berlin "The City of Tomorrow"

Karl Mahler, Albert Wischek, and Hans Schoszberger

Berlin Construction Senator, Karl Mahler, initiated IBA '57, and Albert Wischek and Hans Schoszberger, a well-known exhibition organiser and a Berlin architect, respectively, were commissioned by the Berlin Senate to explore a concept for Interbau Berlin.

Otto Bartning

Otto Bartning, president of the German League of Architects, was chairman of the steering committee for Interbau Berlin. Bartning, along with other architects such as Walter Gropius and Hubert Hoffman, served on committees to oversee and steer the exhibition.

Gerhard Jobst, Willy Kreur, and Wilhelm Schliesser

Gerhard Jobst, Willy Kreur, and Wilhelm Schliesser were awarded first prize for urban planning and design out of thirteen participants in the Interbau Berlin building exhibition competition.

IBA '84/87: "The Inner City as a Place to Live"

Hans Christian Müller

Berlin Senate Building Director, Hans Christian Müller, was an architect and city planner who initiated the idea of IBA '84/87. Müller, along with architects Josef Paul Kleihues and Hardt-Walt Hämer, spearheaded the exhibition. Kleihues managed the new construction of the inner city, and Hämer the redevelopment of the existing blocks.

Government-Funded Housing Timeline

1925: Berlin Building Code

Berlin enacted its own building code in 1925. Prior to this, the city followed the standards of the Prussian state commission for housing and welfare. The newly established Berlin Housing Welfare Office controlled the public funds that were allocated to new housing constructions and that encouraged low-cost housing in low-density settlements. Some of the standards incorporated into law were aimed at humanising housing conditions. During this time, basement and attic dwelling units were prohibited, all dwelling units were required to have cross-ventilation, and at least one room had to have full sunshine.

1930s

Nazi Germany and the Third Reich abolished all funding to state housing projects.

1940s

State-funded housing construction returned after Second World War. There was an immediate need to rebuild the city and to accommodate the many residents whose lives were uprooted during the war.

1950–1960

Roughly 50 percent of state-funded housing stock was built in West Berlin during this time period.

1970s

The city's "redevelopment through demolition" policy angered urban planners, architects, and citizen communities. The programme set out to dismantle and destroy large parts of the city in an effort to erase the scars left by the war. Social upset prompted the government to revise their plan, and to hold discussions leading to new state-funded housing developments and construction; these were undertaken on a smaller scale than in previous years.

Present Day

Berlin block housing remains prevalent in neighbourhoods throughout the city. The Berlin Housing Estates, Interbau Berlin, and IBA '84/87 housing projects have been renovated and are still in use as residences. The three developments were important achievements that elevated the standard of living for all social classes, and continue to influence residential development both locally and internationally. In 1995, the entire area of Hansaviertel became landmark protected and the object buildings are now part of Berlin's architectural heritage. In 2008, Berlin Housing Estates was listed as a UNESCO World Heritage Site. The six estates are now known as Berlin Modernism Housing Estates and their designs have long been celebrated as a great expression of modern architecture during its time. The main developer and housing association of the Berlin Housing Estates, GEHAG, is now known as Deutsche Wohnen, and the organisation remains committed to providing affordable housing and support services to the residents of Berlin.

In recent years, a new approach to housing has emerged. The trend is known as *baugruppen* and it is a group of people, often friends among whom one is an architect, who pool their resources to purchase land or a building in the city to co-own and cohabitate. By acting as their own developers, sharing expenses, and often investing in their own time and labour, the group can afford to live in the city centre close to city amenities and support. The method offers flexibility and affordability and is customised to fit the needs of each individual group or individual group member. The city has recognised the benefits of *baugruppen* housing and has begun to structure public policies to aid the development, and given the housing history of Berlin, the idea may soon influence other developments locally and internationally.

Het Funen

AMSTERDAM

Circa 1990 to 2010
Solitaire and Perimeter Block

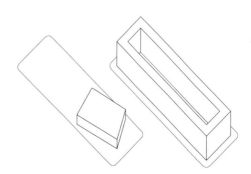

The period from around 1990 to 2010 was a stimulating time for architecture in the Netherlands. In the early 1990s, the need to expand their housing stock and the fierce desire to escape a monotonous pattern of bland brick design forms from decades past prompted the country's highest level of government to take action and to enact policies that endorsed new ideas in architecture. There were ministries, policies, and institutions that administered and mandated an architecture policy that commanded artistic and functional qualities in architectural design, with the objective to elevate Dutch architecture and make it distinctive. During this time, housing constituted much of the Netherlands' construction industry. The new concepts and designs provoked new perceptions on how housing looked and behaved, and it turned the country into a large and fascinating collection of exemplary housing for study.

The name of the country is an indicator of its low-lying physical nature. Roughly half of its land mass of 41,000 square kilometres (15,800 square miles) is at sea level and the other half is below. Throughout much of its history, the Netherlands has had to protect itself from flooding through land management. This highly populated and urbanised country can be divided into two areas, the more elevated south and east and the lowlands in the north and west, with the majority of its 17 million inhabitants reside mostly in the latter.

Perimeter Block Characteristics

The perimeter block building type is a single development that occupies a city block. The key characteristics are:

- Corresponds to individually developed parcels of land

- Building form conforms to the street pattern, height, depth, and other zoning regulations in the city

- Buildings can be single entity or fragmented and divided up by recessed openings or reveals

- Usually has two orientations: street and courtyard

- Courtyards are semi-private green spaces designated for use by residents of the building

- Ground floors can be zoned for retail

Solitaire Characteristics

A solitaire is a fully detached building form. The key characteristics are:

- Building form does not necessarily conform to characteristics of the existing block

- Building appears as autonomous object

- Building receives natural light from all orientations

- Voluminous urban presence usually on its own site

- Smaller in scale than linear blocks and high-rise towers

The Dutch live largely on damp and unstable land. Throughout the millennia, the geography of the western coastline was unpredictable—storm surges broke through the rows of protective coastal dunes regularly and water flooded the rivers and lakes repeatedly. Around the sixteenth century, the Dutch took the offensive and began to build a system of dams and canals to control the relentless turmoil created by the North Sea. They began land reclamation projects, drained swamps, directed dams, and built polders, which are low-lying tracts of land reclaimed from the sea and protected by dikes, to secure solid ground for living and building. These labours have paid off and over the centuries Holland has nearly doubled its original size. Such circumstances dictated the way in which land was managed, used, and inhabited. Since most of the population lived on land that was created artificially, land and space became precious commodities. "Artificial" land was laborious and costly to create and maintain, and so land use and its nature was carefully considered. The practice of regulating the land continued into the twentieth century and as a result, historical maps of medieval and early modern Holland bear little resemblance to the maps of today.

The Dutch have a history of building collective spaces and they are always thinking about optimal strategies to maximise their land and space. Living on a landmass that was and still is somewhat precarious compelled them to work with their land, and it turned them into masters of rebuilding and reusing their space. Dutch architecture up until the 1950s had mostly been humble and commonplace, but the architecture designed and constructed in the 1960s, 1970s, and 1980s fell into a rut of banality. During these years, most buildings seemed to share the same brown brick colour and shape. These uninspiring designs found their way into discussions, and critics ridiculed the mundane architecture and urban landscape. This criticism mobilised the Dutch to do something heroic: they fought back. Their attitude testified to the extensive understanding of their collective space, and like their land-shaping regimen, attested to their taking control of their situation and consequences.

By the late 1980s and early 1990s, Holland had a high population density, a healthy economy, a large demand for housing, the ability to undertake mass building production at relatively low cost, and so the surge of activity and discourse to improve the quality of architecture began to gain momentum. In 1990, Dutch architect Rem Koolhaas organised the symposium "How Modern is Dutch Architecture?" at the Delft University of Technology. Koolhaas disclosed his aspiration to recapture modernism in Dutch architectural design. He believed that the core of the movement was the idea that the architecture and the city need to be, and should always be, new, exciting, and engaging; his presentation was based on his decades' worth of research, theories, and studies. The work of Rem Koolhaas and his firm, Office for Metropolitan Architecture (OMA), investigated, analysed, and developed alternative approaches to high-density living, comprising many different programmes in an urban context. Their research and work paralleled national social dimensions of economics, culture, and politics, and Koolhaas argued that with the majority of the world's population living in urban cities, his theories could easily become reality and the Netherlands would be a great place to explore and realise the concept. The conference proved to be successful in opening up further dialogues and, shortly after, both the public and politicians began to take on a new and keen interest in architecture.

Het Funen

Eastern Docklands – Oostelijke Handelskade

Eastern Docklands

In 1991, the Ministry of Welfare, Health and Cultural Affairs, WVC (*Ministerie van Welzijn, Volksgeznondheid en Cultuur*) and the Ministry of Housing, Spatial Planning and the Environment, VROM (*Ministerie van Volkshuisvesting Ruimtelijke Ordening en Millieu*) jointly drafted a policy paper, Space for Architecture (*Ruimte voor architectuur*), that outlined plans to stimulate interest and upgrade the quality of architecture in the country. The policy paper was an adaptation based on Koolhaas' ideas that architecture should be appealing and engaging. In 1992, the policy paper was accepted and brought into effect by Parliament. It was the first time in Dutch history that the government became directly involved and invested in the aesthetics of architectural design. What began as a concerted effort to stand up and address the country's insipid architectural design had been transformed into an admirable series of resources and support aimed at excellence in architecture, from the country's highest level of power.

The architecture policy helped define the value of building design and quality and measured it in three ways: user value, cultural value, and future value. User value was represented by building designs that their occupants would find useful, comfortable, and attractive; cultural value weighed the architectural expression and how it provided enjoyment to the occupants; and future value was connected to both user and cultural values and placed emphasis on the construction quality as a sustainable investment for the occupants and the environment. The government understood that the design was abstract and that the aim of the policy was to outline objective conditions that promoted high-quality architecture, forged a greater cohesion between quality architectural design and construction, and demanded that in regard to quality architecture design and construction for all new government buildings, the state must lead by example.

Alongside this architecture legislation, the government sponsored other arrangements to advocate its new policy on architecture. One of the first was Architectuur Lokaal, which was a national information centre that promoted the merits of a high-quality built environment to individual citizens and private companies; the Netherlands Architecture Fund distributed financial aid to help stimulate the building of quality architecture; the Dutch Architectural Institute provided architects with funding and awards and the public with information on architecture and urban design; and many other institutions were formed to help extend support for the new national policy on architecture. Local communities were engaged and encouraged to express their views and opinions on the new policy, and the discussions became a cultural activity that imbued the understanding that a healthy built environment will have a positive affect on the well-being of its citizens. The institutions helped generate interest, discussion, and enthusiasm through public events, lectures, exhibitions, and publications. The VROM department provided financing to some key institutions, including the Netherlands Architecture Institute (NAI), which identified and helped guide the city's active architectural politics, and the Netherlands Architecture Fund and Berlage Institute, which offered graduate level architecture schooling.

VROM and OMA were key participants in the instigation, steering, and support of this unique architecture endeavour. VROM coordinated environmentally conscientious public housing and spatial planning in accordance with the newly revised design and planning policy, and OMA became an incubator and think tank that nurtured many young architects. Koolhaas' innovative and experimental theories, designs, and methods on architecture and urban planning were important lessons for the younger generation of architects. His foresight was widely shared and publicised and it cultivated a new era of practitioners. OMA's ideas and work influenced many other architects and urban planners, and many of OMA's employees went on to start their own successful offices, where they continued to hone the skills and craft developed from their former place of employment.

During this same time, the long-awaited residential development in the Eastern Docklands received a substantial amount of funding from the national government to develop housing. The Eastern Docklands, a harbour area located between the IJ and runway A10 in relation to the city's ring of canals, was a former shipping yard and, since the mid-1980s, the city had been trying to re-zone and redevelop the derelict area into a lively residential neighbourhood. The funding was bestowed at an opportune time, but it included a condition, which was that the city needed to act immediately and demonstrate development progress on close to 6,000 dwelling units by 1996. With that lofty target and imminent deadline, the city and VROM quickly initiated a succession of housing design competitions aimed at local architects. The competitions offered an extraordinary opportunity for newly established architecture firms and young architects to launch their careers. It was remarkable that the city believed in, encouraged, and awarded new and young architecture practices and architects for their modern architectural ideas and design.

There was a shortage of land in the city suitable for housing development, and because the city desperately wanted to curb the exodus of city dwellers to the suburbs, the Eastern Docklands was chosen as one of three former shipping yards to be remodelled into residential neighbourhoods. The ambitious initiative to transform defunct industrial areas into liveable spaces was planned for two other neglected areas as well: Westerdok and IJburg. Eastern Docklands is situated between Westerdok and IJburg, and the entire stretch consists of Easterdok, Eastern Islands Funen, Java Island, KNSM Island, Borneo Sporenburg, Entrepot West, and Rietlanden. Of the three rejuvenated areas, the Eastern Docklands district developed the most diverse multitude of housing typologies, the two architecturally prominent types being perimeter block and solitaire.

The perimeter block housing typology was an architectural import of the Second World War when Germany invaded the Netherlands. The solitaire housing typology was new to the Netherlands and was derived from the citizens' disinterest in high-rise housing, but it met the need for the housing conditions set out by the stimulus fund. The Dutch preferred single-family row housing, were accustomed to low- to mid-rise building structures, and though land was limited on the Eastern Docklands, market studies showed that there was more interest in low- than high-rise dwelling typologies. The density calculated for the Eastern Docklands' limited space and its requirement for high-density housing was set at 100 dwelling units per hectare (40 dwelling units per acre), which was equivalent to three times that of conventional Dutch row housing. Though the city could have created artificial land, it was more pragmatic to redevelop the Eastern Docklands and use solitaire as the housing typology. The solitaire housing typology met the density targets without expanding the landmass and best fit the criterion set out by the stimulus fund.

To undertake the Eastern Dockland development, the city assembled a group that comprised representatives from the municipal Urban Planning and Urban Housing departments. The group was responsible for the management of the entire Eastern Dockland project, and swiftly began production that concentrated on Java Island, KNSM Island, and Borneo Sporenburg. Aware that progress had commenced on the Eastern Docklands, a local housing construction corporation approached the city group to assist in its construction. However, the housing construction corporation strongly believed that the entire area should be viewed as a whole and convinced the city to develop all areas simultaneously to achieve a single vision. The resources required to construct the entire Eastern Docklands site were

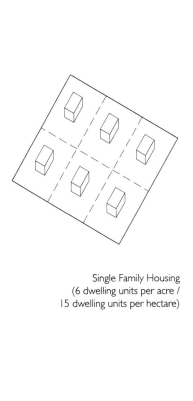

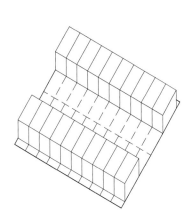

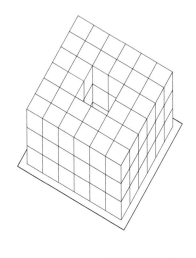

Single Family Housing
(6 dwelling units per acre /
15 dwelling units per hectare)

Row Housing
(20 dwelling units per acre /
50 dwelling units per hectare)

Multi-Unit Housing
(100 dwelling units per acre /
250 dwelling units per hectare)

Housing Density

0.5 FAR

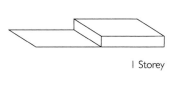

1 Storey

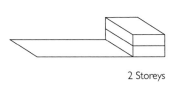

2 Storeys

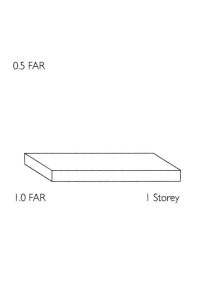

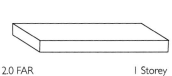

1.0 FAR   1 Storey

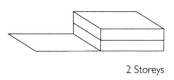

2 Storeys

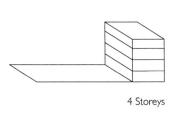

4 Storeys

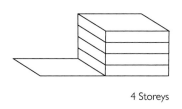

2.0 FAR   1 Storey

4 Storeys

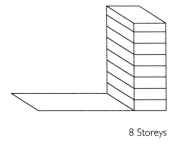

8 Storeys

100% Lot Area Coverage

50% Lot Area Coverage

25% Lot Area Coverage

Floor Area Ratio (FAR)

too great for one construction team, and so the company approached several other local corporations and builders to join forces and work together. An accord was promptly reached among seven building companies, and together they formed a new and sizeable association entitled the New Deal Development Society (*Ontwikkelingsmaatschappij New Deal*) to take on the challenge. More commonly known as New Deal, they began their collaboration with the city and were given exclusive rights to construct all the residential buildings and their facilities on the Eastern Docklands, and in exchange for the privilege, New Deal had to assume all the managerial and financial responsibilities and liabilities associated with the large undertaking.

After the Second World War, much of the housing stock in the Netherlands was either subsidised or rental dwelling units. Housing associations were small, not-for-profit organisations that managed and provided affordable and appropriate housing for the populace. These began during the First World War and proliferated in the mid-1900s. By the early 1990s, 42 percent of the population were housed in a form of social rental sector housing administered by a housing association. There was no stigma or negative connotation attached to living in social housing. The idea that all households had equal access to affordable and adequate housing regardless of their circumstance or phase in life, and in turn, better contributed to an active society, was a shared social responsibility and perspective. In fact, the diversity, quality, and striking architectural design of social housing in the Netherlands made for a diverse coexistence in the community, formed benchmarks for other countries to emulate, and made housing design and standards in the Netherlands unparalleled globally. The Eastern Docklands development was no exception, with the majority of the housing lightly subsidised and remainder heavily financed.

The Eastern Docklands

The Eastern Docklands was one of several artificial peninsulas built to serve passenger and cargo shipping and was the first of three industrial waterfront sites to be developed, followed by Westerdok and IJburg. After the Second World War, the area lost its viability as a port and fell into neglect and abandonment through to the 1970s. In the 1980s, the city determined the area as being suitable for revitalisation and for it to be developed into a mixed-use residential and commercial neighbourhood, but the project stalled. In the early 1990s, the national government injected funding to resuscitate the project and Dutch architects were invited to submit design proposals. Local architect Jo Coenen was selected to design and oversee the master plan of the area; his scheme rejuvenated the islands and increased its population density to meet the government's imposed goals of housing and supporting 100 dwelling units per hectare (40 dwelling units per acre).

To achieve this target population density and maintain a human scale, perimeter block and solitaire housing typologies were introduced into the expanse of row housing that is the common Dutch housing landscape. The buildings were compact, low- to medium-rise in height, the streets were made narrow, and car parking was concealed underground. The residential buildings had to provide dwelling units that comprised a variety of sizes and layouts, to appeal to and accommodate a wide range of residents and lifestyles and to offer private or collective outdoor space. Since much of the land on the Eastern Docklands was long and narrow, there was little opportunity to designate large, open public spaces, and instead the vast acreage of water substituted for the green space. The Dutch principle of "blue for green" was applied, and the resultant concept was that scenic views of the water from each dwelling unit would substitute for park space. All outdoor spaces supported a variety of communal uses and were cherished by everyone and doubled as one large, informal outdoor living room. For those with private outdoor spaces, those areas were highly regarded and used as an extension of internal rooms.

Case Studies: Eastern Docklands

Perimeter Block

Piraeus

Architect: Kantoor Kollhoff
Completed: 1994

The Piraeus was the first of the Eastern Docklands residential development projects. The site is on KNSM Island, and the result is a prominent and severe-looking perimeter block building that consists of 304 dwelling units, 20 ground floor commercial spaces, 2 courtyards and a large underground parking garage. The Piraeus is one of a few developments built by non-Dutch architects. Kantoor Kollhoff, a Berlin-based firm, designed the strong shape that evokes the style of much German perimeter block housing and which paid homage to the warehouses that lined the waterfront. The development was named in reference to the former Greek–Dutch trading ties.

The building site is a 170 by 60-metre (550 by 200-feet) rectangular block and houses a twentieth century building, the former KNSM (Royal Netherlands Steamship Company) administration offices. This became part of the development scheme and was converted and renovated into residential occupancy. The new, larger residential proposal envelops itself around the existing structure, folds and tucks inwards around it, and the new wings create two large inner courtyards. The folding and tucking was a sensitive design response that left the original building as a freestanding historical artefact, and provides access from the waterfront through the building.

The 304 dwelling units, of which 95 percent is social housing and the remaining 5 percent is rental units, accommodate a wide variety of floor plans and are distributed across the building, ranging in height from four to eight storeys. The access system is a complex vertical and horizontal combination served by a single-loaded corridor in the horizontal areas. Each unit is 2.8 metres (9 feet) in floor to ceiling height, 16 metres (52 feet) long, and has access to two external courtyards. The dwelling units present a diverse mix of sizes and layouts. There are one-bedroom to three-storey units on the upper floors, with skylights, and units offer flexible unit arrangements that are suitable for combination and expansion. The concept shows that the architecture can accommodate and engage all types of inhabitant and their demands, and reflects the notion of living in a viable and diversified city.

Each dwelling unit shares a similar basic design of a combined bathroom and kitchen zone. The bathroom facilities are accessed on one side and the kitchen on its opposite side, this grouping being known as "wet core". The wet core enables a corridor with doors on either side to form either a dining area or a separate adjacent space. The grouping is a set block form and is precisely positioned in each unit plan to set the layout for the living room and bedrooms on either side with individual doors, which identifies separate rooms as the typical unit floor plan.

The form is made more solid looking with the use of traditional, locally sourced, handmade, dark brown brickwork and outlines in a continuously edged aluminium roof. The punched windows in the façades fold into a sideways "V" shape that, like the building, forms folds and tucks to open fully and can be used as a winter garden or summer balcony. The building elevation slopes gently from north to south towards the waterfront, enabling better vistas and light for the units on the south of the north wall and into the two internal communal courtyards. The heavy mass also helps protect the courtyards from strong winds and waterside weather elements.

The Piraeus was the first building to be completed on KNSM Island. It has been identified and used as a favourable precedent in the dispute concerning the construction of large-scale developments along the waterfront, and for sensitive, massive brick construction in the rest of Holland in general.

The Whale
Architect: de Architekten Cie
Construction Period: 1998–2000

Located in the Borneo Sporenburg portion of the Eastern Docklands, the Whale was one of the earlier developments in the area and was a New Deal development. The project accommodates 214 dwelling units, 1,100 square metres (11,800 square feet) of ground floor commercial space, an internal courtyard, and 179 underground parking spaces. Of the 214 dwelling units, 150 are designated social housing and 64 are rental units.

The building's enormous size, creased shape, and blue-grey zinc façade is reminiscent of a whale and hence the building's name. The Whale refreshes the definition of a perimeter block, with its upturned ends on the north and south sides of the building making it appear less bulky. The manoeuvre also creates a gradual shift from public to private space, resulting in the private inner courtyard having views over the water on both the north and south sides of the building, and transforms the traditionally private space into a publicly viewable city garden. The sloping rooflines were designed to correspond with the movement of the sun to gain optimal lighting and enable daylight to reach further into the building.

The building's access is split in two, on opposites sides of the building, and is an inverted mirror image of horizontal access with single-loaded corridors. The dwelling units vary in size and layout, with internal doors that separate all the rooms making its typical unit floor plan type separated rooms. The majority of the unit plans are one-bedroom units, and there are three- and four-bedroom units at the four corners of the building. All units are reached via an outdoor gallery that overlooks the courtyard that, along with the inner courtyard, provides views to the shared outdoor space and sky above.

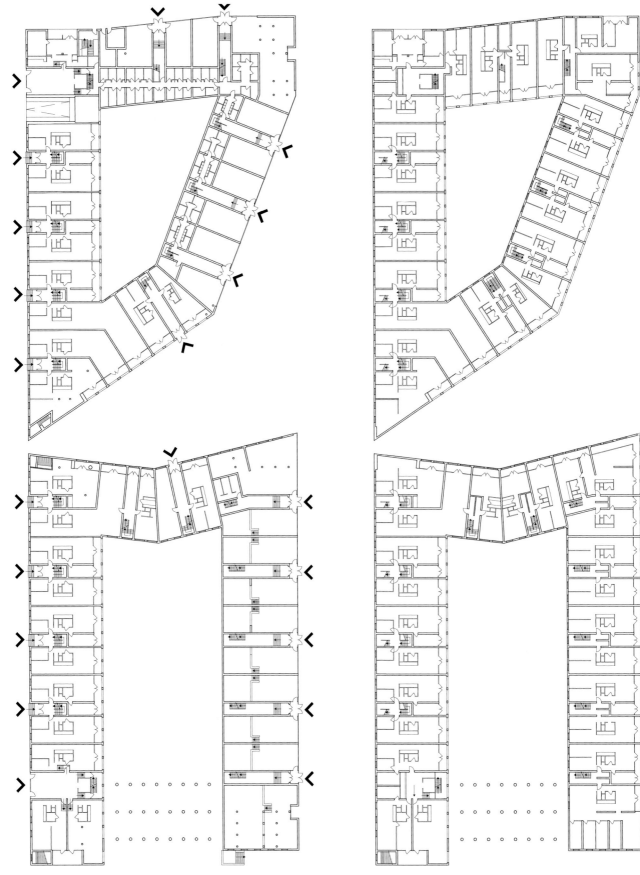

Ground Floor

2nd Floor

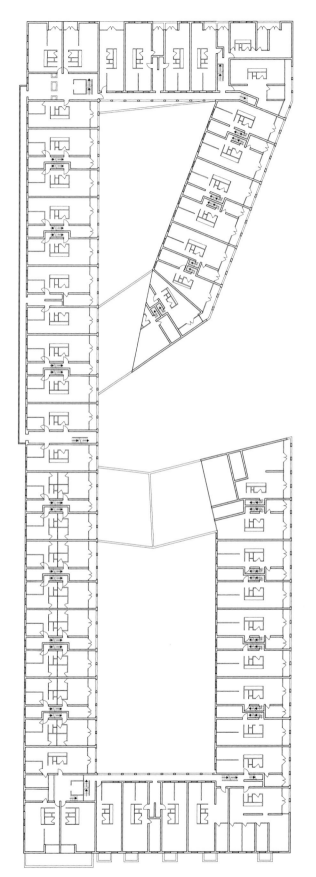

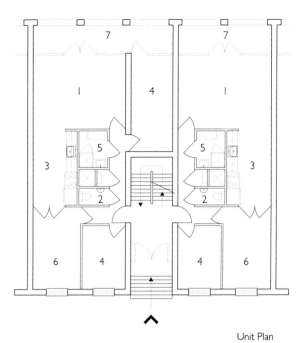

Unit Plan

1 Living Room
2 Toilet
3 Kitchen
4 Bedroom
5 Bathroom
6 Dining Room
7 Balcony

5th Floor

Piraeus

Piraeus

Piraeus

Piraeus

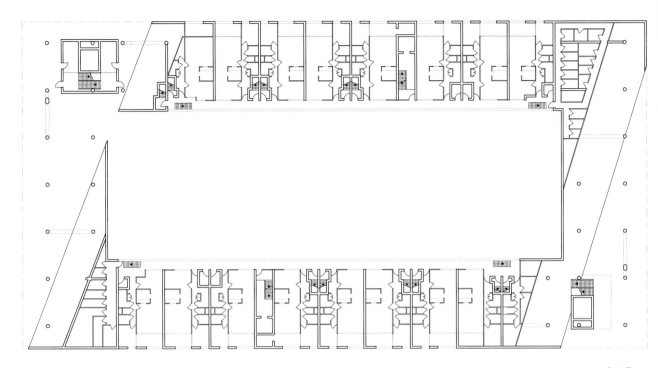

2nd Floor

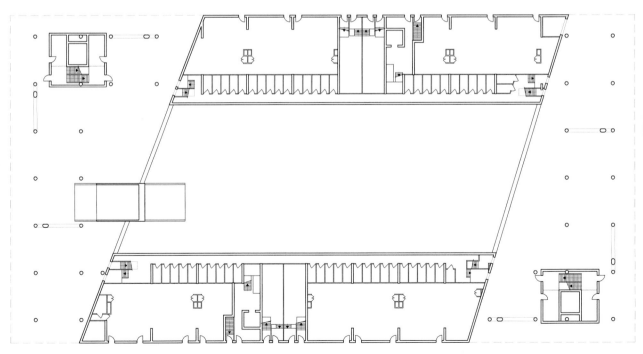

Ground Floor

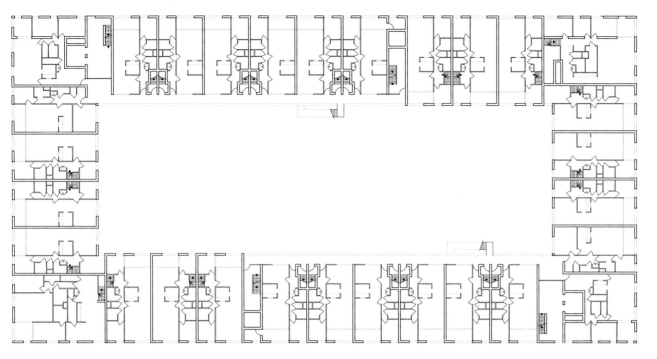

5th Floor

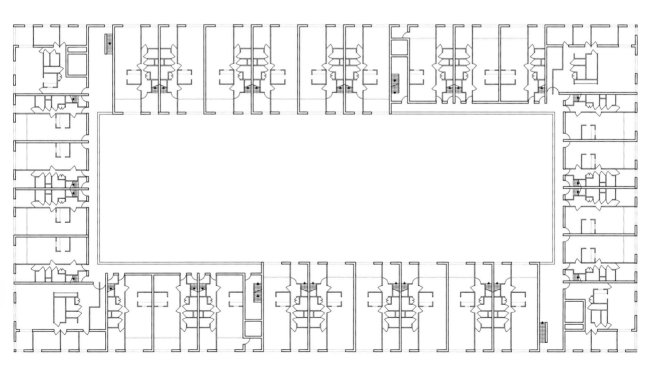

4th Floor

Whale

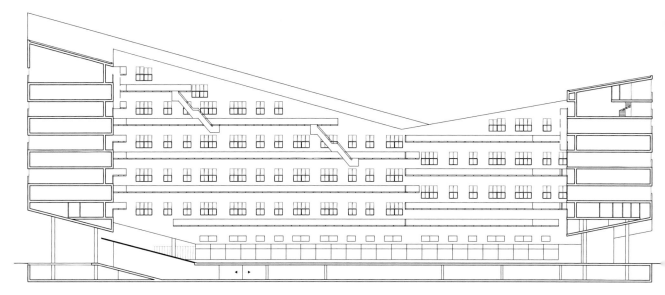

Section

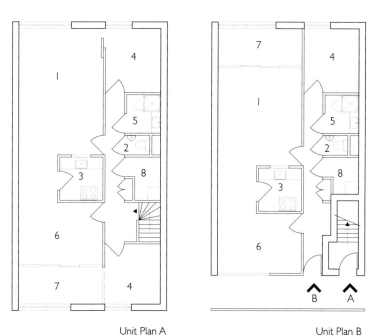

Unit Plan A

Unit Plan B

1 Living Room
2 Toilet
3 Kitchen
4 Bedroom
5 Bathroom
6 Dining Room
7 Balcony
8 Laundry/Storage Room

Whale

Whale

Whale

Solitaire

Het Funen

Architects: Architekten Cie, Geurts and Schulze Architecten, Claus and Kaan Architecten, DKV architecten, KuiperCompagnons, Lafour and Wijk Architecten, Van Sambeek and Van Veen, NL Architects, and Dick van Gameren Architecten
Construction Period: 2000–2005

Located on a triangular site southeast of Eastern Docklands, Het Funen, also referred to as Funenpark, The Funen, or Fyn, is a mixed residential and commercial neighbourhood. The master plan was developed by Dutch architect Frits van Dongen in collaboration with nine architecture offices. The result is a backwards "L"-shaped building designed by Architekten Cie and sixteen solitaire buildings of different shapes and materials, each designed by the other collaborating architects and organised in a grid pattern on the triangular site and separated by large swathes of green space. The housing's different forms and colours are also referred to as "hidden delights", in reference to the assortment of sweets in a single candy box.

The Het Funen area was in the early stages of reuse and was a site that afforded the concept of living in a park. Het Funen embraces the green concept of living around an urban park, rather than closed-off blocks of private green spaces that were common in many residential neighbourhoods in Amsterdam. The park is now free from the traditional closed courts and instead faces open and outwards for all to use. The logic behind Het Funen was to create a lively place where many different types of people and families could reside and, despite the stipulated population density, the open and public green space remained the focus of the development shared.

The sixteen-building development houses 565 dwelling units of various sizes and layouts, 3,000 square metres (32,200 square feet) of commercial space, and 395 underground parking spaces. In the north–south orientation, each building is 20 metres (65 feet) in length and spaced 8 metres (26 feet) apart. The gross area for Het Funen is 3.5 hectares (8 acres); the entire development is intended for urban families, young and old, and the buildings with solar panels, water storage and purification were a testing ground for new techniques in sustainable living and design. Situated close to a train station with elevated tracks, the "L"-shaped building acts as a sound barrier and a defined edge for the 16 residential buildings. The building accommodates commercial programming, 300 residential dwelling units, and the underground car park network that enables the 16 solitaire housing units to be interpreted as individual sculptural objects in the landscape, and also to free up the green and pedestrianised spaces for the inhabitants.

All sixteen solitaire buildings vary in design, materials, and height. The buildings are two to six storeys, comprise between ten and twenty-four dwelling units, and the uniqueness is in the wide variety of floor plans and sizes to suit many different lifestyles. The key programme requirements were that all buildings had main entrances that faced a green space, had a ground-floor level, private outdoor space, and that the building was 50 percent building and 50 percent green roof. Each building is individual, but part of a larger whole. Each is related to another in scale and all are linked by a continuous stone walkway that meanders around trees, planters, and a wide landscaped area.

Blok J/Myriad

Architect: Dick van Gameren
Completed: 2009

Myriad is a six-storey solitaire building that comprises 22 dwelling units, among which are thirteen different unit layouts. The external façade is a three-tier combination of brick and glass. Each tier is two storeys in height; the top and bottom brick façades each house six 2-storey, 3-bedroom units and the middle glass façade houses two floors, each with single-storey units of five, 2-bedroom units. The two-storey units on the ground floor have access to a semi-private outdoor area, while those above share landscaped rooftop access. All units share the use of Funenpark.

Blok K/Verdana

Architect: NL Architects
Completed: 2009

Blok K, also known as Verdana, is one of the sixteen solitaire buildings that make up Het Funen. Blok K stands out from the fifteen other solitaire housing buildings owing to its sculptured swooping roof that visibly outperforms the 50 percent green roof requirement. The entire undulating roof of Blok K was conceived as the fifth façade. It is a vegetated green roof where residents could grow their own herbs and have terraces. The roof's wave shape creates views and vistas from the roof terraces and the unit interiors for maximum light and air.

The overall volume of Blok K compresses and stretches from two to four storeys in height. Blok K is owner-occupied and the 10 units were designed as luxury suites of two-, three-, and four-level accommodation divided equally by volume so all units receive approximately equal levels of usable area and sightlines. Each unit ranges in area from 140 to 180 square metres (1500 to 2000 square feet), has its own ground-level access and private outdoor space, and the parking spaces are shared in the underground lot in the perimeter "L'"-shaped building.

Access to all units is shared at the ground level of the building through an external, covered corridor nicknamed "the alley". The alley tunnels through the centre of the building from one end to the other on a diagonal axis, and entrances to each dwelling unit are aligned and accessed through this corridor. A door immediately adjacent to each unit's entrance door houses that unit's storage space and technical service facilities, such as gas and water meters. The utility services are deliberately installed in the darker zones of the building to provide each unit's habitable areas with more usable space, and the façades are fitted with further windows to provide views and cross-ventilation throughout the unit.

Each unit was designed with a private ground floor and rooftop outdoor space. The concept was to provide each unit with a sense of a single-family dwelling among a multi-unit housing typology. There are no physical or visual dividers or separation between each ground floor outdoor area and, depending on the slope of the roof, many are shallow enough to be looked into from a neighbouring terrace. The building's communal impression is through the visual connection of one neighbour with another.

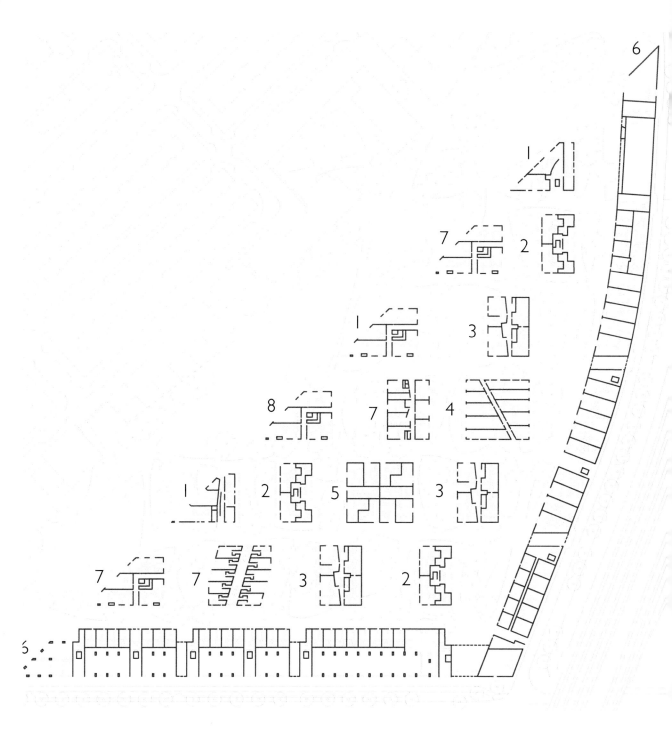

1 Lafour en Wijk   5 Geurst & Schulze Architekten
2 DKV Architekten   6 de Architekten Cie
3 KuiperCompagnons   7 Dick van Gameren
4 NL Architects   8 Claus en Kaan Architekten

Het Funen Site Plan

Het Funen

Het Funen

Het Funen

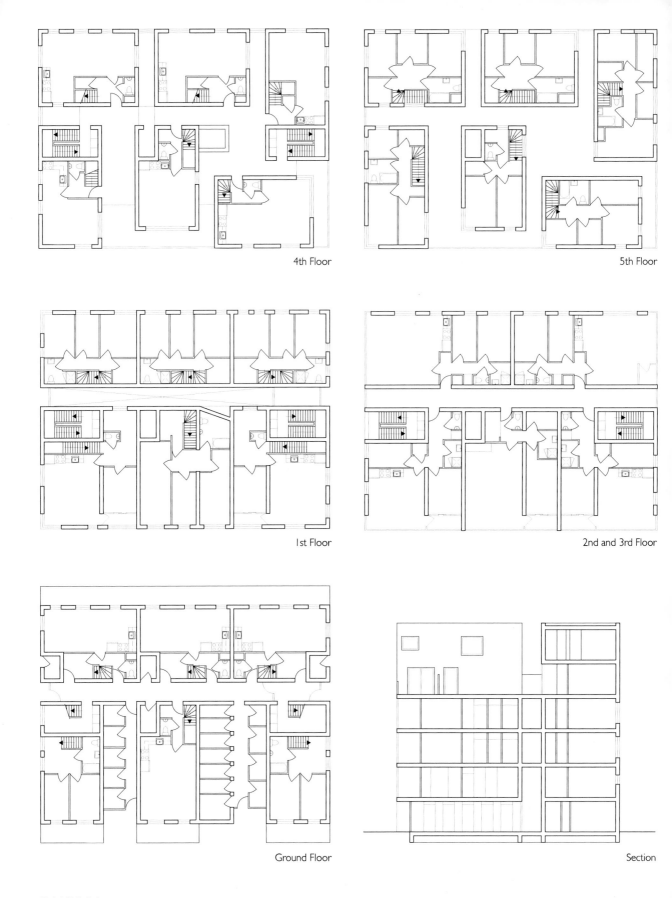

4th Floor

5th Floor

1st Floor

2nd and 3rd Floor

Ground Floor

Section

Blok J / Myriad

Myriad

Myriad

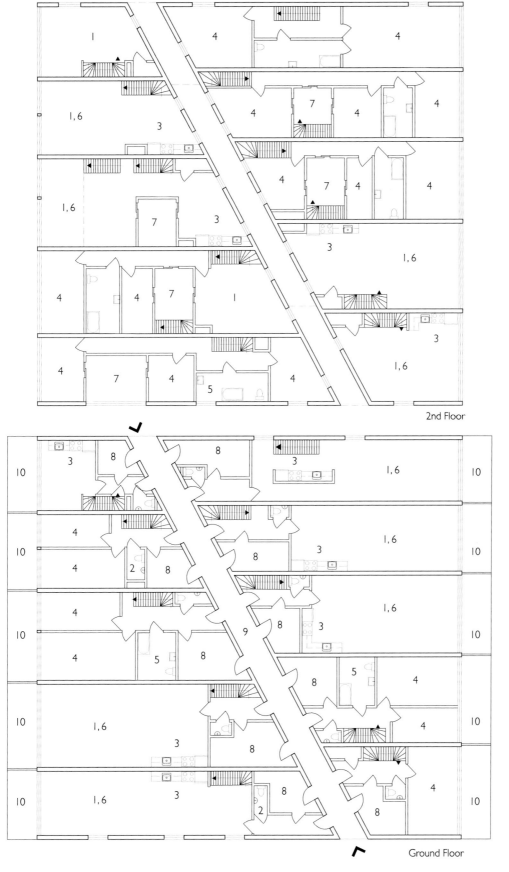

2nd Floor

Ground Floor

1 Living Room
2 Toilet
3 Kitchen
4 Bedroom
5 Bathroom
6 Dining Room
7 Terrace
8 Services and Storage
9 Alley
10 Patio

Blok K / Verdana

Blok K / Verdana

Botania
Architect: de Architekten Cie
Construction Period: 2000–2002

Situated in the Easterdok neighbourhood, Botania is a five-storey, square-shaped building that is owner-occupied property and houses 40 luxury dwelling units, 1,000 square metres (10,700 square feet) of commercial space, and 24 underground parking spaces. The site is located at the intersection of Nieuwe the Herengracht and Entrepotdok canals, and the building's limited 35 by 55 metre (114 by 180 feet) lot is bounded by the water's edge to its north and west sides.

Botania's 40 dwelling units vary in size and layout and are all grouped around a grand and spacious communal atrium that is flanked by two communal access staircases that provide a single-loaded corridor, horizontal access system. There are three large units in the building that span the entire east–west length of the building. These three large units are stepped to create large, three-tiered, private outdoor terraces for each of the large units. Since the three large units are stepped, the undersides of the units form part of the ceilings of the communal access staircases. The three large units have large terraces while each of the other dwelling units have access to their own private outdoor balcony.

The façade material is brick, with white wooden window frames and tinted green glass, in reference to the façades of Amsterdam's traditional canal-side housing. The construction is concrete tunnel form with a steel skeleton. The two methods of construction enable each dwelling unit to be opened up on the entrance side to provide a view into the atrium, and the three large units are fitted with glass access to their large roof terraces.

Typical Unit Floor Plan Type

The majority of the social rental sector buildings are separated rooms.

Access Type

Each building is unique and has its own system that serves the design and purpose of the individual building. The more prominent access types are combination vertical and horizontal.

Construction Materials

The majority of the social rental sector buildings used brick as both a traditional building material and a tribute to the former maritime architecture.

Botania

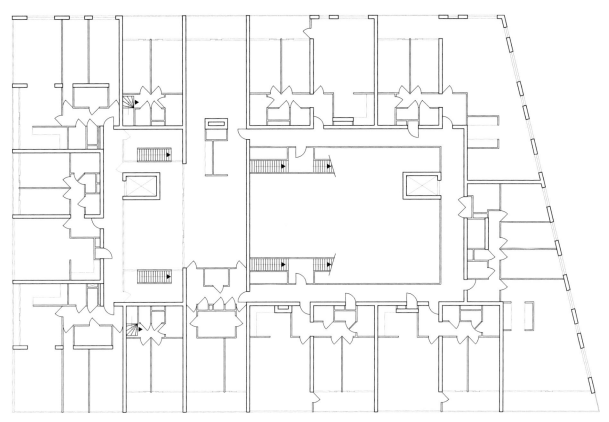

3rd Floor

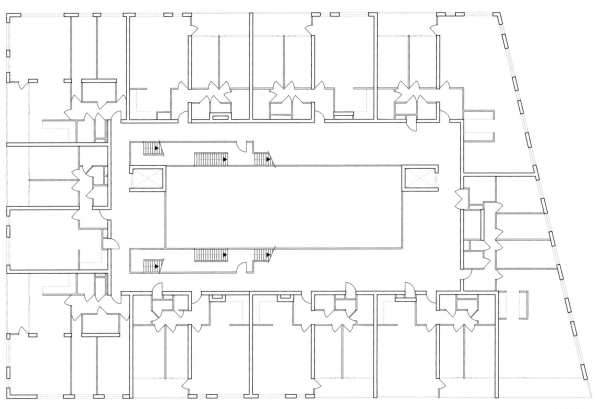

2nd Floor

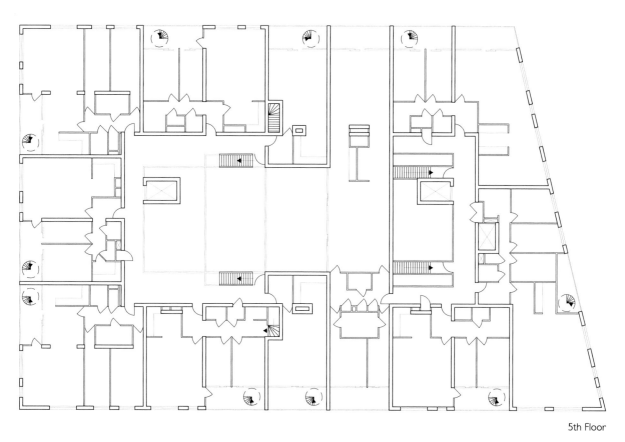

5th Floor

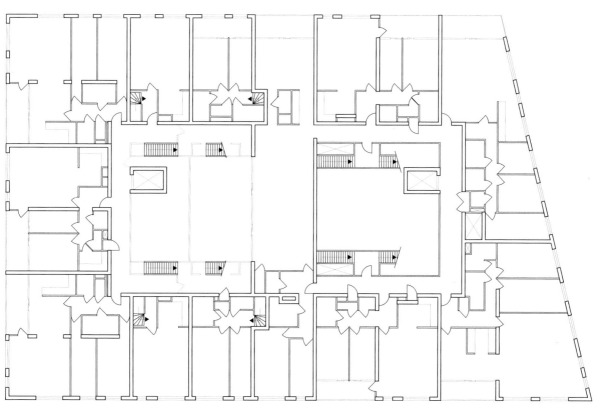

4th Floor

Botania

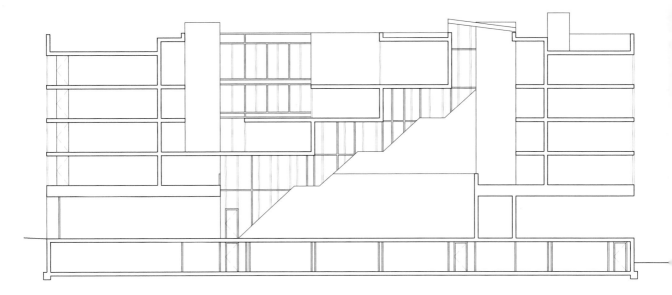

Section

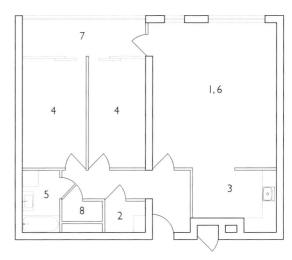

Unit Plan

1 Living Room
2 Laundry Room
3 Kitchen
4 Bedroom
5 Bathroom
6 Dining Room
7 Balcony
8 Storage Room

Botania

Botania

Botania

Botania

Owners, Landlords, Developers, Reformers

Dutch architect Rem Koolhaas was a key figure who instigated, guided, and supported the movement of the architecture policy in the early 1990s. His architecture firm, Office for Metropolitan Architecture (OMA), examined and presented new approaches to high-density living for and in the Netherlands. His theories and work were based on years of research, and he and his firm mentored and nurtured many young architects and ushered in a new generation of innovative practitioners. Today, Rem Koolhaas and OMA are in practice and a leading influence in housing design both locally and internationally.

Government Departments, Policies, and Regulations

Architecture Policy

The Netherlands was the first country in the world to develop a national policy on architecture. The policy began as a proposal in 1991 and was enacted by parliament in 1992. The government recognised the importance of architecture in society and heralded strategies to create quality architecture to last generations for the country. The state created favourable conditions for the design and construction of architectural projects and set in place many institutions to help disseminate and realise the efforts.

The Dutch Parliament had been upholding and upgrading the architecture policy since its conception in 1992. From 1992, supplemental policies by different ministries, some in collaboration with other ministries, were introduced and put into different forms of publication at various times, but all related to architecture and spatial design. Following these publications, several ministries went through name changes or were absorbed into other ministries, but their edict remained focused on how best to use and regulate inhabitable space and the environment in the Netherlands, and on the considered architecture policies.

1982: VROM

The Ministry of Housing, Spatial Planning and the Environment, VROM (*Ministerie van Volkshuisvesting Ruimtelijke Ordening en Millieu*) was formed in 1982 and played an important role in the establishment of the architecture policy. Prior to 1981, the ministry's three sectors were separate and were included in the responsibilities of other ministries. VROM was responsible for housing, sustainable residential environments, and how space was used, preserved, and inhabited nationally. The ministry encompassed a number of governmental departments and formed relationships with other local authorities, social organisations, and the business community to devise their reports and policies on social housing, spatial planning, and the environment. In 1991, VROM initiated an architecture policy paper that was promptly accepted into Dutch legislation and, shortly after the enactment, VROM provided financial support to organisations that helped promote the policy. In 2010, VROM's sectors, tasks, and mandates were redistributed and divided between three different ministries; housing was merged with the Ministry of the Interior, spatial planning with the Ministry of Infrastructure and the Environment, and environment with the Ministry of Economic Affairs.

1991: Space for Architecture

Space for Architecture (*Ruimte voor architectuur*) was a policy paper co-published by WVC (Ministry of Welfare, Health and Cultural Affairs) and VROM. The paper aimed to stimulate interest in architecture in the Netherlands and it initiated discussion on the betterment of architecture nationally.

1992: The Dutch Parliament Accepts Space for Architecture

A year following the Space for Architecture policy paper proposal, the Dutch Parliament formally enacted the policy into legislation. It was the first time in Dutch history that the government had become directly involved and invested in the aesthetics of architectural design. Both WVC and VROM worked jointly to oversee and coordinate new architecture and space planning projects that fell within this new policy.

1993: VINEX

The Fourth Memorandum Spatial Planning Extra (*Vierde Nota Ruimtelijke Ordening Extra, VINEX*) was a supplemental report on Dutch housing published by VROM. The account was part of a larger policy, the Fourth National Policy Document on Spatial Planning, that had been in process since 1988. The VINEX policy outlined goals towards building high-standard, quality, density housing to restrict shortage in the housing stock. VINEX identified the megalopolis Randstad, an area that consisted of the four largest cities in the Netherlands: Amsterdam, Rotterdam, The Hague, and Utrecht, as at risk of overcrowding. VINEX set an original target to develop about 1,000,000 new dwelling units in Randstad between 1995 and 2010. The number of dwelling units was later revised to about 600,000 in 2010. VINEX sites were developed as residential, commercial, and recreational neighbourhoods, and the idea was to provide a distinct identity to each area.

1996: The Architecture of Space: Notes on the Architecture Policy, 1997–2000

Built upon Space for Architecture and issued in 1996 by the Ministry of Education, Culture and Science, OCW (*Ministerie van Onderwijs, Cultuur en Wetenschappen*), the Ministry of Agriculture, Nature and Food Quality, LNV (*Ministerie van Landbouw, Natuurbeheer en Voedselkwaliteit*), and the Ministry of Transport, Public Works and Water Management, VenW (*Ministerie van Verkeer en Waterstaat*), the policy broadened the Space for Architecture policy and planned and managed urban development, landscape, infrastructure, and environmental designs between the years 1997 and 2000.

2000: Shaping the Netherlands: Architectural Policy, 2001–2004

Issued in 2000 by VROM, OCW, VenW, and the Ministry of Agriculture, Nature Management and Fisheries, the policy was an action plan that launched a series of major nationwide projects over the next four years. The projects served as models for future reference and the projects consisted of urban planning, motorway designs, cultural institutions, and government building such as the Delta Metropolis, the Zuiderzee railway line, the Rijksmuseum renovation, two government culture and history departments, and other private initiative projects.

2001: "Making Space Sharing Space", The Fifth National Policy Document on Spatial Planning, 2000–2020

Published by VROM and advised by the Dutch Social and Economic Council, the policy characterised good housing design and quality through seven criteria: (1) spatial diversity, as the physical composition of a housing unit; (2) economic and social functionalities, as community buildings and infrastructure investments; (3) cultural diversity, as a variety of amenities for a community; (4) social equality, as designs in housing development meeting the needs of the community; (5) sustainability, as reducing the environmental footprint of housing development; (6) attractiveness, as the overall appearance of a building within the community; and (7) human scale, as walkable and easily accessible by public transportation.

2004: Action Programme on Spatial Planning and Culture, 2005–2008

Published jointly in 2004 by VROM, OCW, LNV, VenW, the Ministry of Economic Affairs, the Ministry of Defence, and the Ministry of Foreign Affairs, this policy recognised the positive impact of increased development on the country and aimed to integrate and strengthen economic, ecological, and sociocultural ties and values in future spatial planning.

2008: A Culture of Design: Architecture Vision and Spatial Design

Issued by VROM, OCW, LNV, and VenW, this policy further strengthened the role, position, profile, and responsibility of the Dutch government in the country's architecture, urban design, and landscape architecture. It outlined a future for a more beautiful, sustainable, and well-functioning Netherlands.

2012: The Action Agenda for Architecture and Spatial Design, 2013–2016

Issued in 2012 by the OCW, Ministry of Infrastructure and the Environment, the Ministry of the Interior and Kingdom Relations, the Ministry of Economic Affairs, Agriculture and Innovation, and the Ministry of Defence, the policy set out initiatives and tools for the national government to strengthen the position of designs and designers both nationally and internationally. It recognised that Dutch architecture and urban design had developed strongly over the previous 20 years since the launch of the architecture policy, and it would continue to promote architecture and offer opportunities to young architects.

Present Day

The Eastern Docklands, Westerdok, and IJburg developments are complete and house an array of people and services. The developments are a lively mix of people, buildings, and functions. The housing satisfies the city's need to keep inhabitants from moving to the suburbs, keeps the consumer's desire to reside in a low- to mid-rise housing structure; the architecture is bright and interesting and is just the right mix that makes the city attractive. However, many of the VINEX developments, despite the high population density and urban aspirations, have been criticised for a lack of facilities in their built community to serve the populace, and the future of social housing is under debate. The government is questioning its role in a state that has been altered by current economics and societal and political changes. The social housing model has slowly begun to make way for an ownership model, and the existing social rental housing stock may be handed over to private control.

In recent years, a new approach to housing has emerged: a group of people, often friends and future cohabitants, purchase a building in an underdeveloped neighbourhood and hire an architect to renovate the building into dwelling units for themselves to occupy. Those neighbourhoods with newly converted residences have slowly been increasing in value and the residents' risk-taking has rewarded them with an attainable housing alternative in the city. The results have proved positive for neighbourhoods and dwellers and are starting to be seen as a viable dwelling option. With housing prices on the rise in the city, it is a proactive way to be in control of costs, design organisation, and aesthetics, and the most compelling reason—to remain living in the city.

The Dutch have built and earned an international reputation as a proving ground for new ideas in housing, excelling in the challenge of housing design, and offering one of the largest collections of exemplary work for study. The diverse range, high quality, and sheer volume of multi-unit housing in this small country is unrivalled, and Dutch housing ideas have been exported all over the world. The high calibre of housing design, especially for the social rental sector, has been characterised as exceptional, experimental, innovative, bold, quirky, fun, and slightly absurd. Their desire and effort to accommodate a wide variety of residents with a mix of incomes, lifestyles, and attitudes within one building is commendable and inspiring, and demonstrates their knowledge that good architectural design and quality lead to a better standard of living and create healthier and more advanced society.

Jian Wai SOHO Community

BEIJING

Circa 2000 to Present Day
Space-Enclosing Structure

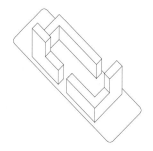

Beijing is one of the oldest, largest, and most populous cities in the world. The city has been continuously inhabited since circa 1045 BC, has a municipal land area of 16,400 square kilometres (6,300 square miles), and a population exceeding 21 million residents. The city has had a long and rich history in housing that dates back over 3,000 years, and the architecture of housing has very slowly evolved throughout this time. More recently, Beijing is now one of the fastest modernising and urbanising cities in the world. In the early 2000s, building construction was accelerating at a rapid pace. Encouraged by local and national governments to shape a new future and rebrand the city's image, and with a boost from being awarded the 2008 Summer Olympics, new large-scale, mixed-use residential developments began to appear in the city and the architectural design of housing evolved remarkably. After the announcement that Beijing was to host the Olympics, the city declared its plan to become a "modernised international city of the first rank" by 2050, and one of its first steps is housing an ever-growing population through new architecture.

According to China's National Bureau of Statistics and the National Development and Reform Commission, 30 percent of the nation's population is currently modernised and living in cities. By 2030, the estimate increases to 60 percent and by 2050, it is projected that 70 percent of the country will be urban. Beijing has been experiencing a monumental shift in its urban landscape and, with the ever-increasing population, there will be more people to house and more housing developments. One of the housing typologies that has been reoccurring and reinterpreted is the space-enclosing structure. This chapter will focus on the space-enclosing structure typology and how Beijing has remade it as its own.

Space-Enclosing Structure Characteristics

A space-enclosing structure is a building or set of buildings that create and enclose open spaces. The key characteristics are:

- A version of linear block that is bent, angular, sinuous, or curved in building form

- Building form envelops a semi-public or private open, outdoor space

- Can be a single building that folds or contours to create one or many open spaces

- Can be a series of similar-shaped buildings that form an enclosure around one or many open spaces

- Building form does not necessarily conform to characteristics of the existing block

Historical Context

In the 1980s, China, economically, enabled foreign trade for the first time, and architecturally, was exposed to Western, industrialised, building techniques. In the 1990s to early 2000s, China allowed the privatisation of businesses including state-owned enterprises. It also reduced tariffs, trade barriers, and regulations and gained a major economic presence. In 2001, the World Trade Organisation approved China for membership. In architecture, the first Chinese architects who left China in the 1980s to 2000s period to study architecture in Western schools returned and were able to initiate their own architectural practices. Prior to this time, the country's architects were employed in Design Institutes, which were large, state-owned firms that supervised the design and development of architectural projects. In the late 1990s, the central government deregulated architecture practices and independent firms were permitted to practice.

In 2001, Beijing was awarded the 2008 Summer Olympics and the planning of the event inundated the city's already rapidly emerging and growing building development and construction plans. In the years 2001 to 2008, Beijing welcomed internationally recognised foreign architects to design and build large-scale, publicly prominent projects to showcase their city as part of the Olympics, as well as for other non-related developments. In 2006, statistics from the China Ministry of Construction revealed that over 1,400 foreign architecture firms had opened satellite offices in China and their design work constituted over 50 percent of the large-scale projects in Beijing.

From 2008 to the present day, China has merged its socialist political system with a capitalist free market economy—and in less than a decade, China managed to double its per capita income and standard of living, outperforming the United States by 40 years and Japan by 23 years. In this short time, China has bared the mark of Western modernity. It has become the second-largest economic power in the world, and the appetite for Western-style consumer goods and architecture has immersed the country with an abundance of adopted merchandise and architectural designs.

Traditional Beijing Courtyard Housing

Historically, housing forms in China were mostly courtyard housing. The *siheyuan* was a type of traditional Chinese courtyard housing that had existed for thousands of years, and for centuries it was the only architectural form of housing. The name *siheyuan* literally translates to "courtyard surrounded by buildings on all four sides", and the housing type was an extensive and illustrious component in the city of Beijing. The courtyard housing development made up a large part of the city's identity, served as a cultural symbol, and was considered an early form of urban housing.

The layout and configuration of Beijing was based on a grid and conceived of as a systematic and orderly organisation. Plots of land were arranged in rectangular and square patterns and streets were aligned in north–south and east–west orientations that resulted in a number of large, rectilinear city blocks. The city was surrounded by a series of fortifications, and walls were used both around and within the city. Internal walls formed neighbourhoods and within the neighbourhoods, the *siheyuan* courtyard housing typology was a walled housing development that grew from its city's urban structure. The urban plan was most evident in the walled Royal Palace of Beijing, which was within the walled enclosure of the Imperial City that was located within the enclosure of the Inner City of Beijing. The distinction between internal and external spaces created the Beijing concept of a city within a city.

Siheyuan was a spacious, single-storey, square or rectangular-shaped courtyard house that was designed to accommodate multi-generations of one family in multi-units within the same housing compound. The typology had a series of domestic spaces, which consisted of a minimum of four separate rooms with its own roof, one for each family member that enclosed a communal family courtyard. The number and size of the courtyards varied, from one modest courtyard for a humble family to numerous large courtyards for the Imperial family, but all comprised the same basic units and brick and stone construction materials.

Section

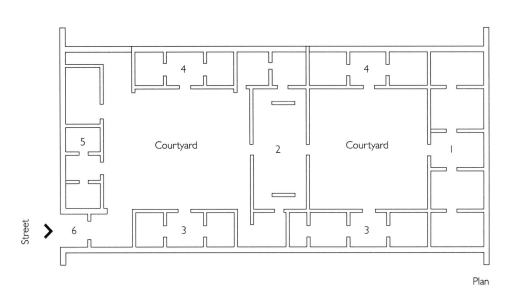

4		4	
5	Courtyard	2	Courtyard	1
6	3	3	

Street

Plan

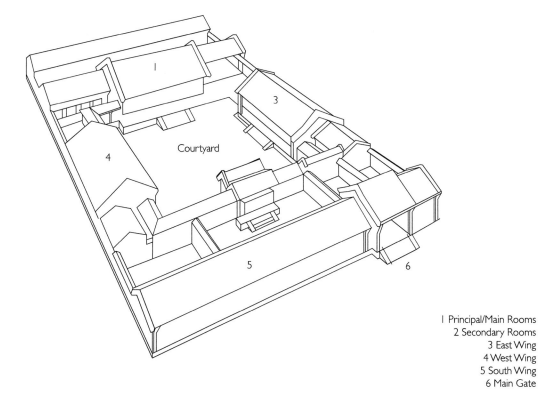

Courtyard

1 Principal/Main Rooms
2 Secondary Rooms
3 East Wing
4 West Wing
5 South Wing
6 Main Gate

Traditional Chinese *Siheyuan* Courtyard Housing

The basic layout of the courtyard house generally consisted of the principal rooms, secondary rooms, corridors, and an enclosed courtyard. The principal rooms were rooms for the family. The main room was reserved and used by the owner of the house and head of the family, the parents, and the east and west wing rooms were for the younger generation, their children. The main room was situated at the north end of the courtyard, oriented in the east–west direction and the main façade faced south. The children's rooms were off to the east and west sides of the courtyard and were orientated in a north–south direction. Secondary rooms were for family gathering and servants' quarters and were located north of the main room or in the south portion of the courtyard. The orientation of the rooms was based on climatic considerations: sheltering the internal courtyard from cold northerly winds and allowing in sunlight. Rooms facing the sun were considered prime rooms and therefore the northern rooms oriented in the east–west direction were generally used as the principal rooms.

The courtyard house was multi-generational housing. Customarily, when the son married, he returned with his wife to live in his parents' courtyard house to begin their new family; when the daughter married, however, she left to live with her husband in his family's courtyard house to start her new family. Essentially, every family grew to become an extended family of in-laws, aunts, uncles, cousins, and grandparents, and the core of family life formed a tight-knit community within itself and the shared living compound — a city within a city.

A wall about 3 metres (10 feet) tall, of vernacular Chinese grey brick or plaster walls, enclosed the courtyard compound. On the outside, the walls created *hutong*s, which were alleyways formed by walls of *siheyuans*. Sloped, tiled roof peaks and leafy trees protruded above the grey walls and provided glimpses of colour and, every so often, a colourful entrance gate to a courtyard house interrupted the continuous grey order. The street façade of the *siheyuan* lacked colour, but the strong use of colours such as red, green, blue, and gold on the entrance gate and in the interiors was common. Inside the courtyard, the painted colours harmonised the space and the outdoor garden's lush and abundant landscaping of trees, plants, and flowers native to Beijing created a sense of calm and tranquil space from the outside city. Such scenery was typical of courtyard housing, and though the entrance gate had doors, these were often left open to allow ready access from the internal private areas to the external outdoor alleyways.

Courtyard House to Space-Enclosing Structure

Beijing's rapid speed towards urbanisation has made it imperative to house its increasing population. Single-storey, multi-generational courtyard housing is no longer a viable housing option, and the time-worn typology is making way for new multi-storey, multi-unit dwelling housing typologies all over the city. The traditional and intimate Beijing courtyard housing of yesteryear is quickly readapting and morphing into modern, large-scale community living. The transformation is realised in many different forms, but the housing typology that has emerged around the city and that best evokes the courtyard housing concept is the recently adopted space-enclosing structure. The new Beijing space-enclosing structure is a massive arrangement that is suited to and tailor-made for the size, layout, and demands of the city.

Shortly after being awarded the 2008 Summer Olympics, Beijing turned into an international, and world's largest, construction site almost overnight. Residential projects of all typologies and scale multiplied along-

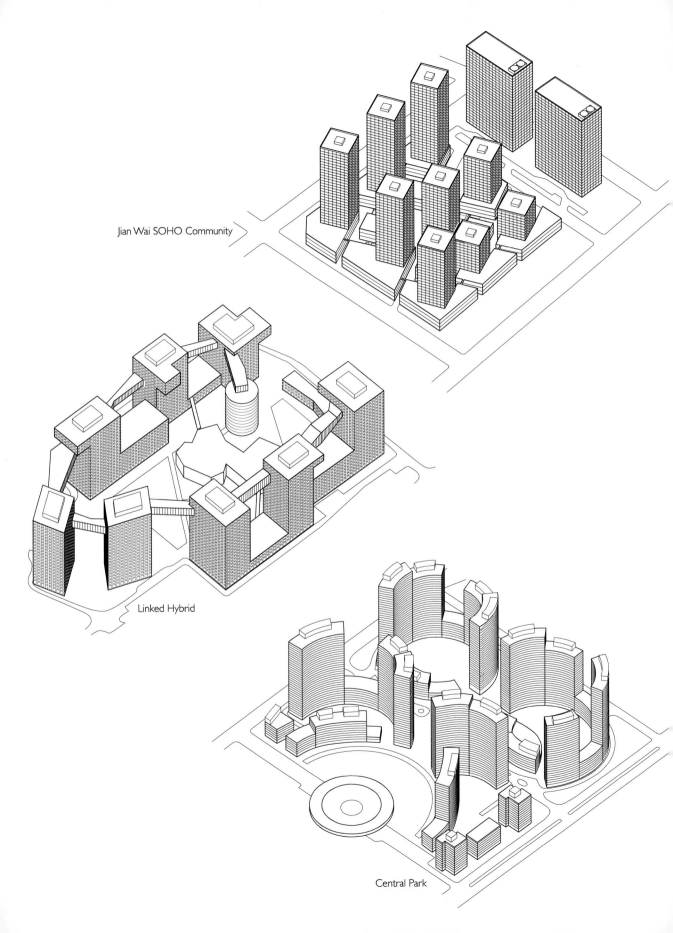

Jian Wai SOHO Community

Linked Hybrid

Central Park

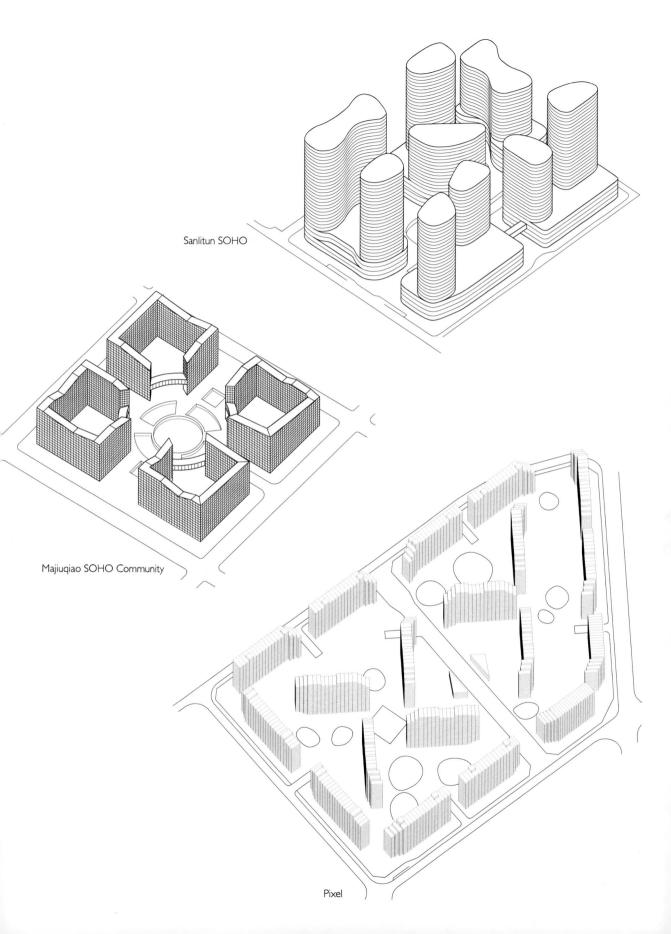

Sanlitun SOHO

Majiuqiao SOHO Community

Pixel

side civic and institutional buildings. Some neighbourhoods with low-density housing were demolished to *tabula rasa* sites and replaced with high-density housing properties, and the space-enclosing structure housing developments were responsible for some drastic neighbourhood conversions. The space-enclosing structure in Beijing has many conceptual similarities to a traditional courtyard house and could be viewed as a modern-day version of the old housing on reconstituted land. Both typologies accommodate multiple families, share communal rooms and outdoor spaces, and form a community—courtyard housing on a much smaller scale and space-enclosing structure on a much larger scale.

The Beijing space-enclosing structure is grand in size and scope. The buildings comprise a minimum 500 dwelling units and occupy at least 10 hectares (25 acres) of land. Alongside the residential component, commercial programming is introduced and it remodels the typology into a large-scale complex that makes the most of the development and creates and encompasses an even larger community than its ancestor typology. The mixed-use housing development is a new housing model for the city and it makes for a very site-specific and appropriate urban typology for the densification of Beijing.

Up until even very recently, foreign architects had been designing the majority of space-enclosing structure complexes in the city. Local state-owned design institutes and private architecture offices act as local representatives and work in company with the Western architecture firms to learn their methods. Western building ideas, designs, practices, detailing, construction, and standards have been imported into Beijing, and Western architecture has become Chinese modernism. As architecture opportunities open up even more in Beijing, there will be increasing cross-collaboration between Western and local architects and the city will become closer to its aspiration to become a modernised international city.

The Beijing space-enclosing structure is more than just housing. The typology is a contemporary form of an elaborate compound that has fashioned a new model of urban space and living. Like its courtyard housing predecessor, the space-enclosing structure is designed to accommodate numerous families; has one or more shared outdoor space; construction materials and palette are coordinated to heighten the sense of community; and the internal shared outdoors spaces are accessible to the outdoor streets. Unlike its predecessor, it is now a multiplex, mixed-use, monumental structure development that incorporates other programming, usually office spaces and retail, parallel to its housing, and all are integrated into one large-scale, mega-city block entity. The housing now accommodates a variety of different people and families, the outdoor spaces are shared among hundreds of people, both residents and users of the other programmes, and the entire mixed-use structure complex wraps itself around the ground-level outdoor areas, which are always accessible by the public from the outdoor streets, physically retaining a notion of community.

For the residential component in a space-enclosing structure, the orientation towards the sun is very important. The direction in which a building or unit faces is established from a general master planning rule for residential areas in China, which stipulates that every citizen has the right to natural daylight. *Feng shui* and market demands have a strong influence, and foreign architects recognise and revere the significance of the sun-facing layouts of the old Beijing courtyard housing.

Space-enclosing structures designed by foreign architects have been designed with foreign standards and conveniences, which are higher-end than those of local norms. Most space-enclosing structures are high-quality buildings, some even being considered luxurious, full of public programming and private amenities, such as swimming pools, fitness rooms, and spas for use by the residents of the private dwelling units. The dwelling units have spacious layouts and are fitted with designer kitchens and appliances, private outdoors balconies or terraces, and modern internal colour schemes, finishes, and fixtures that could pass for any foreign, all-encompassing, high-end dwelling units. The Beijing space-enclosing structure dwelling units are for rent or purchase, and the clientele are usually expatriates in Beijing for business (in the former case) and upper-middle class Chinese (in the latter case).

The new Western space-enclosing structure housing designs are attracting Beijing's rising upper-middle class, who admire Western design, lifestyle, and values. The city's upper-middle class are from a post-Cultural Revolution generation who were raised in China's reform years and consider that non-Chinese cultural references equate to a better way of life. Project briefs reflect this aspiration and desire, and developers and Western architects observed Beijing's, and China's other large cities', "Second Great Leap Forward", this time aiming towards Western ideals and capitalism. The large-scale, Western-designed, space-enclosing projects are concentrated within close proximity to other Western-designed project developments and in prime urban locations, grouping those with similar aspirations and incomes together.

Case Studies

In Beijing, space-enclosing structures can be either one building or a series of connected or disconnected buildings that create and enclose an open public space. From afar, many of the new mega-block developments in Beijing look like a vast city block of high-rises sprouting out of the ground. Upon closer investigation, many of the developments exhibit space-enclosing structure attributes since all the buildings are of the same development—designed, planned, and programmed by one architect, share one design vision throughout, and form a main communal, programmable space for people to gather.

Jian Wai SOHO Community

Architect: Riken Yamamoto
Completed: 2004

Jian Wai SOHO Community is one of the first mega-city block developments in Beijing. Located within close proximity to Tiananmen Square in central Beijing, Jian Wai SOHO Community is a large, mixed-use complex. The project is a shifted orthogonal grid of square residential and commercial towers that total roughly 700,000 square metres (7,500,000 square feet) in gross floor area and cover a site of approximately 17 hectares (42 acres). The complex is designed for pedestrians, and the spaces between the ground floors of the towers form a network of alleyways with several hundred retail shops, restaurants, and cafés. At the centre of the development is a low building enclosed by the tall towers, and serves as an open public space where year-round cultural events take place.

Pedestrian and vehicular traffic is purposely separated in Jian Wai SOHO Community. Cars are directed to underground parking levels that are visible from large openings at the pedestrian level. These openings enable light to reach the lower parking levels and provide visual connection to the multiple, sunken levels below grade and between the towers. The ground level is completely zoned for pedestrians to enjoy the space and services freely and safely. There are several kilometres of retail alleyways for pedestrians to explore. The rest of the spaces are of varying sizes and fitted out with seating and vegetation to be used as open public areas. The rooftops of the towers are occupiable roof gardens and also serve as outdoor public spaces. The entire complex is visually and physically designed for people to have a heightened sense of surroundings and community.

The towers are a combination of residential and offices and differ in height. The buildings all fit onto a chequerboard grid that has been tilted slightly at an angle that correlates to the existing surrounding streets and Tonghui river. The position and separation of the towers allow light and air to infiltrate to the pedestrian level, and each tower can receive sunlight on all four sides. The four sides of each tower in the Jianwai SOHO complex form a modular grid of reflective glass set within white steel frames. Jianwai SOHO houses 2,000 residential dwelling units and at night, when most lights are on in the residential towers, the complex sparkles and glows from the lights reflecting off the glass and the white steel frames.

Linked Hybrid

Architect: Steven Holl Architects
Completed: 2009
Centrally located adjacent to the site of the old city wall of Beijing and within the 2nd Ring of the inner city, Linked Hybrid is a large-scale development that accommodates residential, commercial, educational and entertainment programmes, and underground car parking. The 220,000-square metre (2,368,000-square feet) voluminous complex spreads over a city area of slightly more than 6 hectares (15 acres) and focuses on the pedestrian experience, with a large, landscaped, open space at its ground level accessible to the public from all entrances. The project is a series of eight buildings that vary in height from four to twenty-one storeys, and all link together by multi-levelled glass sky-bridges. The bridges physically connect the buildings and programmes together and embrace the site inward.

Linked Hybrid houses 750 residential dwelling units complete with communal swimming pool, fitness room, café, art gallery, auditorium, and salon for the inhabitants. The remaining programmes are public spaces that contain a hotel, restaurant, retail, Montessori school, kindergarten, cinema and theatre. There are more than 200 different dwelling units that range in area from 60 square metres (645 square feet) to 160 square metres (1,700 square feet) and from layouts of one to four bedrooms. On average, there are four dwelling units per floor and every unit faces two exposures to ensure that living rooms and all bedrooms have windows that are oriented to receive natural daylight, ventilation, and cross-ventilation. The diversity of dwelling units and layouts helps attract and cater to a large clientele, and the variety counters the monotony of living in multi-unit housing.

The project aimed for LEED Gold Certification in advanced technology in geothermal energy was devised and used to service Linked Hybrid. Over 600 geothermal wells at 100 metres (328 feet) below the basement foundation provide Linked Hybrid with its heating and cooling, with approximately 70 percent of the heating and cooling load being covered by this system. The property also uses a grey water system that daily recycles about 220,000 litres (58,000 gallons) of water from all the dwelling units and reuses it for landscaping, green roof irrigation atop the roofs of all eight buildings, and toilet flushing. The sustainable design features in Linked Hybrid set it apart from other similar large scale developments and have made it a viable example of an ecological, large-scale, urban mixed-use development.

The façade of the Linked Hybrid complex is a blocky grid of punched windows with multi-coloured window frames set within a brushed aluminium skin. From a distance, the buildings resemble large, perforated metal panels wrapped into tall, chunky rectangular forms. The façade was inspired by the polychrome of Chinese Buddhist architecture and makes for a uniform and solid presence. The inset window frames and undersides of the glass sky-bridges are painted red, green, and blue and are based on I-Ching and also colours found in ancient Chinese temples. The undersides of the sky-bridges are treated with a coloured membrane that glows at night when lit.

The concept behind Linked Hybrid was a combination of connected public and private spaces that was designed to encourage users to generate spontaneous exchanges and share resources. The idea was to create a city within a city, "streets" in the sky and all around, and an urban oasis to find quiet and green space within the larger city of Beijing, and also to evoke a feeling that one is still in a Chinese village though set in the middle of a bustling city.

Sanlitun SOHO

Architect: Kengo Kuma and Associates
Completed: 2010
Situated in the vibrant neighbourhood of Sanlitun, a popular area with both locals and foreigners with restaurants, retail, and night life, Sanlitun SOHO is a large-scale, mixed-use commercial, retail, and residential development. The project consists of five office and four residential towers, which are connected at various levels, folded around a large outdoor, public space and covering an urban area of 470,000 square metres (5 million square feet). Kuma's idea was to create an organic "tower village" within a natural landscape, and it has resulted in a collection of gentle forms connected by soft greenery and water elements.

The public programmes for the complex include restaurants, cafés, a roller-skating rink, multi-levels of retail and ground-level pedestrian shopping "streets" with underground car parking for close to 2,400 vehicles, and the residential portion of the project is housed in four separate towers labelled Tower A, B, C, and D. The residential towers occupy the south portion of the site to take advantage of the sun, are of various footprints and heights, the tallest reaching just under 100 metres (328 feet), and contain a total of 118,000 square metres (11,000 square feet) of dwelling units. The towers accommodate many different floor plan unit layouts that range in area from 100 square metres (1,000 square feet) to 490 square metres (5,200 square feet), from one to three bedrooms, respectively, and all unit living rooms and bedrooms have access to natural daylight and ventilation. Shared residential facilities include a fitness centre.

All buildings that make up Sanlitun SOHO are voluminous and gently curved in form, and clad in a uniform blue, grey, and white glass and metal curtain wall system. Each sensually rounded entity contributes to form an enclosed "village" or compact neighbourhood that is easily identifiable and unifies the large-scale, urban complex as a whole.

Street

7 Building

8 Building

9 SOHO

8 SOHO

9 Building

4 Building

5 Building

6 Building

5 SOHO

6 SOHO

1 Building

2 Building

3 Building

Street

Street

Street

B

A

Street

1st Floor

7 Building

8 Building

9 Building

8 SOHO

9 SOHO

4 Building

6 Building

5 Building

5 SOHO

6 SOHO

1 Building

2 Building

3 Building

B

A

Typical Floors

Jian Wai SOHO Community

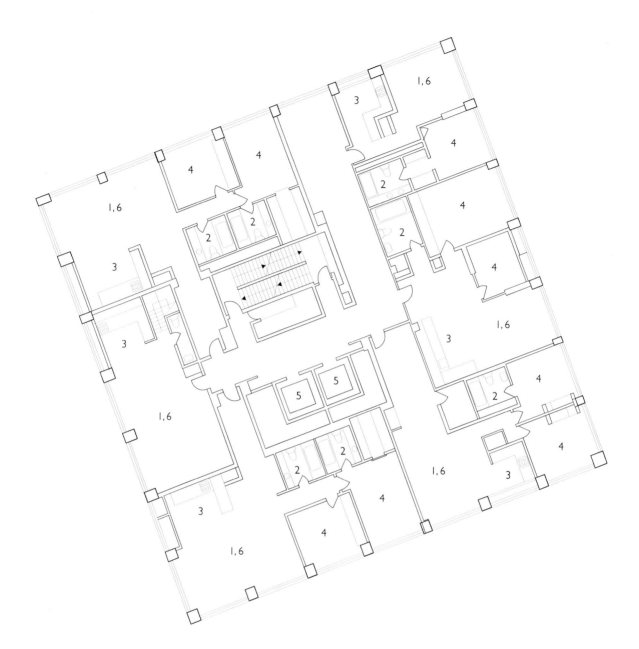

1 Living Room
2 Bathroom
3 Kitchen
4 Bedroom
5 Elevator
6 Dining Room

4 Building
Typical Floors

Jian Wai SOHO Community

Jian Wai SOHO Community

Jian Wai SOHO Community

请勿倚靠栏杆
CAUTION! DANGER!

Jian Wai SOHO Community

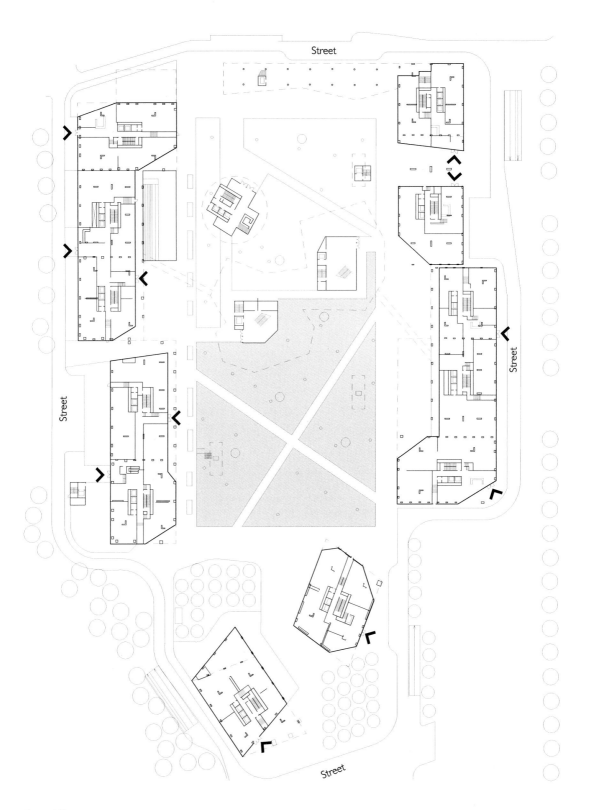

Street

Street

Street

Street

Ground Floor

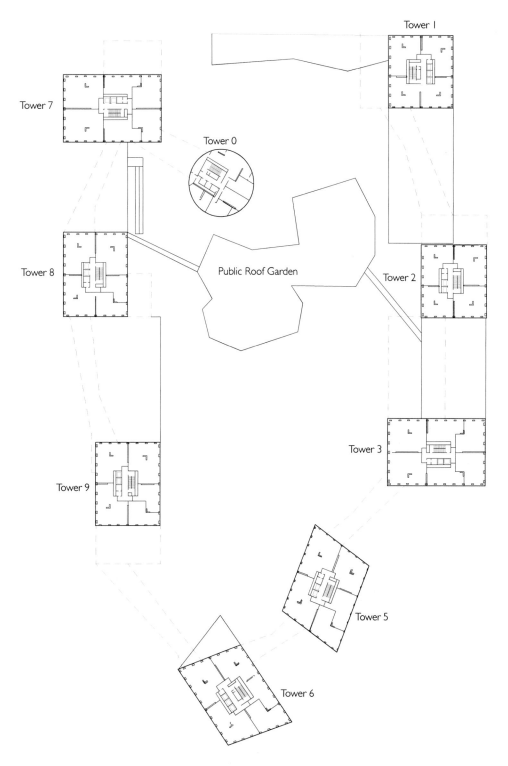

Tower 1

Tower 7

Tower 0

Tower 8

Public Roof Garden

Tower 2

Tower 9

Tower 3

Tower 5

Tower 6

Typical Floors

Linked Hybrid

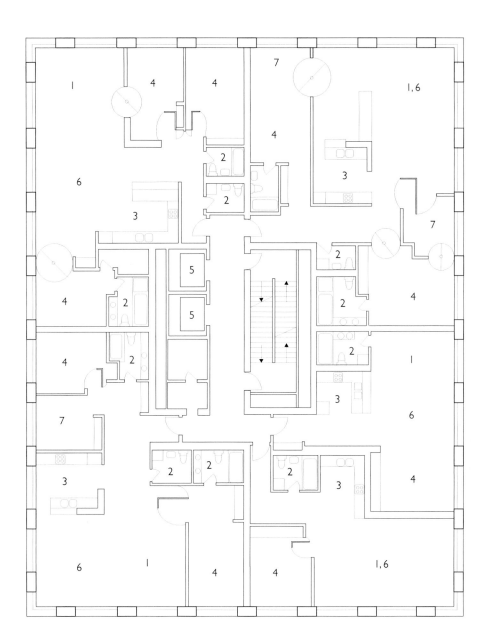

1 Living Room
2 Bathroom
3 Kitchen
4 Bedroom
5 Elevator
6 Dining Room
7 Study

Tower 9
Typical Floors

Linked Hybrid

Linked Hybrid

Linked Hybrid

Linked Hybrid

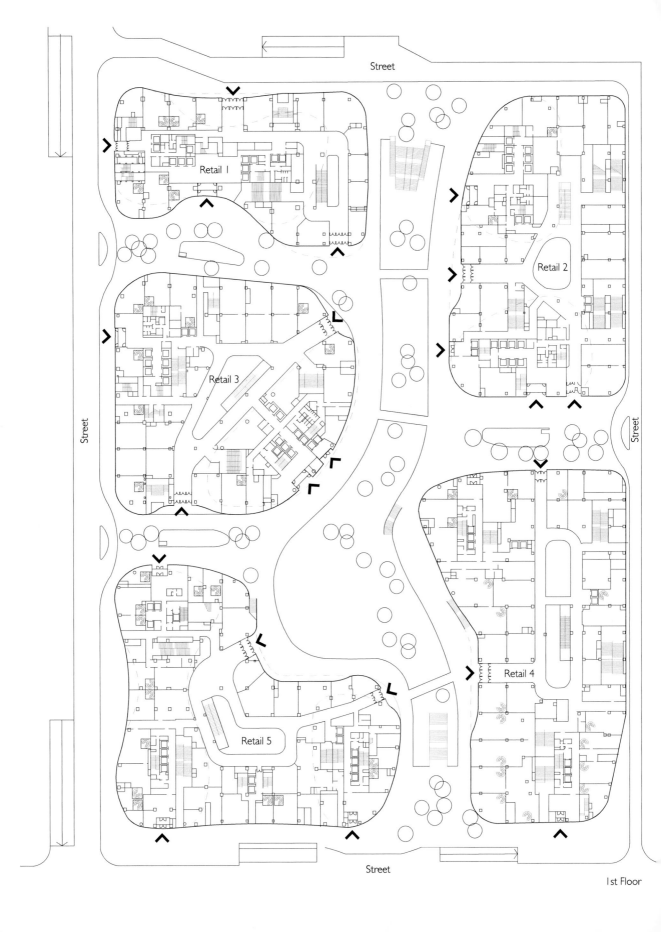

Street

Street

Street

Street

Retail 1

Retail 2

Retail 3

Retail 4

Retail 5

1st Floor

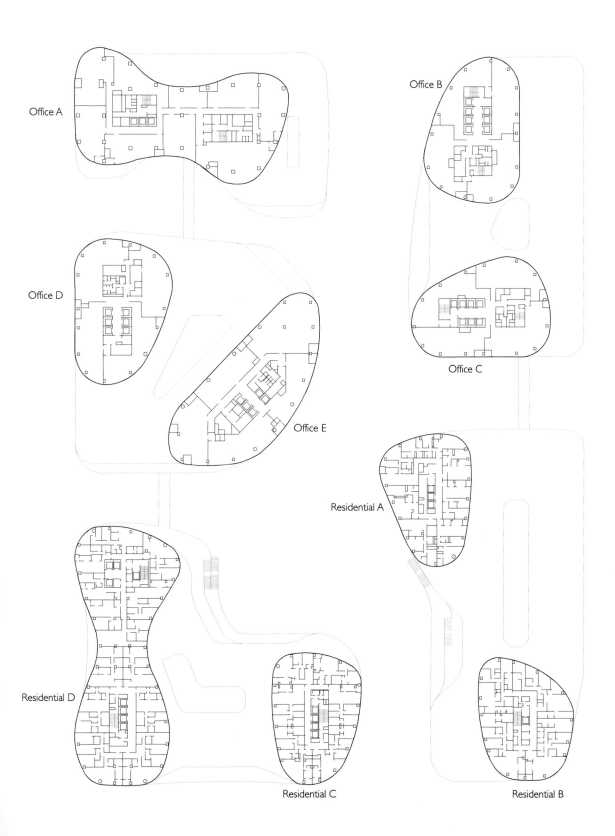

Office A

Office B

Office D

Office C

Office E

Residential A

Residential D

Residential C

Residential B

Typical Floors

Sanlitun SOHO

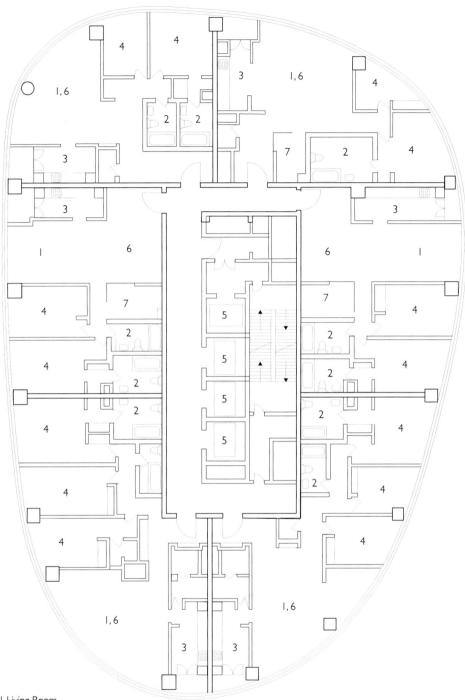

1 Living Room
2 Bathroom
3 Kitchen
4 Bedroom
5 Elevator
6 Dining Room
7 Study

Residential C
Typical Floors

Sanlitun SOHO

Sanlitun SOHO

Sanlitun SOHO

Sanlitun SOHO

Typical Unit Floor Plan Type

The real estate market in Beijing has become more liberal, and this has resulted in marketing to seize a larger share of consumer demand. Space-enclosing structures in Beijing were purposely designed to comprise many different floor plans and layouts to suit and appeal to a broad clientele. There is a wide range of unit floor plan types, from corridor layouts in some smaller units to circular paths and dividing elements in larger units. The units are mostly inhabited by upper-middle class locals who purchase a unit as a primary residence, and by foreigners who rent units for a sojourn working stay in Beijing.

Access Type

The access typology for a Beijing space-enclosing structure is vertical. The buildings are multi-level, with either floor plates stacked atop one another or a series of connected buildings with stacked floors.

Construction Materials

Historically, housing in Beijing used traditional construction systems and materials—cast-in-place solid clay bricks and concrete. Since the influx of foreign architects, who began to design mega-scale projects and brought with them their design methods and techniques, local construction knowledge and quality have grown and improved with each new building development. Currently, the formwork of space-enclosing structures is concrete with the exterior sheathed in metal cladding systems.

Owners, Landlords, Developers, Reformers

SOHO China Ltd.

One of the country's largest real-estate developers is SOHO China Ltd. Founded in 1995 by Pan Shiyi, a former government employee, and his wife Zhang Xin, a former Goldman Sachs employee, SOHO China Ltd. began to develop and own high-profile and branded commercial properties in central Beijing. The company later began to incorporate residential projects in its portfolio and earned a reputation for collaborating with internationally recognised architects to produce architecturally notable, high-quality, landmark developments in prime urban locations: for a space-enclosing housing structures, Japanese architect Kengo Kuma (Sanlitun SOHO) and Dutch architecture firm Rhine Scheme (Majuqiao SOHO Community); and many others for their commercial projects. The company has contributed to Beijing's mixed-use, space-enclosing structures and iconic properties.

Government Departments, Policies, and Regulations

In China, there were five periods of housing policies that were enforced for all cities. The country's housing policies, which began in 1949, opened up housing markets at the beginning of the twenty-first century to welcome the flood of foreign interests and investments, and five short years after, had to begin to address housing shortage and affordability. For Beijing, housing is one of the most difficult problems currently plaguing the city, and the problem is growing in parallel with its density and population.

Building regulations vary from city to city. In Beijing, the main policies applicable to residential developments govern building height, building density, dwelling unit size, sunlight, and earthquake resistance, and vary depending on the proximity to the Forbidden City, the historic urban core. National policies dictated that for urban housing, each person be provided with a minimum of eight square metres (86 square feet) of living space and that at least one main room in each dwelling unit receive a minimum of one hour of sunshine on the day of the winter solstice, 21 December. The sunlight rule is calculated using a mathematical formula that takes into account the distance between buildings, their height, and the angle of the sun on the winter solstice at 11:30 in the morning using solar time. The uniform rule that every dwelling unit must enjoy a minimum of one hour's sunlight across the country was well intentioned. In reality, the rule resulted in wasteful use of scarce urban land, and recently built residential units were no longer required to apply this rule.

With the ingress of both foreign and local wealth in the country, China is struggling to house the majority of its population, which was not a problem until recently. In Beijing, the large-scale, mega-plex, high-end space-enclosing housing complexes cater to a certain type of demographic—foreigners and upper-middle class locals—while housing for the rest of the population is lacking, addressed only in 2005 in the nation's housing policies.

Housing Policies: The Five Periods

1949–1957: Heavily Regulated Urban Housing Markets

Shortly after the People's Republic of China (PRC) was founded in 1949, the government confiscated most private property, assumed state ownership of almost all housing, and controlled the housing rental sector to ensure housing affordability.

1958–1977: Work Unit Housing System

In 1958, the government divided the entire population into urban and rural groups. Urban residents had workers' housing provided by their employer (work unit) according to their office ranking, occupation status, work experience, and other merits. Housing construction was largely initiated and financed by work units.

1978–1997: Reform Experiments of Marketisation in the Housing Sector

The government introduced market forces to the housing sector to reform the state-controlled public housing system, thereby promoting private ownership and the sale of public housing to urban residents. Rent was raised to market levels, and private and foreign investment in housing was encouraged.

1998–2004: Development of Housing Markets

The Work Unit Housing System was terminated and instead a new policy of distributing cash subsidies for housing to newcomers entering the urban workforce began. As a result, a vigorous urban housing market rapidly developed. This reform promoted home ownership and encouraged the development of social rental housing for those who did not want to or could not afford to live in new housing.

2005 to Present: Addressing Housing Affordability and Low-Income Housing

Homeownership has been increasing and so has the supply of housing and its quality, improving the living conditions of a large number of urban households. Housing demand has begun to outpace supply in the big cities, driving housing prices up drastically. Housing has become less affordable to the low-income families and the urban poor, and the government has started to provide affordable housing.

Ministry of Construction

In the 1990s, the Ministry of Construction studied affluent housing abroad and, in 2000, released a guideline entitled *Planning and Design Guidelines for a Sample Residential Area in 2000 for Affluent Housing Engineering*. The study reviewed the living conditions and housing typologies among the upper-middle class abroad, and the research was adopted and published as an outline for Chinese cities. The Chinese outline focused on four areas that would be of importance regarding new building construction in China: community, diversity, sustainability, and property management. Community was a concept used to nurture a new kind of culture and sense of belonging where new social and human relationships could be consciously created; diversity was to create new types of function that would enhance standards of living; sustainability was to encourage conservation at all levels of application; property management looked at property service and management.

Ministry of Housing and Urban–Rural Development

In 2008, the Ministry of Construction was restructured and its name was changed to the Ministry of Housing and Urban–Rural Development. With the quickening pace of building, the country needed a state department to monitor and safeguard fast-moving construction activity in its large, urban cities, specifically with regard to Beijing. This government agency was responsible for the administration of construction projects around the country, to guide the planning and construction of urban and rural areas, to establish national standards of construction, to monitor construction activity, to regulate the construction market, and to manage the housing and real estate industries.

Present Day

Beijing architecture is now in a period of rapid progress and seems to be on its way to reaching its goal of becoming a "modernised international city of the first rank" by 2050. The city has demonstrated a commitment to contemporary ideas and has realised innovative and visionary housing, and foreigners and a certain demographic of Beijingers seem to appreciate the new urban developments that combine different programmes and usage.

Over the past couple of decades, Beijing's rapid progress towards urbanisation and modernisation has seen entire city blocks of neighbourhoods, mostly with *siheyuan* housing, razed to make way for multi-storey dwelling units that can better house the city's fast-growing population. The *siheyuan* housing type is a product of a bygone era and can no longer adequately serve the city's housing needs and modern living requirements; of the *siheyuan* housing deemed worthy of preservation, much has been converted into museums or hotels.

While most locals view these changes as a tremendous advancement and achievement, the speed of construction is exhilarating and some locals and many outsiders are concerned that whole neighbourhoods and livelihoods are being decimated and displaced with yet another mega-scale, foreign-designed—or somewhat Western-looking—development that promises a better future. A closer look at the shiny and glittery space-enclosing structures will reveal that many are looking well worn; courtyard landscapes are not as lush or well maintained as those of their predecessor typology; entrances for public accessibility are guarded or policed so only certain members of the public are allowed passage. It is evident that class segregation has been created; the large scale of such developments is too vast for the creation of any sense of real community or connectivity; residents end up retreating into their own private units and it is rare that there is more than one generation of family living together, gradually eliminating the strong, integrated familial community unit that once existed here.

House NA

TOKYO

Circa 2000 to Present Day
Kyosho Jutaku

Tokyo is one of the world's most populated, dense, and compact metropolises. The city is a mix of high- to mid-rise office buildings, mid- to low-rise multi-unit residential buildings, and a topological and organic ground cover of low-rise, single-family detached houses, all competing for space among narrow streets, winding alleyways, and a tangle of overhead power lines. Due to land constraints and expensive real estate costs, the majority of the single-family detached houses are small in scale and occupy a small footprint. Small-scale living is typical in Tokyo, a city with a land area of about 2,000 square kilometres (800 square miles) and population of around 13 million inhabitants. In the early 2000s, an even smaller version of the single-family house emerged. This new type of single-family detached house, known as *kyosho jutaku*, which translates to micro house, is often less than 100 square metres (1,000 square feet), is ingeniously designed to conform to a micro site, and has gained increasing acceptance both nationally and internationally.

The focus of this book is on multi-storey, multi-dwelling unit housing; however, it is worth making an exception for Tokyo's *kyosho jutaku*. The micro house cannot easily be presented as any true housing typology, as each development is unique in design. Nevertheless, micro houses are so compact, well integrated into the existing surroundings, and readily recognisable throughout Tokyo's urban core, that they could be regarded as its own idiosyncratic interpretation of a high-density urban housing typology. And true to *kyosho jutaku* fashion, it is a housing typology that is attuned to and tailor-made for Tokyo.

Kyosho Jutaku Characteristics

The *kyosho jutaku* is a fully detached building form. The key characteristics are:

- Not informed by the characteristics of any specific block
- Each building is an autonomous object
- Single-family house peculiar to Japan
- Small and often odd-shaped size lot and building footprint
- Building area of 100 square metres (1,000 square feet) or less

Historical Context

The Japanese have long endured crowded cities and scarce living space. In the years following the end of the Second World War, the government advocated the value of home ownership to stimulate the economy and many citizens purchased single-family homes as part of their civic duty. It was also during this time, the 1950s, that houses were unavoidably small due to shortages of building materials and supplies. By the late 1960s, the Japanese economy had fully recovered from the war and the 1970s saw the first housing boom for small-scale urban housing. A magazine entitled *Toshi Jutaku* (Urban Housing) that featured and promoted all small houses was established, and became a staunch public supporter of this trend. In the 1980s, Japan experienced a housing bubble where demand exceeded supply; in the 1990s the bubble burst and brought Japan's financial system to the brink of collapse; and, in the early 2000s the fallout from this experience heralded the introduction of new regulations for future housing in Japan and another small-scale, urban housing boom took effect, especially across the centre of Tokyo.

Urban Scale and Density

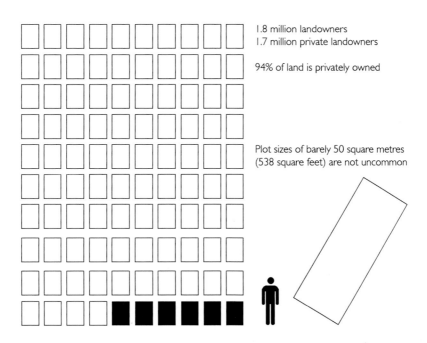

1.8 million landowners
1.7 million private landowners

94% of land is privately owned

Plot sizes of barely 50 square metres
(538 square feet) are not uncommon

Landowners and Plot Sizes

The new building regulations for housing were laws directly passed down by the national government. These favoured new housing construction and gave landowners the rights and freedom to manage their own land. Landowners were able to divide and subdivide their plot of land for sale, and they could demolish and rebuild as they saw fit. New calculations were introduced that enabled buildings to be built taller and narrower, and landowners, especially those planning to build a single-family house, soon began to take advantage of this new approach.

Regardless of a housing surge or crash, for many decades homes in Japan occupied a very limited floor area, and in Tokyo especially, small-scale living was born of necessity due to the city's lack of land that was both affordable and suitable for development. In the early 2000s, the architecture of *kyosho jutaku* became popular throughout the city and was promoted due to increased real estate values and the new housing regulations. Despite the rise in land prices, many opted to make their home in the urban core rather than relocate to the less expensive suburbs. The suburbs usually afforded a larger home, but the gain in floor area was offset by the increased travelling time into the city for work. Many in this generation witnessed or experienced the set-up of the previous generation and preferred to compromise by living in a small house in the city rather than enduring longer travelling times from the suburbs.

Many residents found a novel way to view and appreciate the newly available empty lots around the city. The plots available were often small, irregular, and cast-offs from large industrial or commercial developments whose landowners had capitalised on the new building laws. Some plots were where larger houses had once stood, but because the inheritance taxes in Tokyo were then so steep, the owners were willing to sell off some or even all of their land to pay the fees. With the expertise of an architect, these plots could be redesigned into a habitable site where single-family detached micro houses could be built. With a burgeoning population and increased shortage of land, a vacant lot, no matter how tiny or weirdly shaped, is an attractive lot for those seeking to purchase land on which to build a house.

There is now a government incentive to own and live in a private, single-family house. Most buyers prefer new houses and even if an existing house is purchased, the building is quickly demolished and a new house is built in its place. In Tokyo, demolition is part of the process of owning a single-family detached house, and regardless of how small or odd the lot, with the help of an architect, even a tiny plot of land can accommodate a house that fulfils the needs, style, and budget of the occupant. Since the appearance of the *kyosho jutaku*, although the trend is mostly driven by economics, tiny houses have gained widespread attention and enthusiasm in a country that tends to appreciate everything small, efficient, and singular. It was inevitable that the *kyosho jutaku* would prove irresistible and highly popular.

Micro House

The *kyosho jutaku* represents a completely new view of the single-family detached residential house. The new micro house challenges the conventional perception of what a single-family detached residential house should look like and how it should function. The design and layout of *kyosho jutaku* re-evaluate the spaces and their purposes within a house, and it becomes an experiment not only in architectural design, but also often in structural engineering. The results generally question conventional residential design and explore new ways of dwelling.

The new micro house is a phenomenon peculiar to its time, and perhaps even to the current generation. Japan has a fascination with everything small and cute. It is known as *kawaii* culture, and it is evident throughout Japanese pop culture, beginning in the 1970s with anthropomorphic animal characters. The tight and oddly shaped parcels of land on into which *kyosho jutaku* need to be custom-designed to fit provide an excellent excuse and opportunity to explore something quirky and *kawaii*. Small houses have existed in Tokyo for a long time, but it is this present generation that has taken the influence of Japanese pop design and culture and transformed it into their private piece of architecture.

In Tokyo, many traditional small-scale detached houses are designed by house-makers, which are building companies that sell pre-packaged, mass-produced, stock floor plans made to fit common lot sizes. Unlike the traditional small-scale detached houses, *kyosho jutaku* is site specific and is designed by an architect. Many Japanese architects, from long-established professionals to young, start-up practitioners, include micro house designs in their portfolio. The demand for micro houses has kept some Japanese architects so busy that they are occupied full-time by micro house commissions, and the demand for *kyosho jutaku* has turned this infatuation into a very lucrative construction industry in Japan.

A *kyosho jutaku* is radically different in thought and design from the traditional, single-family detached house. In plot size, *kyosho jutaku* range from as small as 30 square metres (320 square feet) and as narrow as 4.5 metres (15 feet) wide, to 50, 100, or 200 square metres (530, 1,070, or 2,100 square feet, respectively)—the architects of these micro houses are rewriting the definition of house design. In a *kyosho jutaku*, there may be moveable walls to alter the size of a room; rooms may perform two or more functions; furniture may be designed and made to fold into walls or floors when not in use; windows may look out of place on the external façade, interiorly they are positioned for a specific purpose; and the external façade might be a translucent skin, sheer textile, or non-existent, to allow as much natural daylight as possible to permeate the interior. The micro house design emphasises utility and craft, is devised to be highly efficient and functional, and the preconditions of minimum space and maximum usage, all contained within a quirky envelope, make for innovative, delightful, and striking little treasures of showpiece residential architecture embedded around the city.

Traditional Japanese House Elements

The design and construction of a traditional Japanese house include a deep appreciation and veneration for nature, natural materials, and simplicity. Master craftsmen built traditional Japanese houses. The organic elements and techniques found in traditional Japanese arts and crafts were carefully deployed in the making of a house to create a harmonious relationship in the home, and with its inhabitants. Materials, design features, and rooms purposefully function to enrich the peace and tranquillity within the home. According to Japanese art principles, the essence of a Japanese house is that the true beauty of a room is found in the space enclosed by the roof and walls, rather than the roof and walls themselves.

A traditional Japanese house was of wood construction and built on a compact lot. The interior appeared almost empty and emanated a sense of serenity. Internal doors and walls were on wooden sliding track that opened or closed to alter the size of a room or integrate one room with others, and there were no locks on internal doors. There was a connection, either visual or physical, between indoors and outdoors

through a garden. Furniture was usually compact and integrated into the walls. At night, futons were removed from built-in storage cabinets and replaced in the morning to clear floor space for other uses. The rooms, spaces, and systems within a traditional Japanese house were always flexible and adaptable.

Rooms and spaces were measured by *tatami* mats in a traditional Japanese house. The measurement of a *tatami* mat was based on traditional Japanese units and varied slightly depending on the region of the country. This measurement roughly translates in the metric system as 1 by 2 metres (3 by 6 feet), and a typical-size bedroom would be made up of 6 mats, which equates to approximately 10 square metres (100 square feet). The more mats, the larger the room, and room sizes were widely understood by the number of *tatami* mats.

Materials

Bamboo
Prized by craftsmen, carpenters, and builders for its strength and durability—was often used for structure framing such as scaffolding, ceiling rafters, and columns. Bamboo reed was used as external shades to shield the house from the summer sun and heat. The plant was grown in the garden and the clacking of the hollow stems and the rustling of its leaves in the wind were sounds deeply rooted in Japanese culture, and having it as part of the house was a soothing and reminiscent sensory experience.

Mud Walls
Made from a mixture of earth, sand, and hay—were adhered together with glue and plastered over a bamboo meshed frame to form the walls of the house. The mixture was readily available, ecologically beneficial, and had a superior moisture-absorbing ability. When mixed with different grasses, the walls resulted in variable textures and were often painted in neutral colours.

Stone
Mainly used for external pathways and steps to an entranceway. Single large rocks were used to form the focal point of a Japanese garden.

Washi Paper
Was Japanese handmade paper used as a building and decorative material. The paper ranged from translucent to opaque and was used to set a mood or create an atmosphere in the home. The paper was used in *shoji* screens and lamps to cast a delicate glow in rooms at night.

Wood
Traditionally the most common and precious of all materials in traditional Japanese housebuilding. The structural framework of a house was made of wood, while in the interior the use of wood in window and partition screens added warmth to a space. Wood was almost always kept natural and any treatment used was only to bring out and enhance its natural beauty and quality. Pine, cedar, and cypress grew in abundance in Japan and were the types of wood frequently used within and throughout a traditional Japanese house.

Design

Fusuma

Sliding rectangular panels that acted as doors or room partitions that separated or connected rooms in the house. Each was a wood frame covered in heavy, opaque fabric or paper with a round, recessed finger pull, and glided on wooden tracks. Panels were painted with scenes of nature, such as mountains, forests, or animals. *Fusuma* doors were opaque and afforded privacy to the inhabitants of the room.

Shoji

Lightweight sliding rectangular panels that acted as doors or room partitions that separated or connected rooms in the house. Each was a wood frame covered in thin, translucent, plain white rice paper with a lattice structure that supported the paper and glided on wood tracks. The translucent paper in the panel allowed light to filter through and enter into a room. *Shoji* doors were translucent and offered less privacy than *fusuma* doors.

Tatami

A woven rice straw floor covering, this was a core element in the traditional Japanese house. The flooring provided the floor with softness and warmth, especially since the Japanese would remove their shoes while in the home. *Tatami* was more than a floor covering—it was also a form of modular unit measure and regulated the size and dimensions of a room and house. A *tatami* mat was made in standard sizes, with the length twice as long as the width. Room sizes, spaces between columns, and other internal structures were measured in *tatami* mats.

Space

Chanoma

This was the centre of the house: a combined kitchen, living, dining, and sitting room. It is here that the family shared meals and socialised. The furnishings were moveable and could be rearranged as needed. Some pieces were foldable or had multiple functions and made maximum use of the available space.

Engawa

The perimeter walkway on the external edge of the house. It was open to the elements, but the extended roof offered protection from the elements. The walkway bordered the inside and outside of the house and blurred the boundaries of interior and exterior.

Garden

The garden was the connection to nature in a home. It was a miniature landscape, rock garden, or Zen garden as a place of meditation. Alongside trees, bushes, and flowers, gardens also incorporated water, rocks, stones, sand, lanterns, and koi fish.

Kyosho Jutaku Elements

The Tokyo single-family, detached house transitioned through many styles and adaptations. Through all these changes, there have always been certain aspects of the traditional Japanese house design that remained. The new micro house is, to date, smaller in scale than any previous single-family detached house design, and yet it too has inherited and exhibits traits from the traditional Japanese house. Similar to the past, the present is likewise committed to flexible, adaptable, and efficient living and living spaces. New technologies, conveniences, and materials may have changed design, function, and construction to make the tiny house feel much bigger than it actually is, but there is still a deep-rooted tribute to nature, natural materials, and the creation of a harmonious house.

Nature is still an important aspect in the new micro house design, but is now regarded in a different way. Roof gardens, internal courtyards, and visual and physical access to the exterior are still details integrated into the tiny home, but now so is the re-examination of nature and architecture—the boundaries of inside and outside and the relationship between the human body and the space. The new house often considers the user as nature and the house as architecture, and authenticates a way for both to connect and present the same essence of familiarity, comfort, and peacefulness through manoeuvres such as making hard shapes look and feel soft, or complex organisation appear quiet.

Many *kyosho jutaku* are extremely tall, to compensate for a small or oddly shaped lot. Excavating and building underground is expensive in Tokyo, and so the logical solution is to construct vertically. Many micro houses are supported through innovative use of cantilevers, lightweight steel frames, and minimal column structural systems, which generally determine or greatly impact the final building shape. The evolution of, or retreat from, the traditional house design in *kyosho jutaku* involves taking risks, not just on the part of the architect, but also for the clients and consultants. To many architects and structural engineers, *kyosho jutaku* offers an opportunity to test new design ideas and building techniques that can be applied to other projects. Japan is a country of inventive architects, engineers, and craftspeople who pride themselves on finding new methods in design and styles; and in a country that has fabricated Pokémon, *Harajuku* fashion, robot restaurants, and maid cafés, it is easy to see why *kyosho jutaku* would be wholeheartedly embraced by a nation with a penchant for new and unusual things.

The micro houses of Tokyo do not adhere to any style guideline. There is little architectural heritage that needs to be preserved or acknowledged in the city's residential neighbourhoods. The fragments of land that can accommodate a *kyosho jutaku* become *tabula rasa*, and it is acceptable and agreeable that an ultra-small and modern building stands out from a row of older and more muted houses. Micro houses are designed for its inhabitants, but often also with the neighbours in mind. The peculiar window placements, blank elevations, and odd angles are often careful considerations to protect the privacy of and provide light to the inhabitants of the house, and often also to avoid disturbing neighbours' privacy and daylight.

In contemporary Japan, rooms are not measured in *tatami* mats but rather in a unique format of room numbers and letter designators. The abbreviation LDK, which stands for Living, Dining and Kitchen, is used to describe number of bedrooms and common room areas. For example, 4LDK is four bedrooms with living, dining, and kitchen areas. Sometimes there is an "S" to denote a storage, service, or free room, and a house with four bedrooms and a storage room would be termed as 4SLDK.

Small does not mean inexpensive. Generally, the price per square metre to build a *kyosho jutaku* is greater than a larger single-family house that can be purchased directly from a builder. Though the *kyosho jutaku* is very efficient and economical in terms of space design, each house is a customised design that particularly fits the site and the needs of the inhabitants. Even with the high costs, strict building restraints, and self-regulated expiration dates on each house, nowhere else in the world have so many small, varied, and eccentric detached houses been built. This *kyosho jutaku* phenomenon truly makes each house an experiment and individual work of art, and the proximity, quantity, and discernibility of the houses make a case for it in this volume to be considered as a high-density urban housing typology.

The description below of the components of the micro house is not exhaustive, and there are many other design measures available to make a small house useable and enjoyable. It is incredible that a house like the *kyosho jutaku*, which looks as if it defies logic, can actually be a well-functioning and cosy abode.

Materials

Natural and traditional materials can be found in a *kyosho jutaku*, but often many of the interiors are a modern version of the traditional elements and of modern white box design.

Design

Clerestory Windows

These are often found in the first sunken grade level floor, to bring fresh air and light into darker, underground spaces.

Custom Furniture

Built-in and storable furniture helps free up small spaces and creates a smooth transition between spaces. Items not in use are stored away to remove visual and physical clutter. Custom furniture is integrated into the house and adds to a coherent and seamless overall appearance.

Floating Stairs

These are ideal for small spaces because they give the illusion of space. Floating stairs are often used to create a visual connection to the rest of the house. Without risers, the staircase feels more integrated or becomes invisible in a space.

Open Floor

Simply an opening in the floor with a slotted wood floor, secured mesh screen, or translucent glass. The opening allows light through and creates a visual connection to the floor below or other parts of the house. It is used to make a deep and narrow space feel more inviting.

Open Balustrade Handrail

This design method is used to help improve visual connection within a small space to keep it looking light and airy, with no visual interference.

Open Stair Guardrail

A design method to help improve visual connection within a small space to keep that space looking light and airy, with no visual interference.

Sliding Glass Doors

A modernised form of sliding partition to connect the interior with the exterior. Sliding glass doors are usually in seating areas with an adjacent outdoor space; when closed, the doors visually link the internal and external spaces, and when open, they physically draw the two spaces together.

Skylights

These help to bring light from above and often through the house, especially if the house is tall. Many central areas in a *kyosho jutaku* can be dark, and a skylight helps bring optimal daylight and ventilation to those spaces. Skylights also lessen dependency on artificial lighting and heating, which helps reduce the use of electricity.

Tatami

Some residents prefer to have a *tatami* mat room. Such rooms are used as informal spaces, or a more conventional room to hold ritual Japanese tea ceremonies.

Windows

Windows can be sited all over or not at all on a façade. They can be large or small and serve to provide light, frame a view, or prevent direct sightlines from a certain angle or room in which the window is placed.

Spaces

Bedrooms

Bedrooms are used mainly in the evenings and only require morning light; bedrooms are often designed to be on the ground floor of the house to free up daylight for the rest of the spaces to be used throughout the day.

Carport

The carport houses the inhabitant's vehicle, since homeowners must have off-street parking for their cars. Some *kyosho jutaku* have a proper carport or garage, while others have a cantilevered top floor to shelter a car or a slanted wall to carve out a small space for a small car.

Green Space

This can be either on a grade, within the house, or on a roof. Is usually accessible, is used to enhance the connection with nature, and can reduce heating and cooling demands on the house.

Interior Courtyard

A small, enclosed area that incorporates a small garden or tree. The courtyard is open to the elements from above, to provide a connection to nature when viewed from within the house, to extend sightlines, and to allow daylight deep into the core of the house.

Kitchen

Used frequently and occupied often, kitchens can be found on the higher floors in a *kyosho jutaku* where there is the most daylight and views.

Multi-Purpose Room

A modern version of the traditional *chanoma* that combines eating, living, and socializing activities. Furniture is moveable, foldable, and multi-functional for efficient use of the space.

Split Levels

Multiple floor levels create more spaces and provide more useable square area. In a micro house, not all the living spaces can fit on one floor and the introduction of a series of adjoining floor levels, with spatially connected circulation, ensures that many living spaces can be accommodated.

Roof Terrace

An accessible outdoor area on the roof of the house. It provides a seating area or viewing platform since it is usually over the top storey of the house. Roof terraces can reduce energy usage.

Government Departments, Policies, and Regulations

The Japanese Building Standards Law is a complex and complicated model building code that is maintained and published by the Ministry of Land, Infrastructure and Transport. The publication is a set of strict laws, codes, and regulations on housing policy and building development and construction that includes legal language, building, structural, fire and earthquake safety, zoning, planning, project grants, and housing tax systems. To help navigate the documents and facilitate ease of use, the Ministry has simplified some chapters and published those sections in booklet form with colour-coded maps, diagrams, and charts.

Both the country's national and the city's local building laws lack minimum lot size requirements for constructing habitable structures, and this omission has helped facilitate the proliferation of *kyosho jutaku*. Regulations strictly govern building coverage ratio, floor area ratio, setbacks, and height restrictions. For fire safety reasons, houses need to be detached entities and in residential zoned areas, a house proposal is required to fit within a virtual boundary a set distance apart from the roadside and neighbouring property lines. Calculations and projection lines are used to determine where a house may sit on the lot and what shape it may take. The restrictions are an extra challenge to small and tight lot sizes, but the limitations also present an opportunity and freedom for the architects to unleash their creative prowess. The results are evident and commonly seen in the slanted walls and roofs, irregularly shaped massing forms, façades with windows in odd places, and façades devoid of windows altogether, of Tokyo's micro houses.

The "sunshine law" is a reason why many *kyosho jutaku* have angular shapes and volumes. The sunshine law dictates that every citizen has a basic right to sunshine, and limits the shadow that a building may cast onto its surroundings, to ensure that neighbouring buildings and public streets receive daily levels of sunlight on sunny days, even on the shortest day of the year. The "law" is more a courtesy rule of society than a bill of rights, but it does make it unjust and un-neighbourly for new house proposals and constructions to rob or deprive an existing house and citizen of their right to have access to sunshine where they live.

Landowners have the right to use their land and may build, demolish, or rebuild as often, and in any style, as they desire. There are no legal restraints on demolishing a building, and neighbours have no

Neut

F-House

Ring

S House

House Y

House NK

RoomRoom

House in Mishuku II

Crystal Brick

Noh House

Designer House

Stacked House

Cave

Climber's House

Life in Spiral House

House House

Saso House

House NA

Bent House

House in Tamagawa

Ark

House in Daizawa

Plastic Moon

Arrow

Steel House

Transustainable House

Moriyama House

Well

Orange

Park House

The Rose

Monoclinic

House EN

What Categorize the City and Me

House Meguro

Calm

Tunnel House

Reflection of Mineral

Small House

Vista

Fold

Frame

Switch

Burn

Natural Sticks I

63.02

Long Window House

OH House

Matsubara House

House in Matsubara

Small House

1.8 M Width House

House K

Riverside House

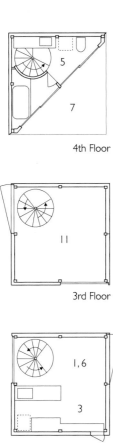

4th Floor

3rd Floor

2nd Floor

Street

1st Floor

Basement

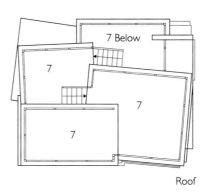

Roof

3rd Floor

2nd Floor

Street

1st Floor

1 Living Room
2 Toilet
3 Kitchen
4 Bedroom
5 Bathroom
6 Dining Room
7 Terrace
8 Foyer
9 Closet
10 Storage
11 Spare Room
12 Family Room
13 Study

Small House – Unemori Architects   Stacked House – Koji Tsutsui Architect and Associates

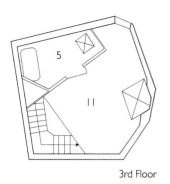

3rd Floor

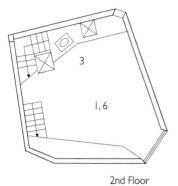

2nd Floor

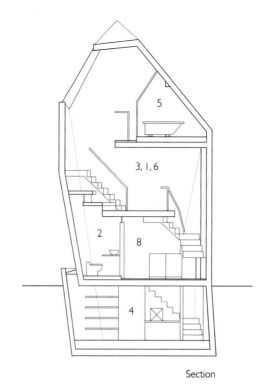

Section

Street

1st Floor

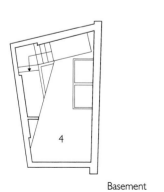

Basement

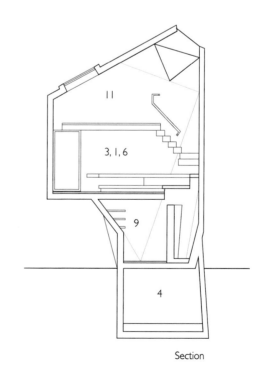

Section

1 Living Room
2 Toilet
3 Kitchen
4 Bedroom
5 Bathroom
6 Dining Room
7 Carport
8 Foyer
9 Closet
10 Storage
11 Study

Reflection of Mineral – Atelier Tekuto

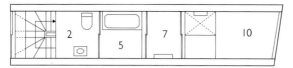

3rd Floor

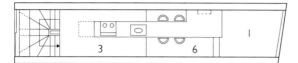

2nd Floor

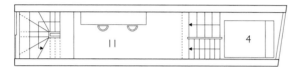

1st Floor

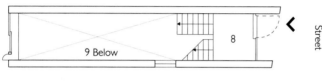

Basement

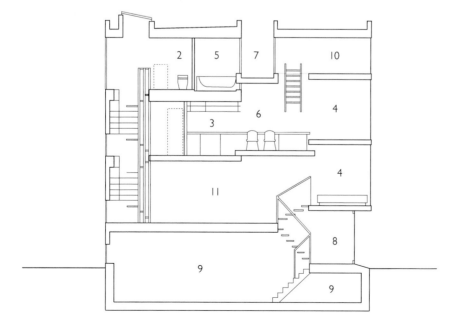

Section

1 Living Room
2 Toilet
3 Kitchen
4 Bedroom
5 Bathroom
6 Dining Room
7 Terrace
8 Foyer
9 Storage
10 Loft
11 Study

1.8 M House - YUUA

1.8M Width House

1.8M Width House

Monoclinic

Riverside House

Small House

Stacked House

Moriyama House

Small House

rights to interfere in a landowner's development. With the scarcity and high cost of land in Tokyo, many lots are passed on from one generation to the next and many families hold onto the property and reconstruct a new house on the lot every generation or sooner. Small, single-family detached houses are often referred to as "disposable architecture" due to their ease of removal and replacement.

For a nation that experiences earthquake tremors on a regular basis, the Japanese government updates the building code every 10 years due to earthquake risks, and a house in Japan has a recommended lifespan of 20 years for wood construction or 30 years for concrete construction. Houses are habitually demolished and rebuilt to ensure the structural stability of the building and the safety of both inhabitants and the public. For homeowners, it is often an excuse to update their house to better suit their current lifestyle and sometimes it is easier to build a new house rather than to have the expense of costly upgrades and retro-fits. In Tokyo, it is the land on which the house sits that is valuable, and usually after 15 years the house built on the land is worth nothing.

Present Day

The *kyosho jutaku* has gained worldwide attention and admiration with its one-of-a-kind designs and odd shapes. The micro house has made Tokyo one of the most dynamic and exciting testing laboratories for new ideas in architecture, and only in Japan have a large number of architects been designing and redesigning tiny, tailored houses. There seems to be no end in sight for the need for these dwelling types and the burgeoning numbers of Tokyoites who want to own and build a house in the city—they want to own and build a *kyosho jutaku* in the city.

Kyosho jutaku can ingratiate itself into an existing neighbourhood in the urban core, has the dexterity to morph into the most challenging of land plots, and maximises every square centimetre of its site and building space. In regard to environmental responsibility, the *kyosho jutaku* can be careless. The replacement of entire housing stocks and the constant need for new buildings has led to considerable construction waste, and the *kyosho jutaku* has been dubbed as "disposable architecture".

The disposal house culture can be blamed on earthquakes, and historically on fires, but also on the indoctrinated illusion that one must achieve home ownership as a way to be patriotic or become a true citizen. Today, building materials and construction techniques are better than they were in past decades, and micro houses could easily last for several more decades than the self-regulated earthquake lifetime. The Japanese government is aware of the situation, and in 2008 parliament demonstrated the need to remedy the culture and enacted the "200-year-home" law. The legislation encourages sustainable and durable buildings through reduced municipal, regional, and national tax reductions based on the age and condition of a house, so the longer and well maintained a house, the lower the taxes paid.

For many architourists, these houses are architectural riches scattered across the city and provide a rewarding treasure hunt. Though the houses are private, with some made known through architectural publications, savvy admirers have located some of the popular houses designed by celebrated architects and treated themselves to photographic documentation made public through photo-sharing websites. Some homeowners have not welcomed the garnered voyeurism and have erected signs to stave off uninvited guests. It is a peculiar predicament: to hire a renowned architect to design an architectural gem of a private space, and the public then takes delight in it, much to the annoyance of the owners.

Condominium Sales Launch

TORONTO

Circa 2007 to Present Day
High-Rise Tower

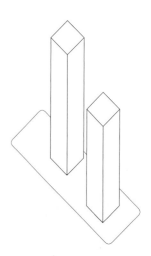

Toronto has been experiencing a hyperactive housing growth, more specifically, a condo boom, never seen before in the history of the city. The city is about a decade into the growth and the movement does not appear to be in decline. There is an observable densification in the skyline of the city, with construction cranes protruding in its horizons and high-rise towers ascending all around, and it is this action that has marked Toronto as the city with the most high-rise construction in North America for several years running. The majority of these new constructions are residential buildings, more definitively, condominiums, and its surge is measured by the municipal government, City of Toronto, in the number of dwelling units within each high-rise development. The arrival of these new housing structures has brought with it more city dwellers and has made Toronto a more dynamic and desirable city in which to reside.

According to Canada Mortgage and Housing Corporation (CMHC), between 2007 and 2016 there were approximately 140,300 new residential dwelling units built in the city. These numbers are increasing and the action is contributing to a housing enrichment that is unprecedented in scale and scope in the city. This housing phenomenon is astonishing and comparable to housing developments in other major international cities during their great expansion.

By definition, a condominium, often shortened to condo, is a form of home ownership. It is not limited to high-rise towers, but to any building where the owner holds title to their own individual unit while sharing title to the land and other common areas of the building with other unit owners. Maintenance and operating costs are shared with other owners through a condominium corporation that jointly represent ownership of the land and entire building. Condominium ownership permits the marketing of individual units in multiple unit buildings, and Ontario was the first province to recognise this form of home ownership, passing the Ontario Condominium Act in 1967. Each condominium declaration has strict building boundaries and outlines owner and condominium corporation building portion responsibilities. For high-rise condominium towers, owners typically own the inside of their unit up to the centre line of any shared walls with neighbours and external façade elements.

High-Rise Tower Characteristics

A building form that is vertical, high in storeys, and stands free from adjacent buildings. The key characteristics are:

- Building appears as autonomous object

- Building receives natural light from all orientations

- Comprises large number of dwelling units

- Stacks the highest possible number of identical or similar floor plans one above the other

- Units are grouped around a central core of elevators and stairwells

- Units usually face one, sometimes two, orientations

- Parking and amenities are generally integrated into the building

Historical Context

A bold decision to protect a vast area of ecologically sensitive site north of Toronto was one of the starts to the high-rise construction momentum. Many cities have experienced rapid condominium construction in the past few years, but none has been as aggressive as Toronto's development. Though the reshaping of Toronto's skyline may seem very sudden, it was, in fact, a progressive manifestation that was aided by timely contributing factors. Many analysts have cited the Government of Ontario's 2005 Places to Grow Act as the primary catalyst for this shift, but it can be traced back even further to the political governing parties of the province in the 1990s: the early to mid 1990s with The New Democratic Party and mid- to late 1990s with The Progressive Conservative Party. In the early 1990s, Oak Ridges Moraine, an extensive, 1900-square kilometre (734-square mile) swathe of ecologically sensitive land situated close to Toronto, was in danger of being bulldozed for building development. In the mid 1990s, single-family dwellings were constructed on portions of the moraine. By the late 1990s, developers targeted an area to propose building large subdivisions, which would house over 100,000 people. For developers, the moraine, with its affordable and manipulable land and proximity to Toronto, was an ideal site to explore. This proposal enraged environmental groups and public support quickly followed, and Oak Ridges Moraine became an extremely controversial and political debate.

The clash over Oak Ridges Moraine continued until the early 2000s. In early 2001, while still under The Progressive Conservative Party, the body declared a six-month ban on any development on the moraine until further studies were conducted. Late in the same year, a land-use plan for the moraine was created and it became the basis for the Oak Ridges Moraine Conservation Act. Under this Act, more than 90 percent of the land mass of the moraine could not be used for development and only projects which had already received zoning and planning approval were allowed to be completed. In early 2003, The Liberal Party became the governing party and promised to abolish any development on the moraine altogether, protect the land from suburban sprawl and development, and declared the moraine a Greenbelt, a permanently guarded area of green space, forests, and wetlands in Southern Ontario, Canada. However, the Liberals failed to stop the more than 6,000 housing units that were already under development on the moraine that were previously approved by the previous political governing party. The developer of this new housing stock boastfully advertised that their project would be the last development on the moraine and that the beauty of the moraine's natural landscape would forever be part of these new homes. This infuriated many people, and accusations that The Progressive Conservative Party had made secret deals with developers that sabotaged the Act and endangered the health of the moraine were rampant.

COMING SUMMER 2016
FOR LEASING INQUIRIES CALL 416.862.0611

South Core and Harbourfront

South Core and Harbourfront

Concord CityPlace

Greenbelt Act and Places to Grow Act 2005

In 2005, the provincial governing party at the time, The Liberal Party, created The Greenbelt Act and Places to Grow Act after learning from the Oak Ridges Moraine Conservation Act, attending to public concern and trying to right a wrong. The political party recognised the pressing need to formulate an official plan for responsible development. The Greenbelt Act was formed to protect about 7,200 square kilometres (2,800 square miles) of environmentally sensitive and agricultural land from the pressures of urban development and sprawl. Currently it is one of the world's largest permanent greenbelts, protecting around 8,000 square kilometres (3,100 square miles) of valuable ecological and hydrological sites, wildlife habitats and sustaining healthy communities. The Places to Grow Act was declared one of North America's most progressive growth plans. It is a legislation created to aid the government in planning and coordinating for growth in a strategic manner. The purpose of the Acts was to enable wise decisions about development and expansion, and its approach favours density and intensification while still supporting the environment, economy, and communities.

Timing and Other Factors

With an extensive greenbelt area being sheltered from development through a series of government policies, existing communities that wish to grow needed to devise new planning procedures. The greenbelt that wraps around Toronto has compelled the city to expand vertically, and the most evident paradigm of the effect from the Acts is the high-rise condominium tower. It is these chronological circumstances that helped shape the Toronto skyline today, and though the saving of the moraine in the 1990s was indeed a major contributory factor in the construction of high-rise condominiums today, it is not its only influence. The greenbelt protection and Places to Grow Act has clearly redefined Toronto's developable land. With a finite range available to expand and construct, what is left of Toronto's buildable land has become precious and costly to develop. Since high-rise towers can house many inhabitants on a smaller parcel of land than single-family houses, the construction of condominium towers has been just a shift in the housing market. There is becoming less land on which to build new single-family housing stock and what adaptable land is left has already begun to be prohibitively costly to develop.

Another factor in the high-rise boom is that Canada's economy remained largely healthy and stable throughout the global financial crisis of 2008. The country's conservatively fiscal strength was seen as a monetary safe refuge that attracted many foreign investors, mostly from China, India, the Middle East, and Russia. Many international buyers recognised that Toronto was a sound place to secure and invest their money, and real estate, especially luxury condos, in Toronto was attainable compared to other major world cities. The mortgage guidelines at some Canadian banking institutions also favoured foreign home buyers by offering exemptions that eased the purchase of Toronto real estate. This type of endorsement, coupled with the vote of confidence in Canada's stable economy, helped feed the city's demand for condo construction. For Toronto, the age of the glass high-rise condominium towers was beginning. High-rise towers are not just being viewed as housing any more. Now, purchasing a unit in a condo can be seen as a tradeable good, in line with stocks and commodities.

During this time, there were two federal government programmes that also furthered the huge interest in condo real estate. The now defunct Immigrant Investor Program and Investor Capital Pilot Program were designed to attract skilled and experienced business immigrants to actively invest, stimulate, and promote growth in the Canadian economy, and in return, the investors and their families received permanent resident status or unconditional residential visas in Canada. While there are no readily available statistics on the number of investors who purchased condos as investments under either programme, the programmes have been cited as major determinants that have propelled Toronto condo construction, sales, and prices.

The timing of condo development also emerged at the right time for two generations of Torontonians, the baby boomers and the millennials. A large portion of Toronto's ageing baby boomers were downsizing their homes, some from the suburbs who wished to move back into the city centre, while at the same time an extensive proportion of the millennial generation were entering the housing market to purchase their first home. For millennials, the shrinking supply of single-family, low-rise houses and the ever-widening price gap between houses and condominiums made buying and owning their first home a challenge. For this generation, purchasing a high-rise unit makes for a more affordable and obtainable first home option. These two very distinct demographical incidences happening around the same time also helped maintain an interest in condo construction.

Economically, high-rise tower construction has become more cost effective. Advanced engineering and building materials are becoming progressively more affordable when applied to high-rise tower design and construction, and the use of mass-produced architectural building components that are stacked repeatedly one on top of another on one single footprint is time and cost efficient. For developers, the high cost of land in Toronto makes it profitable to build high-rise towers and for buyers, the more expensive land and single-family house development are becoming, the more appealing condo purchasing and living are looking.

The Process

A condominium development proposal is a series of actions and negotiations with the city before it becomes realised.

1. Developer acquires land to be developed into a condominium and hires an architect to design the development proposal.

2. Developer hires an architect to prepare Feasibility Study to assess the density the project can yield versus cost of project.

3. Often the study will require rezoning, and a Zoning By-law Amendment Application is prepared and presented to the city.

4. City reviews development proposal, submission proceeds to councillor, community, and public consultations.

5. Public art and Section 37 are considered and may be required for the development proposal.

6. Often the city will respond with revisions to be implemented.

7. If the development proposal satisfies conditions for approval, the proposal receives final approval and registration.

8. If the development proposal does not satisfy conditions for approval, developer may opt to appeal the decision with the Ontario Municipal Board (OMB).

Re-zoning occurs when a development proposal does not conform to the site, significantly alters its land use, or increases its building height and density. The City reviews applications for development proposals that wish to change the zoning by-law and will grant, revise, or reject a proposal.

Section 37 is a clause in the provincial Planning Act. It is an arrangement through re-zoning where a developer can increase the height or density of their development, in exchange for which they provide funding for a community project in the neighbourhood. Each development is reviewed on a case-by-case basis and there is neither precision in the way height or density is appraised, nor clear definitions as to what constitute community benefits. Critics have argued for more rigorous and transparent planning practices where there would not be a need to individually assess bonus settlements. Many councillors have boasted Section 37 funds as leverage to demonstrate how they helped their community, and the achievement can be useful for the purposes of re-election.

The OMB is an independent, apolitical adjudicative body that often assesses appeals on planning processes and disputes in the province of Ontario. The OMB acts in accordance with the city's official plan, and the decision and ruling of the Board is final. The Board has routinely overruled decisions made by the City, been accused of favouritism towards developers, and appeals on their rulings have rarely been reversed. In May 2017, the provincial government gave in to public pressure and announced it will replace the appeal process of the OMB with a committee made up of local planners, the Local Planning Appeal Tribunal.

Tower Floor Plates and Elevator Core

From the Tall Building Design Guidelines, the size of a tower plate area should be 750 square metres (8,072 square feet) or less; this limit, together with exit stairs and elevator cores, are important factors in determining whether the tower plate is economically feasible to develop. The typical elevator core in a tower consists of two, three, or four elevators, the number required in a tower is dependent on the number of storeys and residential units to meet building code requirements and also to achieve an acceptable expected elevator waiting time of approximately forty-five seconds. In order for a tower plate to be economically attractive for development, the ratio of saleable area (area of the units) to gross floor area (area of the tower floor plate) should be around 85 percent.

Building Components and Organisation

Top

The upper floors, including the rooftop, are known as tops in a condo tower. The tops of condo towers house the penthouse units and mechanical units. Some buildings locate an amenity programme at the roof level and then the design for the top of the condo tower has integrated lighting, a cantilever roof to act as shading device, or other design articulation to denote that the top is occupiable.

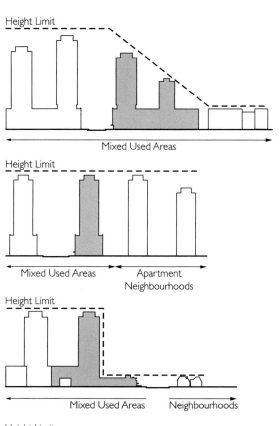

Height Limit

Mixed Used Areas

Height Limit

Mixed Used Areas | Apartment Neighbourhoods

Height Limit

Mixed Used Areas | Neighbourhoods

Height Limit

Mixed Used Areas | Mixed Use Areas

Fit and Transition in Scale

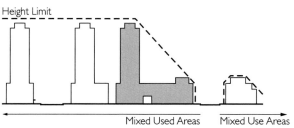

25 m Min.

80% of Right of Way up to 24 m Max.

Right of Way

Separation Distances and Base Building Scale and Height

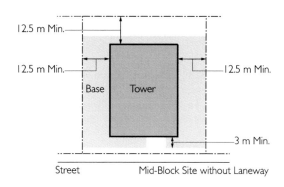

12.5 m Min.

12.5 m Min. — Base | Tower — 12.5 m Min.

3 m Min.

Street | Mid-Block Site without Laneway

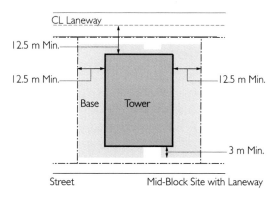

CL Laneway

12.5 m Min.

12.5 m Min. — Base | Tower — 12.5 m Min.

3 m Min.

Street | Mid-Block Site with Laneway

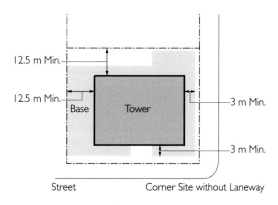

12.5 m Min.

12.5 m Min. — Base | Tower — 3 m Min.

3 m Min.

Street | Corner Site without Laneway

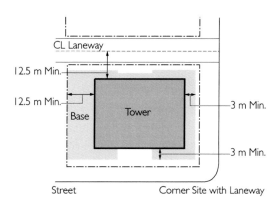

CL Laneway

12.5 m Min.

12.5 m Min. — Base | Tower — 3 m Min.

3 m Min.

Street | Corner Site with Laneway

Separation Distances Small Sites

Tall Building Design Guidelines

Tower

The middle section between the tower top and podium is the tower. The tower houses the typical floor plates and residential units. The scale and separation distance of the tower affect the levels of sky view, wind, sunlight, and shadow at the pedestrian streetscape level below.

Base Building

The base building, also known as the podium, is the lower storeys of a condo tower that house services that support street life and maintain a pedestrian-friendly streetscape. Podiums also act as wind deflectors and reduce winds and tunnel effects caused by the towers.

Amenities

Amenities are a requirement in the Toronto Zoning By-law and are also another alluring selling point. Many condo developers offer familiar luxury conveniences in their buildings that consist of, but are not limited to, fitness rooms, games rooms, guest suites, libraries, multi-media lounges, party rooms, pet services, rooftop terraces, sauna, steam rooms, whirlpools, and swimming pools. Condo amenities that serve only the residents of the building are a scaled-down version of the actual support and services that can be found in an existing neighbourhood. Similar to balconies, amenities are initially desired, but over time many become underused, especially when a condo development is located downtown among full-service gyms, hotels, movies theatres, parks, and restaurants all within walking distance. When a condo development is located in the downtown core, enforcing developers to provide private facilities is counter-productive to the city's grand vision of creating an active and dynamic city life and street presence.

Typical Unit Floor Plan Type

Since 2007, roughly 140,300 new dwelling units have been built in Toronto. Though there is not one typical unit floor plan typology, there are variations of similar floor plans repeated throughout almost all condominium design plans. The most common unit plans in Toronto condos, especially in the downtown core, are studios, one-bedrooms, one-bedroom-plus-dens, and two-bedrooms, and of these layouts, the majority found on a typical Toronto condo floor plate are one-bedrooms. For a condo developer, layouts such as studios and one-bedrooms appeal to a wider group of buyers, the units sell quickly, and the speed of sales helps secure project financing faster. Prices for studios and one-bedrooms are often offered at or under an amount ($450,000 as of 2016) that is eligible for provincial and federal tax rebates, which make the units attainable as entry-level home ownership, or as effortless real estate investment. Smaller units have been selling faster than larger units, and the brisk sales of studio and one-bedroom units have helped developers obtain a loan from lenders more quickly, when approximately 70–80 percent of the units in a condo project must be sold at pre-construction in order to qualify for financing.

In Toronto, architects and engineers design and generate drawings in square metres, yet in the construction and marketing tradition, unit floor plans are understood and sold in square feet.

Studios, One-Bedrooms, and Two-Bedrooms

The variations in each type of unit differ only slightly and the structural bay of the building often determines its size.

Studios

These have zero bedrooms, designed within one structural bay, are the smallest units in a condo building, and are often less than 500 square feet (46 square metres). The areas of eating, sleeping, and living are an open concept and indiscernible. Bathrooms, kitchens, kitchen appliances, and washers/dryers are the same standard sizes as the larger units and occupy a large portion of the unit's square area.

One-Bedrooms

These have an enclosed sleeping area with a door and closet, are designed within one or two structural bays, and are between 500 and 700 square feet (46–65 square metres). One-bedrooms designed within one structural bay are often narrow and long, with the bedroom located inboard and outfitted with sliding glass doors to receive natural light. One-bedrooms designed within two structural bays are wider in proportion. The bedroom has a window and occupies one bay, while the living and eating areas also have a window and occupy the other bay.

One-Bedroom-Plus-Dens

These are similar to the one-bedroom designed within two bays, are between 650 and 750 square feet (60–70 square metres), and have an inboard room without a door, closet, or window that is used as a den or study. Some one-bedroom-plus-dens have a second bathroom. Those units have dens that can accommodate doors and are used as a windowless second bedroom once the unit is occupied. In this one-bedroom-plus-den with two-bath layout, the second bathroom is always a full bath, and can serve different dwelling situations. One common situation is an investment unit where an owner rents to two tenants.

Two-Bedrooms

These have two enclosed sleeping areas with closets, two bathrooms, designed within two or three bays, and are between 750 and 1,100 square feet (70–102 square metres). Both bedrooms can have windows and doors and it is also common that one bedroom has a window and door, while the other bedroom is inboard with sliding glass doors to receive natural light. The two-bedrooms designed within three bays are wider and shallower in proportion. Each bedroom has a window and door and occupies its own bay, and the living and eating areas occupy the other bay. This unit can serve as an investment unit where an owner rents to two tenants.

Three-or-More-Bedrooms

In many downtown neighbourhoods, there is a lack of larger units for families. In 2009, the City of Toronto issued a staff report to implement the development of units for households with children. The report amended the Official Plan and required condominium developers to designate 10 percent of all condo buildings that housed 100 or more dwelling units to be built with three or more bedroom units, or have units that could easily be converted to three or more bedrooms. The downtown core has seen a pattern where young families relocate to the suburbs, partly due to the shortage of family-oriented dwelling units, and the city wanted to curb the exodus to keep downtown a demographically diverse and vibrant place to live. One of the ways to support existing families and attract new ones is to create a greater inventory of housing options that can accommodate a wide range of dwelling lifestyles and circumstances.

The staff report was admirable in theory, but problematic in reality. The Toronto housing market is a free market and housing affordability is one of the greatest challenges for many families who want to live downtown. When the study was conducted in 2009, a dwelling unit containing three or more bedrooms was approximately 1,200 square feet (111 square metres) and, according to the Canadian Mortgage and Housing Corporation, the sale price for a unit of that size was around $600,000, which was unaffordable for most families at that time. For developers, the downtown land costs are expensive and to be forced to build units that may not sell or would be sold at a loss, developers would need to sell the other units at increased prices to make up for the loss. The three-bedroom dwelling units in condos often worked out to be more costly than a single-family house, and for the families who could afford the price of a family-size condo, many opted to purchase single-family houses to have more space.

Currently, the requirement for three or more bedrooms is applied to new residential developments that require re-zoning. Abiding by the requirement is more voluntary than obligatory, but developers have recognised the condition. For three-bedroom units to be profitable for developers and affordable to buyers, the square area of a family unit has been significantly reduced. A three-bedroom, two-bathroom unit has decreased to 800 square feet (74 square metres) and the often poor layout and tight quarters have served an investor renting to three students better than it does for a couple with two children.

Balconies

Balconies are a common design feature and an attractive selling point. From an architectural perspective, balconies are useful as shading for the building and as design features to shape it. For buyers, many seem to favour units with balconies for both private outdoors space and re-sell advantage—fearful their unit will be more difficult to sell without a balcony. Typical condo balconies are shallow in depth and have an unfinished concrete slab. When furnished and finished, most balconies can seat a table set for two, a few plants, and little else. While most balconies are initially desired, over time many become underused and transition into storage space. The Toronto climate also makes a balcony enjoyable only in the warmer months, which is four months out of the year optimistically.

Access Type

The vast majority of Toronto condominiums are high-rise towers and have a central elevator core that provides vertical circulation to each floor. From the elevator core, a corridor provides horizontal access to each unit.

Construction Materials

The most noticeable building material for Toronto condo development is glass. The skyline is punctuated with glass condo towers and the material seems to have become the default standard in design and assemblage. The majority of the new glass condo towers are primarily designed and constructed with window wall systems. From a design and construction point of view, window wall systems are economical and quick to install. From a building science perspective, there has been growing concern among industry experts that the performance of a window wall building envelope is less resilient, less energy efficient, and more susceptible to air and water leakage compared to the more expensive curtain wall or punched window systems. Some specialists have warned that the use of window walls to sheath entire buildings will be problematic, and forecast that these systems will need replacement 15 to 20 years after installation.

In glass condo towers, the balconies are fashioned in tempered glass and its safety became questionable when several downtown condo tower glass balconies shattered and fell from several storeys high to the ground below. Between 2010 and 2011, the recurrence of falling balcony glass compelled city hall to demand developers to secure towers with falling glass in mesh to prevent further accidents. There have been several theories as to why the glass failed, from manufacturer negligence to climate, but the glass was sourced from a variety of manufacturers and the breakages occurred throughout the year. Though there was no definitive answer to the cause of the breaks, developers replaced all balcony glass with laminated glass and the Ontario Building Code was amended to use laminated glass in all new condo balcony construction.

Balcony floor slab design is another common occurrence that has had building science professionals questioning the durability and life cycle of a condo tower. The concrete floor slab of a balcony is often a continuation of the internal concrete floor slab and is not thermally broken to prevent heat loss. In winter, the cold air from the external balcony slab seeps into the warm internal concrete slab and can cause condensation in the internal ceiling and floor. In 2012, the Ontario Building Code required higher standards of energy efficiency and performance for condo buildings.

The construction techniques and colour palette for many condo towers seem to resemble one another. The pleasant and prudent design seems to be a winning formula that sells well and developers have little reason to change it. A Toronto high-rise condo tower built within the last ten years appears to share the same collective language and is easily recognisable. Though there are slight variations in style, most are made up of similar configurations, components, and colours—tall, generic glass and metal cladding, and in agreeable shades of grey.

Developers and Architects

In Toronto, high-rise condo development gives the impression that it is a monopolised business. It seems to be the same developers and architects building and designing very similar projects recurrently in the city. Often it is the same style of branding, artist concept renderings, designs, and colour schemes that dominate, and while no two condo developments are exactly the same, the marking and architecture is very much alike and it is often difficult to distinguish one stylish lobby rendering, concrete construction framework, or sleek glass tower from another.

A small number of developers have been responsible for many of the high-rise condo projects in the city. There are developers who have earned a reputation designing suburban housing for generations and entered the downtown condo boom market in the past ten years, and there are niche offices that were founded during the boom that specialise in downtown condo construction. Similar to developers, there are the same few architectural firms designing high-rise condos in the city. In a city with approximately 780 registered architectural practices, about a dozen architecture offices are repeatedly designing high-rise residential towers in Toronto.

U Condos

ICE Condominiums

Luna Vista

Quartz

Parade 1 and 2

Picasso

Block 32

N Tower

Montage

Murano South Tower

Peter Street Condos

X Condominiums

Casa II

Casa

Spire

Pace Condos

Karma Condos

Maple Leaf Square Condo

Spectra

Gooderham

Radio City

Waterscapes

Market Wharf

Lago

King Charlotte | Theatre Park | Festival Tower | Bisha | Nautilus | Pinnacle Centre

One Bloor | Four Seasons Residences | Aura | Cinema Tower | The Pinnacle on Adelaide | Optima

300 Front | Water's Edge at the Cove | Luna | Charlie | Residences at RCMI | Tableau Condo

Boutique Condos | M5V | Harbour View Estates D | The Bond | Ultra at Herons Hill | Library District Condo

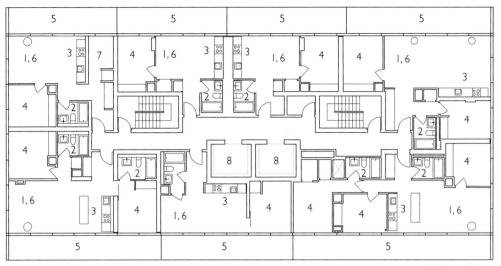

2 Elevator Core
King Charlotte

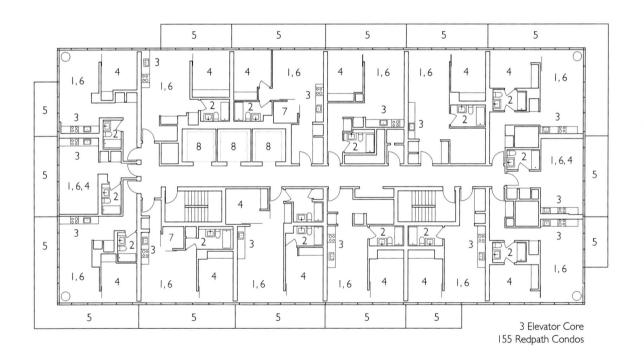

3 Elevator Core
155 Redpath Condos

1 Living Room
2 Bathroom
3 Kitchen
4 Bedroom
5 Balcony
6 Dining Room
7 Study
8 Elevator

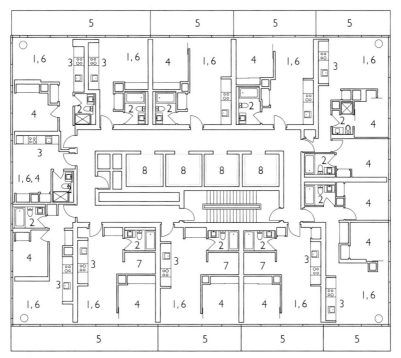

4 Elevator Core
Karma Condos

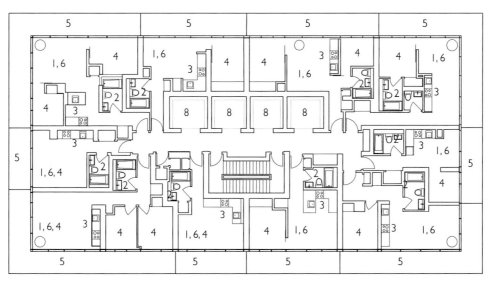

4 Elevator Core
Casa II

Tower Floor Plates

Harbour View Estates SuperClub

Harbour View Estates SuperClub

Spectra

300 Front

Government Policies and Regulations

Official Plan

With the Greenbelt and Places to Grow Acts in place, the City of Toronto underestimated the fever and speed of condominium development and construction that quickly followed. Like other existing cities situated around the greenbelt that needed to grow, it was crucial that Toronto re-examine their planning policies and devise new procedures. The City of Toronto has an Official Plan in place and its intent is to ensure that the city evolves, improves, and realises its full potential in areas such as land use development, transit, and the environment.

The City of Toronto Official Plan is a strategy designed to aid in the development of the city. It is a vision for where and how the city can best grow to the year 2031 and covers areas of transportation, land-use development, and the environment. The Plan forecasts city growth trends and includes goals, standards, and policies to help guide decisions to build a sustainable and successful city for tomorrow.

The Plan also contains amendments that address the ever-evolving needs of the city today. The condo boom has caught the city by surprise and the Official Plan has been vulnerable to the sharp increase in density in the short amount of time. The City of Toronto reviews almost all new condo development proposals on a case-by-case basis and makes amendments to the Plan on an as-needed basis. This improvisation to the updating of the Plan has made its presence felt on existing infrastructure that has been struggling to keep pace with the new demand.

City of Toronto Zoning By-Law

The City of Toronto Zoning By-law governs types of buildings permitted, lot sizes and dimensions, building heights, setbacks, parking requirements, and amenities. This by-law is applied to the entire City of Toronto and each condo tower development is reviewed on a case-by-case basis—a conversation and negotiation between the developers and city councillors, with the recommendation from the planning department. The downtown urban environment and lifestyle is acutely different from other less dense areas of the city and is not reflected in the current zoning by-law.

Tall Building Design Guidelines

The Tall Building Design Guidelines were introduced in 2013 and are the consolidation of and replacement for the Design Criteria for Review of the Tall Buildings Proposal of 2006 and the Downtown Tall Building Vision and Performance Standard Design Guidelines of 2012. The Tall Buildings Guidelines were developed to help formulate new directives and standards to explicitly address the high concentration of condo tower application for development in the downtown core and rapid building typology transforming the city skyline. The Tall Buildings Design Guidelines are used as part of a framework alongside the Official Plan. The guide is a unified set of performance measure for the evaluation of all tall building development applications citywide and focuses on how their design will best fit within their context. This guide is currently in use today.

According to the Tall Building Design Guidelines, tall buildings are generally defined as "buildings with height that is greater than the width of the adjacent street right-of-way or the wider of the two streets if located at an intersection. Since street right-of-way width varies across Toronto, typically between 20 and 36 metres, this definition reinforces the importance of site context in determining the threshold for when a building is considered tall and when these Guidelines will apply". Based on these criteria, most of buildings over seven storeys are to be considered tall buildings, disregarding the mass distinction between a seven-storey building and, for example, a fifty-storey building. The guidelines read to be more of set of reactionary parameters to mitigate the presence of a tall building on a site rather than a visionary scheme to prepare for a dynamic city of the future.

The Tall Buildings Guidelines divide the building in three parts: base building, middle (tower), and top; the majority of the recommendations are focused on the base of the building, aiming to protect the existing building context and provide comfort level at the pedestrian realm. The list includes: (1) provide appropriate transition from a tall building mass to a lower-scale building; (2) locate the base of the buildings to frame the edges of the street; (3) ensure building entrances on the street are well defined; (4) locate back of house areas away from the public view; (5) provide comfortable, safe, and accessible pedestrian and cycling routes through and around the site; (6) align the height of the base of the building with the height of the existing context buildings; (7) protect views to heritage buildings; (8) provide five hours of sunlight on the opposite side of the street at the equinox; and (9) minimise adverse wind conditions on the adjacent street.

The recommendations for the tall part of tall buildings include: (1) limit the size of the tower plate area to 750 square metres (8,072 square feet) or less; (2) provide 3 metres (10 feet) setback to the street or edge of the base of the building; and (3) provide 25 metres (82 feet) setback between towers or 12.5 metres (41 feet) to the property line or centre of adjacent laneway. The recommendations also touch on the use of balconies to minimise the impact of the mass of the building on the site.

Present Day

The high-rise condominium towers in Toronto have maintained their pace of development. Sales and construction have not appeared to be on the decline and line-ups and buying frenzy at new condominium presentation sale centres remain active. New ways have been found to attract clientele: invitation-only parties, exclusive pre-sales events, and celebrity-endorsed affairs are now part of sales centres or have replaced the old sales centre formula. The viewing and purchasing of dwelling units has become a fashionable social scene in the city, complete with media coverage. Towers have remained popular despite predictions that the condo boom is going to burst at any moment, and the warnings by building science experts on their inferior construction practices. The City would like to think that vertical growth of the high-rise condominium towers has helped restrain urban sprawl and added another housing option to the existing and ageing rows of semi-detached, single-family houses that line most of Toronto's residential streets.

There is worry among market research analysts that Toronto's multi-unit dwellings are being developed faster than the rate of the projected population growth and that increases in public transit, infrastructure, and services have not matched its pace. The city has been welcoming the growth and opportunities that the new dwelling units bring, but has been slow at providing support and amenities for the new inhabitants. There are no substantiated records to understand the demographics, data on the number of storeys a building has, or single bedroom units versus family-oriented units. Information on storeys and unit types is required by developers when filing a Zoning By-law Amendment Application, and yet the City of Toronto is only now in the process of indexing this information. Statistics Canada and CMHC have begun collecting information on condo towers in Toronto in the last four years, but their categories are general and dependent on the accuracy of the citizens filling out the surveys. It seems like Toronto lacks proper tools to measure the condo phenomenon, and this basic information is essential to help plan and design for today so that high-rise towers can serve the interests of the city and its residents tomorrow.

In the first three months of 2017, there has been serious concern that the real estate market was out of control. Toronto saw housing prices increased by more than 30 percent compared to the previous year, and the provincial government was forced to step in to try to cool the market. In April 2017, the government introduced a 15 percent foreign buyers' tax and will authorise a vacancy tax on uninhabited homes. Despite considering foreign investors as being among the culprits for such an increase, there was actually little evidence collected to support this charge. To date, most of the necessary information has come from Toronto's private real estate board. The board estimated that foreign investors comprised less than 5 percent of all homebuyers in 2016, and they acknowledged that the accuracy of their surveys is unreliable. As part of the plan to curb absentee foreign buyers, the provincial government will begin to develop a regulation to gather data on the buyer's citizenship or residency status and whether the buyer intends to live in or rent out the home. Another monitoring plan will be to collaborate with Canada Revenue Agency to access buyers' taxes to ensure that those who purchase floors of new condo towers as investment and then re-sell the units before the deal closes are paying legitimate land transfer taxes. For foreign buyers, if they become a Canadian citizen or permanent resident within four years of purchasing a property, or if they are a full-time student for a minimum of two years after the purchase of a home, or if they legally worked full-time in Ontario for one year after acquiring home ownership, they will be entitled to tax exemptions. There is already speculation that buyers will find loopholes to circumvent the system, and many contest that the measures will have little to no impact on repressing the booming market. Despite the new rules for foreign investors, many real estate agents have voiced that the foreign clients they represent would consider the additional 15 percent a small price to pay to buy into the safe and stable financial haven of Toronto.

The provincial government measures had to be politically calculated. This represents an interesting dilemma: it has to control a heated market, maintain housing prices attainable by young and first-time buyers, and yet at the same time, it cannot afford to scare off new investments and instigate a housing meltdown. The measures must be seen like they do not affect those who already own a home, which is a great part of Toronto as homeowner is synonymous with investor, not just for living, but buying a second or third property in the city for investment is not uncommon. Toronto has transformed the notion of housing from a place of residence to a stock in the commodity market, and architecture and the city becoming goods being used by developers and buyers. The Toronto condo phenomenon is just over a decade old. It will take some time to see how the typology matures and evolves, and it will be interesting to see whether the high-rise tower can accommodate the future changing housing needs of a diverse population, or whether it is mostly suited for investors and short-term living.

In May 2017, when the changes to the OMB were announced, many local resident groups and not-in-my-backyard (NIMBY) activists celebrated the news as a step to curb intense densification. Those in the development and construction industries were concerned that the move will suppress and deprive the city of development and advancement, especially that high-rise residential towers would take longer to be approved and built.

At present, condominiums are still viewed as merchandise goods and some condo buyers purchase their unit on pre-construction floor plans and resell the unit right after construction. Buyers refer to their purchases as investments, whether or not they are renting their units to tenants or living in the units themselves. In the earlier start of the condo boom, some buyers faced deficiencies in their buildings, were dissatisfied with their investment, and created resident Facebook groups to complain and commiserate their discontent about their building and developer. The pages started out as open public forums, but owners quickly realised that publicly posting disdain about their building and developer was harming their resale value and negatively affecting their investment. The condo Facebook pages are in existence today, but are set as private forums reserved only for the residents of the building.

It is an exciting and transformative time for Toronto at present. Housing development is at a record prosperity and the city is racing to update its planning and building regulations to counterbalance the new reality and surprise good fortune. In the current case-by-case review of high-rise residential projects, it is likely that the Toronto planning and building laws will be standardised when the condo boom has passed. In 2013, a foreign journalist covering a story in Toronto noted that the city was full of high-rise construction sites, that all finished sites were glass towers that looked the same, and that the city should look great when it's finished!

Karl Lagerfeld for Art Shoppe Lofts + Condos

IMAGE CREDITS

Please note all drawings within this book were a collaboration between Katy Chey, Javier Viteri, Zainab Abbasi, Bohden Tymchuk, Jiawen (Carmen) Lin, Xinting Fan and Roseanne Imee Reyes Barbachano, unless otherwise noted.

New York

p. 84
Bain News Service, LC-B22-351-4, Library of Congress Prints and Photographs Division Washington, D.C. 20540

pp. 92–93
Detroit Publishing Co., LC-D401-12683, Library of Congress Prints and Photographs Division Washington, D.C. 20540

p. 95
Top Jacob Riis

p. 99
Maggie Land Blanck

p. 100
Jacob Riis

p. 101
Jacob Riis

p. 102
Detroit Publishing Co., LC-D4-18616, Library of Congress Prints and Photographs Division Washington, D.C. 20540

p. 103
Detroit Publishing Co., LC-D4-71269, Library of Congress Prints and Photographs Division Washington, D.C. 20540

p. 104
Top Underwood & Underwood, c.1915, LC-USZ62-16068, Library of Congress Prints and Photographs Division Washington, D.C. 20540

p. 104
Bottom Detroit Publishing Co., LC-D418-9350, Library of Congress Prints and Photographs Division Washington, D.C. 20540

p. 105
Top Collection of the Lower East Side Tenement Museum

p. 105
Bottom LC-USZ62-72444, Library of Congress Prints and Photographs Division Washington, D.C. 20540

p. 109
Top Detroit Publishing Co., LC-D4-36490, Library of Congress Prints and Photographs Division Washington, D.C. 20540

p. 109
Bottom LC-USZ62-51301, LC-USZ62-51302, Library of Congress Prints and Photographs Division Washington, D.C. 20540

Hong Kong

p. 112
Image by Mark Kauffman © Time Inc.

p. 117
CO 1069-444-23, The National Archives UK, The Institute Of Historic Building Conservation

p. 120
Image by Mark Kauffman © Time Inc.

p. 121
Image by Mark Kauffman © Time Inc.

p. 122
LC-USZ62-120618 Prints and Photographs Division, Library of Congress, Washington D.C.

p. 123
LC-USZ62-118528 Prints and Photographs Division, Library of Congress, Washington D.C.

p. 124
LC-USZ62-118535 Prints and Photographs Division, Library of Congress, Washington D.C.

p. 125
Photographer Unknown

p. 132
Top Peggy Tao

p. 132
Bottom Peggy Tao

p. 133
Top Left Toby Chey

p. 133
Bottom Left Toby Chey

p. 133
Top Right Toby Chey

p. 133
Bottom Right Toby Chey

Berlin

p. 136
Julia Neubauer

p. 145
Top F Rep. 290 (01) Nr. 0271582, Photographer k.A., Landesarchiv Berlin

p. 145
Bottom F Rep. 290 (01) Nr. 0271587, Photographer Arthur Köster, Landesarchiv Berlin

p. 147
Top Ben Buschfeld, Tautes Heim

p. 147
Bottom Ben Buschfeld, Tautes Heim

p. 148
F Rep. 290-01-30 Nr. 411, Photographer Otto Hagemann, Landesarchiv Berlin

p. 149
F Rep. 290-01-30 Nr. 775, Photographer Otto Hagemann, Landesarchiv Berlin

p. 151
ART530771, bpk Bildagentur / Art Resource, NY

pp. 152–153
ART530768, bpk Bildagentur / Art Resource, NY

p. 155
Top ARKM.1970-103-031-06, Arkitektur-och designcentrum, Digitalt Museum

p. 155
Bottom F Rep. 290 (01) Nr. 0122737, Photographer Hans Seiler, Landesarchiv Berlin

pp. 158–159
ART530769, bpk Bildagentur / Art Resource, NY

p. 160
ARKM.1970-103-031-15, Arkitektur-och designcentrum, Digitalt Museum

p. 242
Top Oski Collado. Collection of van Dongen-Koschuch Architects and Planners

p. 242
Bottom Oski Collado. Collection of van Dongen-Koschuch Architects and Planners

p. 243
Top Oski Collado. Collection of van Dongen-Koschuch Architects and Planners

p. 243
Bottom Oski Collado. Collection of van Dongen-Koschuch Architects and Planners

Beijing

p. 248
Luc Nadal/ITDP

p. 263
Top Eric Firley

p. 263
Bottom Rob Deutscher

pp. 264–265
Jian Wai Soho, Beijing, Photographer Thomas Spier / apollovision

p. 269
Philippe Brysse

p. 270
Philippe Brysse

p. 271
picturenarrative

p. 275
Evan Chakroff

p. 276
David Brennwald

p. 277
VIEW Pictures Ltd/Alamy Stock Photo

Tokyo

p. 282
Iwan Baan

pp. 288–289
Jonas Aarre Sommarset

p. 296
From Left to Right, Top Row: Neut, Apollo Architects & Associates, Photographer Masao Nishikawa; F House, Hashimoto Yukio Design Studio Inc., Photographer Yoshio Shiratori; Ring, Apollo Architects & Associates, Photographer Masao Nishikawa

From Left to Right, Middle Row: S House, Komada Architects' Office, Photographer Sobashima Toshihiro; House Y, Kochi Architects Studio, Photographer Daici Ano; House NK, Miyahara Architect Office

From Left to Right, Bottom Row: RoomRoom, Takeshi Hosaka Architects, Koji Fujii Nacasa & Partners Inc; House in Mishuku II, Nobuo Araki/The Archetype, Photographer Shimizu Ken; Crystal Bricks, Atelier Tekuto, Photograph Makoto Yoshida

p. 297
From Left to Right, Top Row: Noh House, Koji Tsutsui Architect and Associates, Masao Nishikawa; Industrial Designer House, Koji Tsutsui Architect and Associates, Masao Nishikawa; Stacked House, Koji Tsutsui Architect and Associates, Photographer Iwan Baan

From Left to Right, Middle Row: Cave, Apollo Architects & Associates, Photographer Masao Nishikawa; Climber's House, Komada Architects' Office, Photographer Toshihiro Sobashima; Life in Spiral House, Hideaki Takayanagi Architects, Photographer Takumi Ota

From Left to Right, Bottom Row: House House, Taku Sakaushi + OFDA, Photographer Hiroshi Ueda; Sasao House, Klein Dytham Architecture, Photographer Koichi Torimura; House NA, Sou Fujimoto. Photograph Javier Viteri

p. 298
From Left to Right, Top Row: Bent House, Koji Tsutsui Architect and Associates, Iwan Baan; House in Tamagawa, Case Design Studio; Ark, Apollo Architects & Associates, Photographer Masao Nishikawa

From Left to Right, Middle Row: House in Daizawa, Nobuo Araki/The Archetype, Photographer Shimizu Ken; Plastic Moon, Architect Norisada Maeda, Photographer Toshihiro Sobajima; Arrow, Apollo Architects & Associates, Photographer Masao Nishikawa

From Left to Right, Bottom Row: Steel House, Funinori Nousaku Architects; Transustainable House, SUGAWARADAISUKE, Photographer Jérémie Souteyrat; Moriyama House, Ryue Nishizawa. Photograph Javier Viteri

p. 299
From Left to Right, Top Row: Well House, Architecture Atelier Akio Takatsuka, Photographer Mr. Hiroyasu Sakaguchi; Orange, Architect Norisada Maeda, Photographer Studio Dio; Park House, another APARTMENT, Photographer Koichi Torimura

From Left to Right, Middle Row: Calm, Apollo Architects & Associates, Photographer Masao Nishikawa; The Rose, Architect Norisada Maeda; Monoclinic, Atelier Tekuto, Photographer Toshihiro Sobajima

From Left to Right, Bottom Row: House EN, Miyahara Architect Office, Photographer Mitsumasa Fujitsuka; What Categorize The City and Me, Ondesign; House Meguro, Key Operation Inc./Architects, Photographer KOP+Hattori

p. 300
From Left to Right, Top Row: Makiko Tsukada Architects, Photographer Shinkenchiku-sha; Atelier Tekuto, Photographer Makoto Yoshida; Kasuyo Sejima. Photograph Javier Viteri

From Left to Right, Middle Row: Apollo Architects & Associates, Photographer Masao Nishikawa; Apollo Architects & Associates, Photographer Masao Nishikawa; Apollo Architects & Associates, Photographer Masao Nishikawa

From Left to Right, Bottom Row: Apollo Architects & Associates, Photographer Masao Nishikawa; Apollo Architects & Associates, Photographer Masao Nishikawa; Tokyo Architects, Photograph Jon Cummings

p. 301

From Left to Right, Top Row: Schemata Architects, Photographer Takumi Ota; another Apartment Ltd., Photographer Koichi Torimura; Atelier Tekuto, Photographer Toshihiro Sobajima

From Left to Right, Middle Row: Hiroyuki Ito Architects, Photographer Masao Nishisawa; Ken'ichi Otani Architect, Photographer Koichi Torimura; Small House, Unemori Architects, Photographer Ken Sasajima

From Left to Right, Bottom Row: YUUA architects and Associates, Photographer Toshihiro Sobajima; Hiroyuki Shinozaki Architects, Photographer Kai Nakamura; Mizuishi Architect Atelier, Photographer Hiroshi Tanigawa

p. 305

Left YUUA architects and Associates, Photographer Toshihiro Sobajima

p 305

Right YUUA architects and Associates, Photographer Toshihiro Sobajima

p. 306

Top Atelier Tekuto, Photographer Toshihiro Sobajima

p. 306

Bottom Mizuishi Architect Atelier, Photographer Hiroshi Tanigawa

p. 307

Top Unemori Architects, Photographer Ken Sasajima

p. 307

Bottom Koji Tsutsui Architect and Associates, Photographer Iwan Baan

p. 308

Top Javier Viteri

p. 308

Bottom Bjorn Lundquist

Toronto

p. 310
Jack Landau

pp. 314–315
Jimmy Wu

pp. 316–317
Jack Landau

p. 317
Right Javier Viteri

p. 326
Javier Viteri

p. 327
Javier Viteri. One Bloor and Aura, John Vo

p. 330
Top Core Architects

p. 330
Bottom Core Architects

p. 331
Top Amanda Yang

p. 331
Bottom Ivan Silin

p. 335
George Pimentel Photography

BIBLIOGRAPHY

General

Broto, Carles. *Social Housing*. Barcelona: Links International, 2014.

Curtis, William J.R. *Modern Architecture since 1900*. London: Phaidon, 2000.

Di Palma, Vittoria, Diana Periton, and Marina Lathouri. *Intimate Metropolis*. London; New York: Routledge, 2009.

Ebner, Peter. *Typology+*. Basel: Birkhäuser Architecture, 2005.

Firley, Eric and Caroline Stahl. *The Urban Housing Handbook*. Chichester, UK; Hoboken, NJ: Wiley, 2009.

Frampton, Kenneth. *Modern Architecture: A Critical History*. London: Thames and Hudson, 2007.

French, Hilary. *New Urban Housing*. New Haven, CT: Yale University Press, 2006.

French, Hilary. *Key Urban Housing of the Twentieth Century: Plans, Sections and Elevations*. New York: W.W. Norton, 2008.

French, Hilary. *New Urban Housing*. London: Laurence King, 2009

Gausa, Manuel. *Housing: New Alternatives, New Systems*. Basel; Boston: Berlin Birkhäuser, 1998.

Gibberd, Frederick and F.R.S. Yorke. *The Modern Flat*. The Architectural Press, 1937.

Lane, Barbara Miller. *Housing and Dwelling: Perspectives on Modern Dwelling Architecture*. London; New York: Routledge, 2007.

Leupen, Bernard and Harald Mooij. *Housing Design: A Manual*. Rotterdam: NAi, 2012.

Macsai, John. *High Rise Apartment Buildings: A Design Primer*. Chicago: University of Illinois, 1972.

Mornement, Adam and Annabel Biles. *Infill: New Houses for Urban Sites*. London: Laurence King, 2009.

Mostaedi, Arian. *Apartment Architecture Now*. Barcelona: Carles Broto & Josep Ma Minguet, 2003.

Oliver, Paul. *Dwellings: The Vernacular House World Wide*. London; New York: Phaidon, 2003.

Perks, Sydney. *Residential Flats of All Classes, Including Artisans' Dwellings: A Practical Treatise on Their Planning and Arrangement, Together with Chapters on Their History, Financial Matters, Etc., with Numerous Illustrations*. London: B.T. Batsford, 1905.

Pfeifer, Gunter and Per Brauneck. *Freestanding Houses A Housing Typology*. Berlin: Birkhauswer 2010.

Ravetllat, Pere Joan. *Block Housing a Contemporary Perspective*. Barcelona: Editorial S.A., 1992.

Schittich, Christian. *Best of Wohnen Housing*. Munchen: Edition Detail, 2012.

Schneider, Friederike and Oliver Heckmann. *Floor Plan Manual Housing*. Basel: Birkhauser Architecture, 2004.

Schoenauer, Norbert. *6000 Years of Housing*. New York: W.W. Norton, 2000.

Segantini, Maria Alessandra. *Contemporary Housing*. Milan; New York: Distributed in North America by Rizzoli International, 2008.

Sherwood, Roger. *Modern Housing Prototypes*. Cambridge, MA: Harvard University Press, 1978.

Site (Patricia Phillips and James Wines). *Highrise of Homes*. New York: Rizzoli, 1982.

Team X. *Team X in Search of a Utopia of the Present 1953–81*. Rotterdam: NAi, 2006.

Zhou, Jingmin. *Urban Housing Forms*. Amsterdam; Boston, MA: Elsevier/Architectural Press, 2005.

Birmingham

Chapman, Stanley. *The History of Working-Class Housing*. Newton Abbot, UK: David and Charles, 1971.

Darra Mair, Ludovic William. *Report on Back-to-Back Houses*. London: H.M. Stationery Office, 1910.

Schoenauer, Norbert. "Back-to-Backs, Tenements and Bylaw Housing", *6000 Years of Housing*. New York: W.W. Norton, 2000.

Upton, Chris. *Living Back-to-Back*. Chichester, Uk: Phillimore, 2005.

London

Beattie, Susan. *A Revolution in London Housing: LCC Housing Architects & Their Work 1893–1914*. London: Greater London Council/The Architectural Press, 1980.

Chapman, Stanley D. *The History of Working-Class Housing*. Newton Abbot, UK: David and Charles, 1971.

Conlin, Jonathan. "The Restless House", *Tale of Two Cities: Paris, London and the Birth of the Modern City*. London: Atlantic, 2013.

Gauldie, Enid. *Cruel Habitations: A History of Working-Class Housing 1780–1918*. London: Allen & Unwin, 1974.

Gillian, Darley. *Octavia Hill: Social Reformer and Founder of the National Trust*. London: Francis Boutle, 2010.

Hickmott, Arthur. "Houses for the People", *The London County Council: What it is and What it does*. London: Fabian Society, 1897.

Hill, Octavia and Robert Whelan. *Octavia Hill and the Social Housing Debate: Essays and Letters by Octavia Hill*. London: St Edmundsbury, 1998.

Metcalf, Priscilla. *Victorian London*. New York: Praeger, 1973.

Schoenauer, Norbert. "Back-to-Backs, Tenements and Bylaw Housing", *6000 Years of Housing*. New York: W.W. Norton, 2000.

Tarn, John Nelson. *Working-class Housing in 19th Century Britain*. London: L. Humphries for the Architectural Association, London, 1971.

Wise, Sarah. *The Blackest Streets: The Life and Design of a Victorian Slum*. London: Bodley Head, 2008.

Paris

Carmona, Michel. *Haussmann: His Life and Times, and the Making of Modern Paris*. Trans. Patrick Camiller. Chicago: I.R. Dee, 2002.

Chapman, J.M. and Brian Chapman. *The Life and Times of Baron Haussmann: Paris in the Second Empire*. London: Weidenfeld and Nicolson, 1957.

Conlin, Jonathan. "The Restless House", *Tale of Two Cities: Paris, London and the Birth of the Modern City*. London: Atlantic, 2013.

Dennis, Michael. *Court and Garden: From the French Hotel to the City of Modern Architecture*. Cambridge: MIT, 1986.

Jordan, David P. *Transforming Paris: The Life and Labours of Baron Haussmann*. New York: Free Press, 1995.

Kirkland, Stephane. *Paris Reborn: Napoleon III, Baron Haussmann and the Quest to Build a Modern City*. New York: St. Martin's, 2013.

Loyer, Francois. *Paris Nineteenth Century: Architecture and Urbanism*. Trans. Charles Lynn Clark. New York: Abbeville, 1998.

Marcus, Sharon. "Enclosing Paris, 1852–1880", *Apartment Stories: City and Home in Nineteenth-Century Paris and London*. Berkeley, CA: University of California Press, 1999.

Marshall, Bruce. *Building Paris: Creating the World's Most Beautiful Capital City*. London: Endeavour, 2009.

Olsen, Donald J. "The New Paris", *The City as a Work of Art: London, Paris, Vienna*. New Haven, CT: Yale University Press, 1996.

Olsen, Donald J. "Inside the Dwelling: The Paris Flat", *The City as a Work of Art: London, Paris, Vienna*. New Haven, CT: Yale University Press, 1996.

Panerai, Philippe, Jean Castex, Jean Charles Depaule, and Ivor Samuels. "Chapter 1 Haussmannien Paris: 1853–82", *Urban Forms: The Death and Life of the Urban Block*. Oxford; Woburn: Architectural Press, 2004.

Shapiro, Ann-Louise. *Housing the Poor of Paris, 1850–1902*. Madison, WI: University of Wisconsin Press, 1985.

Sutcliffe, Anthony. *Paris: An Architectural History*. New Haven, CT: Yale University Press, 1993.

New York

Dolkart, Andrew S. *Biography of a Tenement House*. Santa Fe, NM: Centre for American Places, 2007.

Plunz, Richard. *A History of Housing in New York City: Dwelling Type and Social Change in the American Metropolis*. New York: Columbia University Press, 1990.

Riis, Jacob. *The Battle with the Slum*. New Jersey: Patterson Smith, 1969.

Riis, Jacob. *How the Other Half Live: Studies among the Tenements of New York*. New York: Dover, 1971.

Schoenauer, Norbert. "Back-to-Backs, Tenements and Bylaw Housing", *6000 Years of Housing*. New York: W.W. Norton, 2000.

Seitz, Sharon. *A Tenement Story: The History of 97 Orchard Street and The Lower East Side Tenement Museum*. New York: Lower East Side Tenement Museum, 2004.

Hong Kong

Bristow, Roger. *Land-use Planning in Hong Kong: History, Policies and Procedures*. Hong Kong; New York: Oxford University Press, 1984.

Chu, Cecilia. "Between Typologies and Representation: The Tong Lau and the Discourse of the 'Chinese House' in Colonial Hong Kong", *Colonial Frames, Nationalist Histories: Imperials Legacies, Architecture and Modernity*. Ed. Mrinalini Rajagopalan and Madhuri Desai. Farnham; Burlington: Ashgate, 2012.

Lee, Ho Yin. *Pre-war Tong Lau: A Hong Kong Shophouse Typology*. Hong Kong: Faculty of Architecture, University of Hong Kong, 2010.

Leeming, Frank. *Street Studies in Hong Kong: Localities in a Chinese City*. Hong Kong; New York: Oxford University Press, 1977.

Magnago Lampugnani, Vittorio. *Hong Kong Architecture: The Aesthetics of Density*. New York; Munich: Prestel, 1993.

Owen, Norman G. *The Heritage of Hong Kong: Its History, Architecture and Culture*. Hong Kong: FormAsia, 1999.

Pryor, E.G. *Housing in Hong Kong*. Hong Kong; Oxford: Oxford University Press, 1983.

Shelton, Barrie, Justyna Karakiewicz, and Thomas Kvan. *The Making of Hong Kong from Vertical to Volumetric*. London; New York: Routledge, 2011.

Wong, Luke S.K. *Housing in Hong Kong: A Multi-Disciplinary Study.* Hong Kong: Heinemann Educational Books, 1978.

Berlin

Bader, Ingo and Martin Bialluch. "Gentrification and the Creative Class in Berlin-Kreuzberg", *Whose Urban Renaissance?: An International Comparison of Urban Regeneration Strategies.* Ed. Libby Porter and Kate Shaw. London; New York: Routledge, 2009.

Bingham, John. *Weimar Cities: The Challenge of Urban Modernity in Germany, 1919–1933.* New York; London: Routledge/Taylor & Francis Group. 2008.

Borsi, Katharina. "Drawing and Dispute: The Strategies of the Berlin Block", *Intimate Metropolis: Urban Subjects in the Modern City."* Ed. Vittoria Di Palma, Diana Periton, and Marina Lathouri. London; New York: Routledge, 2009.

Buddensieg, Tilmann. *Berlin 1900–1933: Architecture and Design = Architektur und Design.* New York: Cooper-Hewitt Museum, Smithsonian Institution's National Museum of Design, 1987.

Buschfeld, Ben. *Bruno Taut's Hufeisensiedlung.* Berlin: Nicolai Der Hauptstadtverlag GmbH, 2015.

Haspel, Jörg and Annemarie Jaeggi. *Housing Estates in the Berlin Modern Style.* Munich: Deutscher Kunstverlag GmbH, 2007.

Gameren, Dick van. *Woningbouwtentoonstellingen = Housing Exhibitions.* Rotterdam: nai010 uitgevers, 2013.

Kleihues, Josef Paul. *Internationale Bauausstellung Berlin 1984 Die Neubaugebiete Dokumente Projekte 2.* Berlin: Bauausstellung Berlin: Siedler, 1981.

Loeb, Carolyn. "The Politics of Public and Private Space: Housing and Urbanism in Divided Berlin", *The Housing Question: Tensions, Continuities, and Contingencies in the Modern City.* Ed. Edward Murphy and Najib B. Hourani. Farnham, UK: Ashgate, 2013.

Nakamura, Toshio. "IBA: International Building Exhibition Berlin 1987", *Architecture and Urbanism.* Tokyo: a+u Publishing , 1987.

Nalbach, Gernot and Johanne Nalbach. *Berlin Modern Architecture Exhibition Catalogue.* Berlin: Senatsverwaltung für Bau und Wohnungswesen Berlin, 1989.

Siedlungen der Berliner Moderne: Eintragung in die Welterbeliste der UNESCO = Berlin Modernism Housing Estates: Inscription on the UNESCO World Heritage List. Berlin: Braun, 2009.

Weitz, Ewald and Jürgen Friedenberg. *Interbau Berlin 1957: Internationale Bauausstellung im Berliner Hansaviertel, 6. Jul ibis 29. September.* Berlin: iwag, 1957.

White, Ian Boyd and David Fisby. *Metropolis Berlin: 1880–1940.* Berkeley, CA: University of California Press, 2012.

Wiedenhoeft, Ronald. *Berlin's Housing Revolution: German Reform in the 1920s.* Ann Arbor, MI: UMI Research Press, 1985.

Amsterdam

Baeten, Jean Paul, Jaap van den Berg, and Véronique Patteeuw. *Living in the Lowlands: The Dutch Domestic Scene 1850–2004.* Rotterdam: NAi, 2004.

Betsky, Aaron and Adam Euwens. *False Flat: Why Dutch Design is So Good.* London: Phaidon, 2004.

Cousins, Matthew. *Design Quality in New Housing: Learning from the Netherlands.* Taylor & Francis, 2009.

Galle, Maaike and Ettjen Modderman. "VINEX: National Spatial Planning Policy in the Netherlands during the Nineties", *Netherlands Journal of Housing and the Built Environment*, Volume 12, Issue 1. Delft: Delft University Press, 1997.

Ibelings, Hans. *20th Century Urban Design in the Netherlands.* Rotterdam: NAi, 1999.

Koster, Egbert. *Oostelijk Havengebied Amsterdam = Eastern Docklands.* Amsterdam: Architectura & Natura, 1995.

Lebesque, Sabine. *Along Amsterdam's Waterfront: Exploring the Architecture of the Southern IJ Bank.* Amsterdam: Valiz, 2006.

Leupen, Bernard and Harald Mooij. *Housing Design A Manual.* Rotterdam: NAi, 2012.

Lootsma, Bart. *Superdutch: New Architecture in the Netherlands.* New York: Princeton Architectural Press, 2000.

Maar, Birgitte de. *A Sea of Houses: The Residences from New Deal on Borneo/Sporenburg = Een Zee van Huizen: De Woningen van New Deal op Borneo/Sporenburg.* Bussum: THOTH, 1999.

Netherlands. Ministry of Education, Culture and Science. Ministry of Housing, Spatial Planning and the Environment. Ministry of Agriculture, Nature and Food Quality. Ministry of Transport, Public Works and Water Management. *The Architecture of Space: Notes on the Architecture Policy 1997–2000.* 1996.

Netherlands. Ministry of Welfare, Health and Cultural Affairs. Ministry of Housing, Spatial Planning and the Environment. *Dutch Government Policy on Architecture.* 1991.

Netherlands. Ministry of Education, Culture and Science. Ministry of Housing, Spatial Planning and the Environment. Ministry of Transport, Public Works and Water Management. Ministry of Agriculture, Nature Management and Fisheries. *Shaping the Netherlands: Architectural Policy 2001–2004.* 2001.

Netherlands. Ministry of Education, Culture and Science. Ministry of Housing, Spatial Planning and the Environment. Ministry of Agriculture, Nature and Food Quality. Ministry of Transport, Public Works and Water Management. Ministry of Economic Affairs. Ministry of Defence. Ministry of Foreign Affairs. *Action Programme on Spatial Planning and Culture.* 2005.

Netherlands. Ministry of Education, Culture and Science. Ministry of Housing, Spatial Planning and the Environment. Ministry of Agriculture, Nature and Food Quality. Ministry of Transport, Public Works and Water Management. *A Culture of Design: Architecture Vision and Spatial Design.* 2008.

Netherlands. Ministry of Infrastructure and the Environment. Ministry of Education, Culture and Science. Ministry of Interior and Kingdom Relations. Ministry of Economic Affairs, Agriculture and Innovation. Ministry of Defence. *Action Agenda for Architecture and Spatial Design 2013–2016: Building on the Strength of Design.* 2012.

Oosterman, Arjen. *Woningbouw in Nederland: Voorbeeldige Architectuur van de jaren Negentig = Housing in the Netherlands: Exemplary Architecture of the Nineties.* Rotterdam: NAi Uitgevers, 1996.

Ouwehand, André and Gelske van Daalen. *Dutch Housing Associations: A Model for Social Housing.* Delft: DUP Satellite Delft University Press, 2002.

Rodolfo, Machado. *Residential Waterfront Borneo Sporenburg, Amsterdam: Adriaan Geuze, West 8 Urban Design & Landscape Architecture.* Cambridge, MA: Harvard University Graduate School of Design, 2006.

Beijing

Buurman, Marlies and Maarten Kloos. *Dutch Architects in Booming China.* Amsterdam: ARCAM, 2005.

Dawson, Layla. *China's New Dawn: An Architectural Transformation.* Munich; New York: Prestel, 2005.

Gili, Mónica, Guim Costa, Moisés Puente, and Miguel Ruano. "Instant China: Notes on an Urban Transformation", *2G* N.10, Barcelona: 1999.

Liang, Samuel. *Remaking China's Great Cities: Space and Culture in Urban Housing, Renewal, and Expansion.* London; New York: Routledge, 2014.

Lu, Junhua and Peter Rowe. *Modern Urban Housing in China 1840–2000.* Munich; New York: Prestel, 2001.

Lu, Xin. *China, China . . . Western Architects and City Planners in China.* Ostfildern: Hatje Cantz, 2008.

Ruan, Xing. *New China Architecture.* Singapore: Periplus, 2006.

Shan, Deqi. *Chinese Vernacular Dwellings.* Cambridge, UK; New York: Cambridge University Press, 2011.

Wang, Mark Y., Pookong Kee, and Jia Gao. *Transforming Chinese Cities.* London; New York: Routledge, 2014.

Xue, Charlie Q.L. *Building a Revolution: Chinese Architecture since 1980.* Hong Kong: Hong Kong University Press, 2006.

Zhu, Jianfei. *Architecture of Modern China: A Historical Critique.* London; New York: Routledge, 2009.

Tokyo

Asensio, Paco. *Tokyo Houses.* New York: Dusseldorf: teNeues, 2002.

Black, Alexandra. *The Japanese House: Architecture and Interiors.* Tokyo; Rutland, VT: Tuttle, 2011.

Brown, Azby. *The Very Small Home: Japanese Ideas for Living Well in Limited Space.* Tokyo; New York: Kodansha International, 2005.

Habuka, Takao. *Modern Japanese Style Architecture: Refined Technique of Classic Architecture.* Tokyo: hatsubaijo Rikuyosha, 2006.

Ishido, Takeshi. *Contemporary Japanese Houses 1985–2005.* Tokyo: Toto Shuppan, 2005.

Iwatate, Marccia and Geeta K. Mehta. *Japan Houses.* North Clarendon, VT: Tuttle, 2005.

Japan. Ministry of Land, Infrastructure and Transport. *Introduction of Urban Land Use Planning System in Japan: Outline of City Planning System, Urbanization Promotion/Control Area, Land Use Zone and Regulation, Building Control, Incentive System and District Plan.* 2003.

Jodidio, Philip. *The Japanese House Reinvented.* New York: Monacelli, 2015.

Mehta, Geeta K. and Deanna MacDonald. *New Japan Architecture: Recent Works by the World's Leading Architects.* North Clarendon, VT: Tuttle, 2011.

Nuijsink, Cathelijine. *How to Make a Japanese House.* Rotterdam: NAi, 2012.

Pollock, Naomi. *Modern Japanese House.* London: Phaidon, 2005.

Pollock, Naomi. *Jutaku: Japanese House.* London: Phaidon, 2015.

Sacchi, Livio. *Tokyo: City and Architecture.* New York: Universe, 2004.

Wagner, George. *Tokyo from Vancouver.* Vancouver: School of Architecture, University of British Columbia, 2005.

Toronto

Ibelings, Hans and Partisans. *Rise and Sprawl.* Montreal; Amsterdam: The Architecture Observer, 2016.

Kesik, Ted. *The Glass Condo Conundrum.* University of Toronto John H. Daniels Faculty of Architecture, Landscape and Design, 2011.

Toronto (Ont.) Toronto City Council. *Tall Building Design Guidelines.* Prepared by HOK Canada and Urbana Architects Corporation. Toronto: Toronto City Council, 2006.

Toronto (Ont.) Toronto City Council. *Final Report—Official Plan Amendment to Encourage the Development of Units for Households with Children.* Prepared by Toronto: Toronto City Council, 2009.

Toronto (Ont.) Toronto City Council. *Tall Buildings: Inviting Change in Downtown Toronto.* Prepared by Urban Strategies Inc and Hariri Pontarini Architects. Toronto: Toronto City Council, 2010.

Toronto (Ont.) Toronto City Council. *Downtown Tall Buildings: Vision and Supplementary Design Guidelines.* Toronto: Toronto City Council, 2012.

Toronto (Ont.) Toronto City Council. *Tall Building Design Guidelines.* Toronto: Toronto City Council, 2013.

Toronto (Ont.) City of Toronto, City Planning. *Trends Issues Intensification Downtown Toronto.* Written by Thomas Ostler. Toronto: City of Toronto, City Planning, 2014.

INDEX

Note: italic references denote images.